**MALMARNA &
FURTHER AFIELD**
See pages 100–133

**EXCURSIONS FROM
STOCKHOLM**
See pages 140–151

LILLA VÄRTAN

DJURGÅRDEN

SALTSJÖN

DJURGARDEN
See pages 84–99

0 metres	500
0 yards	500

EYEWITNESS TRAVEL
STOCKHOLM

EYEWITNESS TRAVEL
STOCKHOLM

Main contributor: KAJ SANDELL

LONDON, NEW YORK,
MELBOURNE, MUNICH AND DELHI
www.dk.com

PRODUCED BY Streiffert Förlag AB, Stockholm
CHIEF EDITOR Bo Streiffert
PROJECT EDITOR Guy Engström
EDITORS Monica Nilsson, Guy Engström
DESIGNER Bo Streiffert
PICTURE RESEARCH Guy Engström

Dorling Kindersley Ltd
MANAGING EDITOR Anna Streiffert
ART DIRECTOR Gillian Allan

MAIN CONTRIBUTOR Kaj Sandell

CONTRIBUTORS
Lisa Carlsson, Jan & Christine Samuelson
Christina Sollenberg Britton, Stockholm Visitor's Board

MAPS Stig Söderlind

PHOTOGRAPHERS
Jeppe Wikström, Erik Svensson

ILLUSTRATIONS
Urban Frank, assisted by Jan Rojmar

ENGLISH TRANSLATION
Philip Ray

Reproduced by PDC Tangen, Norway
Printed and bound by South China Printing Co. Ltd., China

First published in Great Britain in 2000 by Dorling Kindersley Ltd
80 Strand, London WC2R 0RL
Reprinted with revisions 2001, 2004, 2007

Copyright 2000, 2007 © Dorling Kindersley Ltd, London
A Penguin company

ISBN 978 1 40531 695 8

FLOORS ARE REFERRED TO THROUGHOUT IN ACCORDANCE WITH EUROPEAN
USAGE; IE THE "FIRST FLOOR" IS THE FLOOR ABOVE GROUND LEVEL.

Front cover main image: Riddarholmen, Gamla Stan, Stockholm

◁ **Dawn at Skeppsbron, on the eastern side of Gamla Stan**

CONTENTS

**Wooden sculpture on the
17th–century warship *Vasa***

INTRODUCING
STOCKHOLM

**Kaknästornet, Stockholm's tallest
building at 155 m (508 ft)**

Late winter walk along the shores of Kungsholmen

A packet of traditional round Swedish crispbread

The renovated Royal Chapel at the Royal Palace

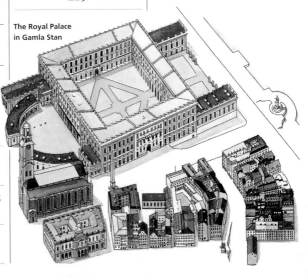
The Royal Palace in Gamla Stan

INTRODUCING
STOCKHOLM

FOUR GREAT DAYS IN STOCKHOLM

In Stockholm you are never far from water. Between them, the city's 14 islands offer a beguiling mix of culture and nature – there is something for everyone here. As well as being beautiful seen from the water, this city is also a pleasure to explore on foot, particularly around Gamla Stan's medieval lanes and

Hercules outside Drottningholm

alleys and the leafy island of Djurgården. To help you to make the most of your visit, here are ideas for four themed days out. All the sights are accessible using public transport. Prices include travel, food and admission charges. Family prices are for two adults and two children.

Looking over the Nordiska Museet towards the city centre

MUSEUMS MEANDER

- **A sunken ship and Swedish history on Djurgården**
- **Lunch near Kungsträdgården park**
- **Skeppsholmen – "museum island"**

TWO ADULTS allow at least 300 kr

Morning
Start the day on the island of Djurgården at the **Vasamuseet** *(see pp92–4)*. The impressive 17th-century warship *Vasa* is worth at least 90 minutes, and try not to miss the informative video. Next door, the **Nordiska Museet** *(see pp90–91)* gives a glimpse into Swedish life over the centuries. Allow two hours. Leaving the island over **Djurgårdsbron** *(see p88)*, turn left and a 15-minute waterside walk down Strandvägen brings you to

Kungsträdgården (see p64). Around this park are plenty of places for a lunch break.

Afternoon
Refreshed, head for Skeppsholmen, passing the stately **Grand Hotel** *(see p79)* and the **Nationalmuseum** *(see pp82–3)*. Once there, you can choose between the **Moderna Museet** *(see pp80–81)* and the **Arkitekturmuseet** *(see p78)*. Finish with a late *"fika"* (coffee break) in the museum café, or try the restaurant with its view over the water.

PALACES AND WATERWAYS

- **Kungliga Slottet (the Royal Palace)**
- **The city from the water**
- **Drottningholm Palace**

TWO ADULTS allow at least 380 kr

Morning
Start the day with a touch of royalty at **Kungliga Slottet** *(see pp50–53)*, the Royal Palace, in Gamla Stan. Choose any combination of tours – the Royal Apartments, the Tre Kronor Museet or Gustav III's Museum of Antiquities – which will take up most of the morning. Then, just before noon, step outside for the Changing of the Guard, complete with full horse parade over Norrmalm Bridge. Afterwards, take a gentle walk through the cobblestone streets of Gamla Stan to **Stortorget** *(see p54)* for lunch at any one of the cafés lining the square. The charming Chokladkoppen is an excellent choice, popular with tourists and locals alike. During the winter holidays, one of the oldest *Julmarknad* (Christmas Markets) is held here.

Drottningholm Palace by boat

Afternoon

After lunch it is onto the water. A one-hour canal cruise to **Drottningholm Palace** *(see pp146–9)*, the residence of the Swedish royal family, also provides a waterfront view of the city on the way to the palace just outside of town. Be sure to visit the Chinese Pavilion and the beautiful summer gardens in the palace grounds. "Under the Bridges of Stockholm" is another popular canal tour, which takes two hours and passes all of the city's major landmarks. Coffee and cakes are available on board. For both tours, it is worth booking in advance during peak times *(see pp204–5)*.

The busy Stortorget square in the heart of Gamla Stan

A WALK FROM NATURE TO CULTURE

- **The mountain park of Vita Bergen**
- **Shopping and eating in trendy SoFo**
- **Old Södermalm and the Katarinahissen lift**

TWO ADULTS allow at least 300 kr

Morning

Begin on the island of Söder-malm at **Vita Bergen** *(see p130)*, a beautiful mountain park. Here you will find allotment-gardens, worker's houses from the early 18th century and the monumental **Sofia Kyrka** *(see p130)*. Then head down-hill and into trendy "SoFo" (the area south of Folkungagatan). A variety of boutiques and cafés are

located here, with Folkunga-gatan itself leading towards **Medborgarplatsen** *(see p131)*. Traditional Swedish lunch can be had at an outdoor restaurant on the square.

Afternoon

From Medborgarplatsen it is not far to **Katarina Kyrka** *(see p128)* and the characteristic 18th-century cottages of old Södermalm. For a more contemporary view of Söder, the stretch of Götgatan between Medborgarplatsen and Slussen has an eclectic mix of shops, many selling Swedish design. The area east of here is **Mosebacke** *(see p128)*. Here you will find the **Södra Teatern** *(see p176)* and a public terrace, offering amazing views of the city. A more glamorous viewing point is the cocktail bar right at the top of **Katarinahissen** lift *(see p127)*, accessible from **Slussen** *(see p126)*.

A FULL FAMILY DAY

- **A trip to the Skansen zoo and open-air park**
- **Amusements at Gröna Lund**
- **The world of Pippi Longstocking and a theatre visit at Junibacken**

FAMILY OF 4 allow at least 900 kr

Morning

Start the day at the world's oldest open-air museum and zoo of Scandinavian wildlife, **Skansen** *(see pp96–7)*, on the

Children having fun at Skansen, on the island of Djurgården

island of Djurgården. Here you can visit period houses preserved and transported from all over Sweden, watch traditional glass blowing, and walk through a typical Swedish town, complete with market and post office. After such a busy morning, take a well-deserved break in one of the many cafés in the grounds of the park.

Afternoon

On to **Gröna Lund** *(see p95)*, an amusement park where you can ride one of the roller coasters, float through the Tunnel of Love or relax on the Ferris wheel. Alternatively, enter the world of beloved children's author Astrid Lingren at **Junibacken** *(see p88)*. This centre is dedicated to her many characters, including Pippi Longstocking, Alfie Atkins and Old Man Festus. It also has one of Sweden's leading children's theatres.

People enjoying picnics at Nytorget in "rustic chic" SoFo

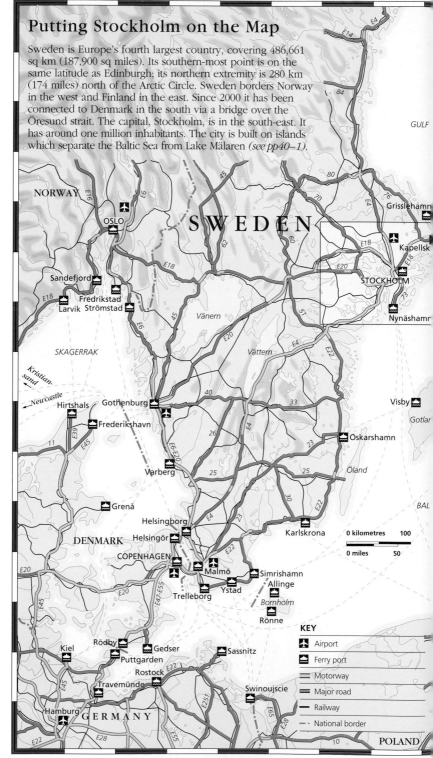

Putting Stockholm on the Map

Sweden is Europe's fourth largest country, covering 486,661 sq km (187,900 sq miles). Its southern-most point is on the same latitude as Edinburgh; its northern extremity is 280 km (174 miles) north of the Arctic Circle. Sweden borders Norway in the west and Finland in the east. Since 2000 it has been connected to Denmark in the south via a bridge over the Öresund strait. The capital, Stockholm, is in the south-east. It has around one million inhabitants. The city is built on islands which separate the Baltic Sea from Lake Mälaren (*see pp40–1*).

NORWAY

OSLO

SWEDEN

GULF

Grisslehamn

Kapellsk

STOCKHOLM

Sandefjord

Fredrikstad

Larvik Strömstad

Vänern

Nynäshamr

SKAGERRAK

Vättern

Kristian-sand

Newcastle

Hirtshals

Gothenburg

Visby

Frederikshavn

Gotlar

Varberg

Oskarshamn

Öland

Grenå

BAL

Helsingborg

Helsingör

Karlskrona

DENMARK

0 kilometres   100

COPENHAGEN

0 miles   50

Malmö

Simrishamn

Allinge

Trelleborg   Ystad

Bornholm

Rönne

KEY

Kiel   Rödby   Gedser   Sassnitz

✈ Airport

Puttgarden

⛴ Ferry port

Rostock

Travemünde

Swinoujscie

Motorway

Major road

Hamburg   GERMANY

Railway

National border

POLAND

◁ **View of Stockholm from Mosebacke, painted in 1787 by Elias Martin**

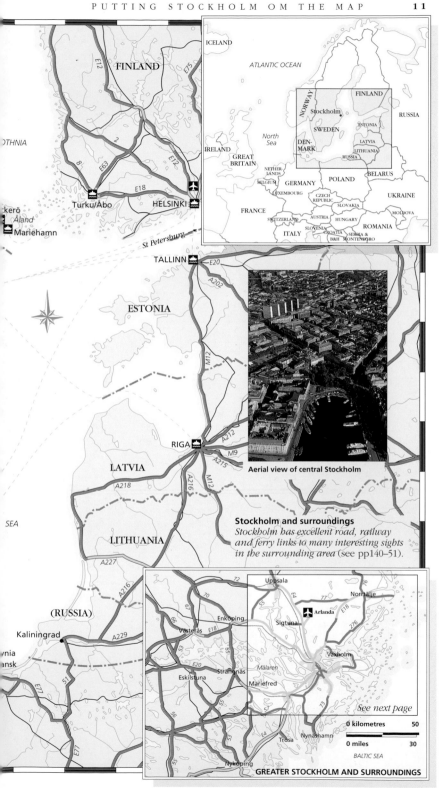

Aerial view of central Stockholm

Stockholm and surroundings
Stockholm has excellent road, railway and ferry links to many interesting sights in the surrounding area (see pp140–51).

See next page

0 kilometres 50

0 miles 30

BALTIC SEA

GREATER STOCKHOLM AND SURROUNDINGS

Stockholm and Surroundings

Stockholm's first buildings were erected on a small island in the narrow Strömmen channel between the Baltic and Lake Mälaren. When the town started to expand, buildings sprang up on the "Malms", the areas on either side of Strömmen. Today Stockholm stretches over 14 islands, with high-rise suburbs sprawling almost all the way out to the royal country palaces. The network of underground and suburban trains, buses and ferry services offers easy transport to sights beyond the city centre *(see pp140–51)*.

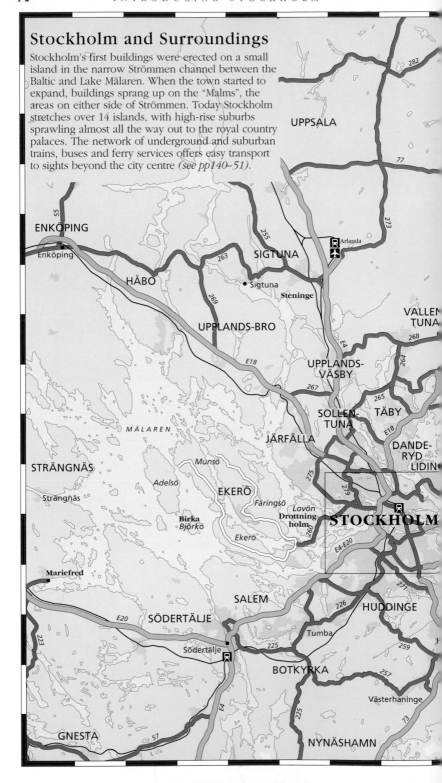

UPPSALA

282

77

ENKÖPING

Enköping

55

255

263

SIGTUNA

Sigtuna

Steninge

Arlanda

273

HÅBO

269

UPPLANDS-BRO

E18

E4

UPPLANDS-VÄSBY

267

VALLEN-TUNA

268

264

265

SOLLEN-TUNA

TÄBY

E18

MÄLAREN

JÄRFÄLLA

DANDE-RYD

LIDIN

STRÄNGNÄS

Strängnäs

Munsö

Adelsö

275

279

EKERÖ

Färingsö

Lovön

Drottning-holm

STOCKHOLM

Birka
Björkö

Ekerö

260

E4·E20

Mariefred

SALEM

226

271

HUDDINGE

E20

SÖDERTÄLJE

Tumba

259

223

Södertälje

225

BOTKYRKA

257

225

Västerhaninge

73

E4

GNESTA

57

NYNÄSHAMN

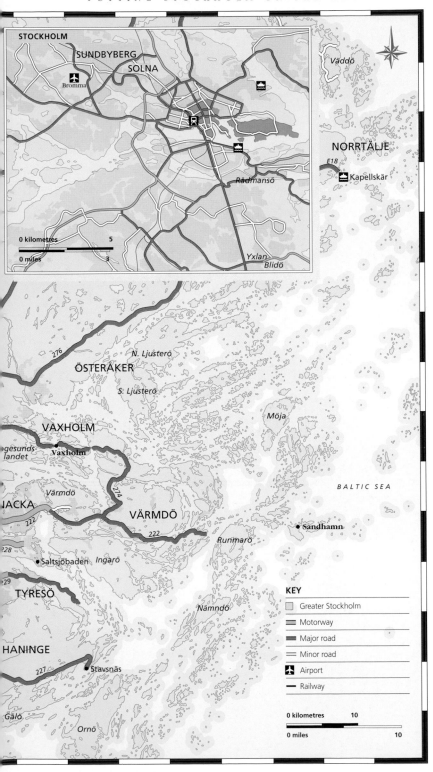

STOCKHOLM
SUNDBYBERG
SOLNA
Bromma
Väddö
NORRTÄLJE
E18
Kapellskär
Rådmansö
Yxlan
Blidö

0 kilometres   5
0 miles   3

276
N. Ljusterö
ÖSTERÅKER
S. Ljusterö
Möja
VAXHOLM
gesunds-
landet
Vaxholm
BALTIC SEA
Värmdö
274
IACKA
VÄRMDÖ
222
222
Runmarö
Sandhamn
228
Saltsjöbaden   Ingarö
229
TYRESÖ
Nämndö
HANINGE
227
Stavsnäs
Galö
Ornö

KEY
Greater Stockholm
Motorway
Major road
Minor road
Airport
Railway

0 kilometres   10
0 miles   10

THE HISTORY OF STOCKHOLM

egends and theories about Stockholm's origins have been many and varied, and sometimes even contradictory. But they have a common factor – control over the waterways. The generally accepted founder of Stockholm is the 13th-century regent Birger Jarl who, according to the medieval Erik's Chronicle, wanted to build a fortress to protect Lake Mälaren from marauding pirates.

A thousand years ago the waters around the island now known as Gamla Stan were busy with warships , trading vessels and pirate ships using the narrow channel between the Baltic and Lake Mälaren. In those days boat was the quickest and safest method of travel.

Stockholm's oldest preserved city seal (1296)

In the first literary mention of what was to become Stockholm, the Icelandic poet and saga writer Snorre Sturlasson (1178–1241) described a barrier of piles across a waterway which he named Stocksundet, the present Norrström.The island formed by this piling became known as Stockholm. Excavations in the late 1970s revealed the remains of a large number of piles in the water dating from the 11th century. Snorre also mentioned a 12th- century castle tower which would have predated Birger Jarl's fortress, the predecessor of the present Royal Palace.

Documents show that Stockholm was already a city in 1252, four years after Birger Jarl became regent. Many towns in Sweden started to expand in the early 13th century. Stockholm was a late starter but soon caught up. A document from 1289 describes

Stockholm as the biggest place in the kingdom. But it was not the capital city, because the king was always on the move. Birger Jarl's son, King Magnus Ladulås, did not regard Stockholm as his capital either. For a long time the city's importance lay in its role as a trading centre. It became an important port for the German-dominated Hanseatic League, which controlled Swedish overseas trade from the 13th century until the late 17th century.

The frontiers of the Nordic countries remained undefined for some time, but with a background of similar languages and cultures, Sweden, Norway and Denmark signed the Kalmar Union in 1397. Finland at that time was still part of Sweden. The era of union became one of conflict and violence. At the battle of Brunkeberg in Stockholm in 1471 the Danish king tried to take control of Sweden, but was defeated by the regent Sten Sture. A new Danish campaign in 1520 culminated in the notorious Stockholm Bloodbath at Stortorget *(see p54)*, when more than 80 Swedish noblemen were executed.

TIMELINE

1008 Olof Skötkonung converts to Christianity and is baptized in Västergötland	*Birger Jarl, Stockholm's founder*		**c.1250** Birger Jarl founds Stockholm	**1364** Albrecht of Mecklenburg chosen as Sweden's King		
			1350 Code of Magnus Eriksson replaces provincial laws		**1397** Kalmar Union links the Nordic countries	
1000	**1100**	**1200**	**1300**	**1400**	**1500**
800–975 Vikings settle and trade at Birka *(see p144)*	**1275** Magnus Ladulås chosen as Sweden's king at Mora	**1280** Ordinances of Alsnö give nobility freedom from taxation	**1349–50** Plague ravages Sweden	**1520** Swedish noblemen executed in Stockholm Bloodbath
	1101 Three Kings' Meeting fixes Scandinavian frontiers		**1471** Sten Sture the Elder defeats the Danish King Kristian at Brunkeberg	

◁ **Painting in Storkyrkan (Stockholm's cathedral) depicting a remarkable light phenomenon seen in 1535**

The newly chosen king, Gustav Vasa, making his ceremonial entry into Stockholm, Midsummer Day 1523

THE VASA ERA

One of those who managed to avoid execution in the Stockholm Bloodbath was the young nobleman Gustav Eriksson. At the end of 1520 Gustav organized an army to oust the Danish King Kristian from Sweden. Gustav was successful and on 6 June 1523 – later to become Sweden's National Day – he was named king with the title Gustav Vasa.

When Gustav Vasa took the throne he discovered a nation in financial crisis. He called on Parliament to pass a contro-versial law transferring the property of the Church to the State, which then became the country's most important source of economic power. Another important result of this policy was the gradual separation from Catholicism and the adoption of the Luth-eran State Church.

During his reign Gustav Vasa implemented tough economic policies in order to concentrate central power in Stockholm. This effective dictator-ship also resulted in the Swedish

**Portrait of
Erik XIV (1561)**

Parliament's decision in 1544 to make the monarchy hereditary.

Descendants of Gustav Vasa oversaw the rise of Sweden into one of Europe's great powers. During the reign of Gustav's son Erik XIV, there were wars against Denmark, Lübeck and Poland. His brothers dethroned him and he died in prison, probably of a pea soup poi-soned by his brother Johan III. During the reign of Karl IX, the third son, Sweden waged war against Denmark and Russia.

GUSTAV II ADOLF AND KRISTINA

When the next king, Gustav II Adolf, came to power in 1611, Sweden was involved in wars against Russia, Poland and Denmark. Under his rule Sweden steadily increased its influence over the Baltic region. Stockholm started to develop into the country's political and administrative centre. In 1630 Gustav II Adolf, to-gether with his influential chancellor Axel Oxenstierna, decided to inter-vene in the Thirty Years War on the

TIMELINE

1523 Gustav Vasa chosen as king in Strängnäs and marches into Stockholm	**1542** Nils Dacke and supporters stage a peasant revolt in Småland	*Vasa dynasty's coat of arms*	**1560** Gustav Vasa dies	**1568** Erik XIV imprisoned by his brothers at Gripsholms Slott **1577** Erik XIV dies, probably poisoned	**1611** Gustav II Adolf comes to power

1525		**1550**		**1575**		**1600**

1527 Reformation, Parliament con-fiscates Church property	**1544** Heredi-tary monarchy established for Gustav Vasa's male descen-dants	**1561** Eric XIV is crowned king and his brothers' powers curbed **1569** Johan III crowned in Stockholm	**1570** Nordic Seven Years War ends **1587** Johan III's son Sigismund chosen king of Poland	**1612** Axel Oxenstierna named State Chancellor

side of the Protestants, using religious motives as a pretext. Sweden had some notable military successes during the war, but paid a heavy price for winning the bloody battle at Lützen in 1632 as the king was killed in action.

Gustav II Adolf's only child, Kristina, came to the throne at the age of six. During her reign (1633–54), life at the court was influenced by the world of science and philosophy. Kristina corresponded with leading academics and invited the French philosopher René Descartes, who died in 1650 only a few months after arriving in Stockholm. The Tre Kronor castle became the permanent royal residence. Kristina's reluctance to marry resulted in her cousin, Karl Gustav, becoming Crown Prince. Kristina abdicated and left for Rome, where she converted to Catholicism.

Karl XII with the widowed queen on his arm leaving the burning Tre Kronor fortress

the frozen waters of the Great Belt (see p19). Karl XI (1660–97) secured the southern Swedish provinces, and divided the land more evenly between the crown, nobility and peasants.

While the body of Karl XI lay in state at Tre Kronor in 1697 a fire broke out which destroyed most of the building. The new monarch was the teenage Karl XII (1697–1718). He faced awesome problems when Denmark, Poland and Russia formed an alliance in 1700 with the aim of crushing the power of Sweden. Karl XII set off to battle.

Denmark and Poland were soon forced to plead for peace, but Russia resisted. A bold push towards Moscow was unsuccessful and the Swedish army suffered a devastating defeat at Poltava in 1709. This marked the beginning of the end for Sweden as a great power.

Karl XII, the most controversial Swedish monarch, returned to Sweden in 1715 after an absence of 15 years. His plans to regain Sweden's position of dominance never came to pass and he was killed in Norway in 1718.

By now, Sweden was in crisis. Crop failures and epidemics had annihilated one-third of Stockholm's population and the state's finances were drained.

Queen Kristina, fascinated by science and corresponding with leading scientists

THE CAROLIAN ERA

Karl X Gustav (1654–60) was the first of three Karls to reign. At the height of Sweden's era as a great power and in one of the most audacious episodes in the history of war, he conquered Denmark by leading his army across

1617 Death penalty introduced for conversion to Catholicism		**1654** Kristina abdicates and Karl X Gustav crowned king		**1697** Tre Kronor castle destroyed by fire; 15-year-old Karl XII crowned
1632 Gustav II Adolf killed at battle of Lützen	**1633** Six-year-old Kristina becomes queen; guardians rule	**1655** Kristina converts to Catholicism and is ceremonially greeted in Rome		
1625	**1650**	**1675**		**1700**
1618 Thirty Years War starts in Germany	**1648** Peace of Westphalia gives Sweden new territories	**1658** Swedish army crosses the Great Belt and acquires new territory under Peace of Roskilde	**1680** Karl XI starts the era of Carolian autocracy and limits powers of the nobility	**1709** Swedish army defeated by Peter the Great at Poltava
Gustav II Adolf				**1718** Karl XII dies

Sweden's Era as a Great Power

For more than a century (1611–1721) Sweden was the dominant power in northern Europe, and the Baltic was effectively a Swedish inland sea. The country was at its most powerful after the Peace of Roskilde in 1658, when Sweden acquired seven new provinces from Denmark and Norway. Outside today's frontiers the Swedish Empire covered the whole of Finland, large parts of the Baltic, and important areas of northern Germany. Over 111 years as a great power Sweden spent 72 of them at war when many treasures were brought back to the new palaces. It was also an era of cultural development and efficient government.

SWEDISH EMPIRE

☐ *Sweden's empire after the Peace of Roskilde, 1658*

The Tre Kronor Castle
Built as a defensive tower in the 1180s, the Tre Kronor castle was the seat of Swedish monarchs from the 1520s and became the administrative centre of the Swedish Empire. It was named after the three crowns on the spire which burned down in 1697.

The columns of troops
ride out over the shifting ice
towards Danish Lolland.

THE THIRTY YEARS WAR

A major European war raged between 1618–48, largely on German soil. Sweden entered the war in 1631 in an alliance with France. Gustav II Adolf was a fine military leader and had modernized the Swedish army which immediately had major successes at the battles of Breitenfeld (1631) and Lützen (1632), where the king, however, was killed. Later the Swedes pressed into southern Germany and also captured and plundered Prague (1648). Some rich cultural treasures were brought back to Sweden from the war. In 1648 the Peace of Westphalia gave Sweden several important possessions in northern Germany.

The death of Gustav II Adolf at the Battle of Lützen in 1632

Stockholm in 1640
The city's transformation from a small medieval town into a capital city can be seen in the network of straight streets, similar to the present layout.

Karl XI's Triumphs
The roof painting in Karl XI's gallery at the Royal Palace (1693) by the French artist Jacques Foucquet shows in allegoric form the king's victories at Halmstad, Lund and Landskrona.

The Powerful Nobility
The nobility were very influential in the Empire era and many successful soldiers were ennobled. The Banér family coat of arms from 1651 is adorned by three helmets and barons' crowns.

Count Carl Gustaf Wrangel *(see p56).*

King Karl X Gustav himself leads the Swedish army of 17,000 men.

Bondeska Palatset
One of the leading buildings of the era (1662–73), this palace was designed by Tessin the Elder and Jean de la Vallée for the State Treasurer Gustav Bonde (see p58).

CROSSING THE GREAT BELT
When Denmark declared war on Sweden in autumn 1657, the Swedish army was in Poland. Marching west, Karl X Gustav captured the Danish mainland, but without the navy, he could not continue to Copenhagen. However, unusually severe weather froze the sea, making it possible for the soldiers to cross the ice of the Great Belt, and the Danes had to surrender.

Karl XII's Pocket Watch
The warrior king's watch-case dates from 1700. It shows the state coat of arms, as well as those of the 49 provinces that belonged to Sweden at that time.

Karl XII's Last Journey
After being hit by a fatal bullet at Fredrikshald in Norway (1718), the king's body was taken first to Swedish territory then on to Uddevalla for embalming. Painting by Gustav Cederström (1878).

Gustav III with the white armband he wore when mounting his *coup d'état* in 1772

THE AGE OF LIBERTY AND THE GUSTAVIAN ERA

A new constitution came into force in 1719 which transferred power from the monarch to parliament. As a result, Sweden developed a system of parliamentary democracy similar to that of Britain in the early 18th century.

The "Age of Liberty" coincided with the Enlightenment, with dramatic advances in culture, science and industry. The botanist Carl von Linné became one of the most famous Swedes of his time. Another was the scientist, philosopher and author Emanuel Swedenborg. The production of textiles expanded in Stockholm, and Sweden's first hospital was constructed on Kungsholmen.

Changes in the balance of power around 1770 gave the new king, Gustav III, an opportunity to strike in an attempt to regain his monarchical powers. On 19 August 1772 Gustav accompanied the guards' parade to the Royal Palace where, in front of his life-guards, he declared his intention to

mount a bloodless *coup d'état*. The guards and other military units in Stockholm swore allegiance to the king, who tied a white handkerchief round his arm as a badge and rode out into the city to be acclaimed by his people. Absolute power had been restored.

Gustav III was influenced by the Age of Enlightenment and by French culture, which had a great effect on Swedish cultural life *(see pp22–3)*. But over the years opposition grew to the king's absolute powers, largely because of his costly war against Russia. In 1792 he was murdered by a nobleman, Captain Anckarström, during a masked ball at the Opera House *(see p23)*.

Gustav III was succeeded by his son, Gustav IV Adolf. During his reign Sweden was dragged into the Napoleonic wars. After a war against Russia in 1808–9, Sweden lost its sovereignty over Finland, which at the time accounted for one-third of Swedish territory. The king abdicated and left Stockholm to flee the country.

THE ERA OF KARL JOHAN AND BOURGEOIS LIBERALISM

By the early 19th century the absolute powers of the monarch had been removed for all time, and the privileges

Napoleon's former marshal, Jean-Baptiste Bernadotte, as King Karl XIV Johan surrounded by his family

TIMELINE

1719 New constitution transfers power from the king to Parliament	**1741** Carl von Linné appointed professor at Uppsala	**1754** Royal family moves into Royal Palace **1780s** Immigrants are given wide religious freedom		**1790** Swedish defea over Russia at battle of Svenskund **1792** Gustav III murdered
1720	**1740**	**1760**	**1780**	**1800**
1738 Parliamentary power is established in the Age of Liberty as the "Hat" party wins elections *Carl von Linné (1707–78)*		**1772** Gustav III crowned and mounts *coup d'état* giving the king absolute power	**1786** Swedish Academy founded **1778** National costume decreed. Death penalty removed for some crimes	

Newspaper readers outside the *Aftonbladet* office in 1841

Norwegians were reluctant to unite with Sweden, but a union between the two countries was agreed which lasted from 1814 to 1905. A long era of peace began and with it came a dramatic increase in the country's population, which grew by 1 million to 3.5 million by 1850. Many Swedes were driven into poverty because there was not enough work to go round. Mass emigration followed. From the 1850s to the 1930s about 1.5 million people left Sweden. Most of the emigrants travelled to North America in search of a better life.

of the aristocracy were undermined even more in 1809 with a new constitution that divided power between the king, the government and parliament.

With a new class structure and the effect of the French Revolution, a new middle class emerged which also wanted to be more influential. One of the best-known newspapers founded around this time was the liberal mouthpiece, *Aftonbladet*.

Difficulties in finding a suitable new monarch led eventually to the choice of one of Napoleon's marshals, Jean-Baptiste Bernadotte, who took on the more authentic Swedish name of Karl Johan. Founder of the present royal dynasty, Karl XIV Johan continued to speak French and never fully learned the Swedish language. His French wife, Queen Desideria, found Stockholm a cultural backwater compared with Paris.

In 1813 a Swedish army with Karl Johan at its head became involved in a campaign against Napoleon. The Battle of Leipzig ended in defeat for France, but more significantly Denmark had to hand over Norway to Sweden. The

FOLK MOVEMENTS AND INDUSTRIALIZATION

As Sweden was transformed from an agricultural society into an industrialized country the problems posed by the population surplus were gradually tackled. Its industrial revolution started around 1850, gathering momentum in the late 19th century, and the textile, timber and iron industries provided the main sources of employment. In 1806 the nation's first steam-driven mill, Eldkvarn, was built on the site of the present-day City Hall in Stockholm. It continued production until destroyed by fire in 1878.

Folk movements sprang up in the 19th century which still play an important role in Swedish life. A temperance movement emerged against a background of alcohol abuse – in the 1820s annual consumption of spirits was 46 litres (80 pints) per person.

Stockholm's Eldkvarn mill, destroyed by fire in 1878

The Era of Gustav III

Gustav III (1771–92) is one of the most colourful figures in Swedish history. The king's great interest in art, literature and the theatre made the late 18th century a golden age for Swedish culture, and several prestigious academies were founded at this time. After a bloodless revolution in 1772 Gustav III ruled with absolute power and initiated a wide-ranging programme of reform. But his attacks on the privileges of the nobility and his adventurous and costly foreign policy made him powerful enemies. In 1792 he was murdered during a masked ball at Stockholm's Opera House.

The Swedish Academy
The academy was founded by Gustav III in 1786 to preserve the Swedish language. Members received a token depicting the king's head at every meeting.

A courtier entertains by reading aloud.

Gustav III's Coronation, 1772
The coronation of the all-powerful monarch in Stockholm's cathedral was a magnificent ceremony, portrayed here by C G Pilo (1782). Every detail was overseen by Gustav himself, who used his flair for the dramatic in politics as well.

Gustav III studies architectural designs.

COURT LIFE AT DROTTNINGHOLM

Hilleström's painting (1779) gives an insight into court life at Drottningholm, where the king resided between June and November. In the present-day Blue Salon, Gustav III and Queen Sofia Magdalena socialized with their inner circle. Behaviour was modelled on the French court and etiquette was even stricter at Drottningholm than at Versailles.

The Battle of Svenskund
Gustav III was not known as a successful warrior king, but in 1790 he led the Swedish fleet to its greatest victory ever, when it defeated Russia in a major maritime battle in the Gulf of Finland.

Life in the Inns
The city abounded with inns, frequently visited by the 70,000 inhabitants. J T Sergel's sketch shows a convivial dinner party.

Murder at the Masked Ball

In 1792 Gustav III fell victim to a conspiracy at the Opera House. He was surrounded by masked men and shot by Captain Anckarström on the crowded stage. He died of his wounds 14 days later.

Gustav III's Mask and Cocked Hat

Despite his mask, Gustav III was easy to recognize since he was wearing the badges of two orders of chivalry. The drama intrigued the whole of Europe and inspired Verdi's opera Un Ballo in Maschera.

Flogging of the King's Murderer

Among the conspirators, only Anckarström was condemned to death. Before he was taken to his execution in Södermalm he was flogged on three successive days on the square in front of Riddarhuset.

Queen Sofia Magdalena does her needlework.

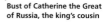

Bust of Catherine the Great of Russia, the king's cousin

GUSTAVIAN STYLE

The mid-18th century saw the emergence of Neo-Classicism, with the focus on antiquities and Greek ideals. Gustav III embraced this trend with great enthusiasm and supported the country's talented artists and authors. He established his own Museum of Antiquities *(see pp52–3)* with marble sculptures which he brought home from Italy. In handicrafts, the sweeping lines of Rococo elegance were replaced by the stricter forms of what has become known as Gustavian Style. Rooms at the Royal Palace were renovated with decoration and furnishings adapted to suit this style.

Chair designed in Gustavian Style

Swedish Court Costume

In 1778 Gustav III introduced a costume based on French lines to restrain fashion excesses. This is the male court costume for daily wear.

UNIVERSAL SUFFRAGE

Sweden's population reached 5 million around 1900 despite mass emigration to America. Many people moved to the towns to work in industry, and by the early 20th century Stockholm's population was about 300,000, a fourfold increase since the year 1800.

Increasing social awareness and the rise of the Social Democrat and Liberal parties in the early 20th century gave impetus to the demands for universal suffrage. Radical authors like August Strindberg became involved. A political battle ensued which was not resolved until 1921 when universal suffrage was introduced for both sexes.

Another question which was hotly debated in the 19th century was the role of the king and the extent of his powers. In his "courtyard speech" at the Royal Palace in 1914 King Gustav V called for military rearmament. This led to a constitutional crisis and the resignation of the Liberal government. After the 1917 election the king was forced to accept a government which contained repub-

Branting and Gustav V in conversation, 1909

lican-friendly Social Democrats, including the future prime minister, Hjalmar Branting. By then it was parliament, not the king, that decided what sort of government Sweden should have.

THE GROWTH OF THE WELFARE STATE

In 1936 the Social Democrats and Farmers' Party formed a coalition which developed what was to become known as the welfare state. The Social Democrat prime minister, Per Albin Hansson (1885–1946), defined the welfare state as a socially conscious society with financial security for all. Reforms introduced under this policy included unemployment benefit, paid holidays and childcare. As a result, poverty in Sweden virtually disappeared during the 1930s and 1940s.

The right of everyone to good housing was also part of welfare state policy. Under the principle of "work-home-centre" a new Stockholm suburb, Vällingby, was planned and built in the early 1950s. The idea was to transform the dormitory suburbs into thriving communities where people would both live and work. The concept was unsuccessful. It soon became apparent that the people who lived there still worked somewhere else, and vice versa. The great shortage of housing in the 1960s led to the "million" programme, which involved the building of a million homes in an extremely short time. These areas soon became known as the "new slums" despite high standards of construction.

Calls for democratic reforms in June 1917 led to riots like this one outside the parliament building in Stockholm

TIMELINE

1914 Gustav V gives his "courtyard speech".

1921 Universal suffrage for men and women

1932 Suicide of industrial magnate Ivar Krueger is followed by stockmarket crash

1940 Sweden-German agreement on transit of German military personnel

1955 Obligatory national health insurance

1958 Women can be ordained as priests

1967 R[...] hand dr[...] introd[...]

1920

1940

1960

Selma Lagerlöf, winner of the Nobel Prize for Literature

1930 Rise of Functionalist style in architecture, stimulated by the Stockholm Exhibition

1939 Sweden has coalition government and declares neutrality in World War II

1950 First public TV broadcast in Sweden

1964 Art exhibition at Moderna Museet shows works by Andy Warhol, Roy Lichtenstein and Claes Oldenburg

THE WAR YEARS

Sweden declared its neutrality during both World War I and II. Its policy of continuing to trade with nations involved in the conflict during World War I provoked a number of countries into imposing a trade blockade on Sweden. The situation became so serious that hunger riots broke out in some towns.

World War II produced an even more difficult balancing exercise for Swedish neutrality, largely because its Nordic neighbours were at war. With a combination of luck and skill, Sweden remained outside the conflict, but the concessions it had to make were strongly criticized both nationally and internationally.

Neutrality stamp issued in 1942

THE POST-WAR ERA

Although the Social Democrats dominated government from the 1930s to the 1970s the socialist and non-socialist power blocs in Swedish politics have remained fairly evenly matched since World War II.

The policy of non-alignment has not proved an obstacle to Swedish involvement on the international scene, including the United Nations. The country has offered asylum to hundreds of thousands of refugees from wars and political oppression. Prime minister Olof Palme (1927–86), probably the best-known Swedish politician abroad, was deeply involved in questions of democracy and disarmament, as well as the problems of the Third World. He was renowned for condemning undemocratic acts by dictators. Palme's assassination on the streets of Stockholm in 1986 sent a shock wave across the world, but strangely the murder has still not been solved.

Important changes took place during the closing decades of the 20th century. These included a new constitution in 1974 which removed the monarch's political powers. In 1995 Sweden joined the European Union after a referendum approved entry by only the narrowest of majorities.

The start of the new millennium marked a change in the role of the church in Sweden, which severed its connections with the state after more than 400 years.

Sveavägen, the site of Palme's murder, 1986

As Stockholmers enter the third millennium, the country shows signs of economic crisis, even though most people still lead a good life. Rapid technical developments and globalization have provided Sweden both with new job opportunities and new inhabitants, as well as a leading international role in information technology.

The centre of Vällingby, which attracted attention among city planners worldwide in the 1950s

1974 The monarch loses all political powers	**1980** New constitution gives women the right of succession to the throne	**2000** Swedish Church separated from the State		**2003** Foreign minister Anna Lindh murdered in Stockholm
		1986 Prime minister Olof Palme murdered in Stockholm		
1980			**2000**	
1974 ABBA pop group wins Eurovision Song Contest		**1995** Sweden joins European Union	**2000** Öresund bridge opens between Denmark and Sweden	
1973 Gustav VI Adolf dies and is succeeded by grandson, Carl XVI Gustaf	*Crown Princess Victoria*			

STOCKHOLM THROUGH THE YEAR

Stockholm's heart never misses a beat despite the vagaries of the climate. Although summer is a glorious time to visit the capital, the city shimmering in ice and snow is also an amazing experience, and numerous popular events take place throughout the year. Stockholm's countless sporting fixtures attract top-class international stars. Its many concerts, both pop and classical, indoor and outdoor, feature performers from around the world. Sweden's national festivals are celebrated in the traditional way in Stockholm and are always popular attractions for both locals and visitors alike. The capital's proximity to the surrounding countryside and water provides an extensive range of opportunities for all kinds of outdoor activities throughout the year.

Crocus, a sure sign of spring

SPRING

As in all the Nordic countries, people long for spring after the dark days of winter, and it has a big impact on life in the capital. Sun-lovers sit on the steps of Konserthuset (Concert Hall) and Kungliga Dramatiska Teatern (Royal Dramatic Theatre); people work on their boats; football competes with ice hockey for attention; spring flowers come into bud in Kungsträdgården; and the traditional *semla* cream buns go on sale to break the Lenten fast.

Semla bun

MARCH

Stockholm International Boat Show *(early Mar)*. The spring's major boat exhibition at Stockholm International Fairs in Älvsjö.
Outdoors Fair *(Mar)*. Camping, tourism, and outdoor equipment fair at Stockholm International Fairs in Älvsjö.

Spring sun-bathers at Djurgårdsbrunnsviken

Kuriosa *(early Mar)*. Fair for antiques and collectables at Sollentuna Exhibition Centre.
Sewing Festival *(late Feb/ early Mar)*. Needlework fair at Sollentuna Exhibition Centre.
Garden Fair *(Mar)*. Everything for the gardener on show at Stockholm International Fairs in Älvsjö.
Stockholm Art Fair *(Mar)*. Works of art for sale at Sollentuna Exhibition Centre.
Spring Salon *(Jan– Mar)*. Annual art show mainly featuring new artists at Liljevalchs Konsthall (gallery) on Djurgården.

APRIL

Gröna Lund *(last weekend in Apr)*. Djurgården's amusement park opens for the season.
Swedish Football Championship *(last weekend in Apr)*. Series starts at Råsunda and Söder stadiums.
Walpurgis Night at Skansen *(30 Apr)*. Traditional celebrations with massed standard bearers, folk dancing, torchlight procession, student choirs, bonfire and fireworks.
The King's Birthday *(30 Apr)*. The king is greeted at Kungliga Slottet (Royal Palace) with a military parade, and children hand over flowers and gifts.

MAY

Round Lidingö Race *(2nd Sat in May)*. Long-distance sailing race with hundreds of boats of all shapes and sizes.
Hat Parade *(mid-May)*. The parade starts at Nordiska museet and finishes at

Walpurgis Night bonfire at Evert Taubes Terrass, Riddarholmen

Skansen, where the "hat of the year" is chosen.
Circus Princess *(May)*. A series of circus performances by female artists, the best of whom is chosen as the year's Circus Princess.
Archipelago Fair *(late May)*. Second-hand leisure boats for sale, purchase or exchange.
"Tjejtrampet" *(last weekend in May)*. 45-km (28-mile) cycling competition at Gärdet with 7,000 female cyclists.
Historical Festival *(last weekend in May)*. Wide range of programmes in Gamla Stan, and on Riddarholmen and Helgeandsholmen.
Elite Race *(last weekend in May)*. Trotting competition at Solvalla with top horses from all over the world.
Theatre in Hagaparken *(late May)*. Outdoor theatre in the old palace ruins.
Kungsträdgården *(late May)*. The programme of summer entertainment in the park starts on the main stage.
Gärdet Race *(late May)*. Veteran cars in friendly competition at Gärdet.

AVERAGE DAILY HOURS OF SUNSHINE

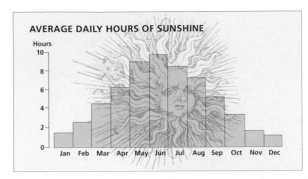

Hours
10 –
8 –
6 –
4 –
2 –
0 –

Jan Feb Mar Apr May Jun Jul Aug Sep Oct Nov Dec

Sunshine Chart
Stockholm's climate can vary markedly from hot, sunny days followed by a cooler rainy spell during the summer to winters with freezing temperatures and snow. From mid-June to mid-July it never really gets dark. Winter days are very short, although there can still be a strong sun at times.

SUMMER

Stockholm shows its best face at this time of year. Although May can be warm, summer does not really start until early June when the schools break up. In late June the sun shines almost round the clock, and with it comes a vibrant outdoor life with picnics and street festivals. The capital gets a bit emptier at peak holiday-time in July. When the schools go back in late August, Swedes celebrate the arrival of two annual culinary delights: crayfish and fermented Baltic herring.

Traditional Midsummer celebrations at Skansen, the open-air museum

JUNE

Stockholm Marathon *(first Sat in Jun)*. One of the world's 10 biggest marathons with around 13,000 runners.
Restaurant Festival *(early Jun)*. Kungsträdgården becomes the world's largest outdoor restaurant.
Archipelago Boat Day *(early Jun)*. Classic steamboats assemble at Strömkajen near the Grand Hôtel for a round trip to Vaxholm.
Riddardamen *(Jun)*. Regatta for female sailors at Riddarfjärden.
Stockholm Grand Prix *(Jun)*. Season's second-largest racing event at Täby racecourse with an international field.
National Day *(6 Jun)*. Celebrations at Skansen take place in the presence of the royal family.
Midsummer Eve *(next to last Sat in Jun)*. A major Swedish festival celebrated at Skansen over three days. It starts at 2pm on Midsummer Eve with

the traditional raising of the maypole and ring dancing.
Music at the Palace *(Jun–Aug)*. Summer concert season starts in the Hall of State and the Royal Chapel at Kungliga Slottet (Royal Palace).
Drottningholms Slottsteater *(Jun–Aug)* Season of concerts, opera and dance throughout the summer in the 18th-century court theatre.
Palace Gala *(mid-Jun)* Concerts featuring the popular classics as well as more modern music played by international stars in the park at Ulriksdals Slott.
Boules Festival *(mid-Jun)*. Boules enthusiasts gather in Kungsträdgården.

Crayfish

JULY

Round Gotland Race *(first week in Jul)*. Major international sailing event, with start and finish at Sandhamn.
DN Gala *(Jul)*. Major international athletics competition at Stockholm Stadion.

Stockholm International Jazz & Blues Festival *(third week in Jul)*. Great artists from around the world play in a fantastic outdoor setting on Skeppsholmen.

AUGUST

Midnight Race *(early Aug)*. Night-time running over 10 km (6 miles) in Söder with around 16,000 participants.
"Recykling" *(second week in Aug)*. A festival of environmentally-oriented events of 4,000 cyclists at Kungsträdgården.
Philharmonikerna i det Gröna *(2nd Sun in Aug)*. Royal Philharmonic Orchestra performs free for picnicking music-lovers on the lawn by Sjöhistoriska Museet.
"Tjejmilen" *(last Sun in Aug)*. About 25,000 female runners compete in a 10-km (6-mile) event at Gärdet.
Crayfish Season *(last week in Aug)*. Swedes eat crayfish and sing "schnapps songs".

AVERAGE MONTHLY RAINFALL

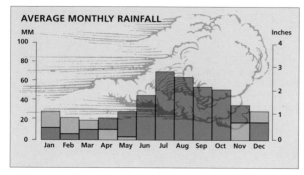

MM
100
80
60
40
20
0

Jan Feb Mar Apr May Jun Jul Aug Sep Oct Nov Dec

Inches
4
3
2
1
0

Rainfall Chart

Some years Stockholm can have very rainy summers, but in other years the weather can be dry for several weeks at a time. Heavy snowfall in winter may lie until March, but some winters have been known to be virtually free of snow.

■ Rain (from the baseline)
▨ Snow (from the baseline)

AUTUMN

Early autumn mornings can be crisp and clear, but summer often stages a successful and lengthy last-ditch stand, and the trees explode in a cascade of colours.

Globen and other indoor arenas draw increasingly large attendances, and cultural activities in theatres and art galleries get under way again, although many outdoor events continue well into the autumn, weather permitting.

Chanterelles

SEPTEMBER

Now is the time to pick mushrooms in the forests, or apples, pears and plums in the garden. The summer cottages are shut and the boats are laid up for the winter, but there is still a lot going on in the capital.
Riddarfjärden Regatta *(first weekend in Sep)*. About 100 fine old wooden boats compete in this regatta.
Stockholm Cup *(first weekend in Sep)*. Horse race at Täby course with an international field.

Elite Series *(first weekend in Sep)*. The season's first ice-hockey matches at Globen.
Swedish Army Tattoo *(first weekend in Sep, even-numbered years)*. Military bands and display groups perform at Globen.
Stockholm Race *(last weekend in Sep)*. Fun-run round the city centre starting from Stadion.
Pet Fair *(last weekend in Sep)*. Pets of all kinds on show at Soluntuna Exhibition Centre.
Lidingö Race *(end of Sep)*. The world's largest cross-country race with tens of thousands of competitors of all ages, including elite runners, senior citizens and children.

OCTOBER

This is a busy time for theatres, cinemas, restaurants and clubs. There are fewer outdoor events, instead people head for the parks and forests for autumn strolls.
Stockholm Open *(mid-Oct)*. ATP tennis tournament at Kungliga Tennishallen.
Popcorn *(mid-Oct)*. An eight-day film festival at cinemas in the city centre.

Annual Stockholm International Horse Show at Globen

NOVEMBER

As darkness falls over the city, there is a wide selection of events to choose from.
Autumn Antiques Fair *(mid-Nov)*. Notable antiques fair with a chance of some real finds at Wasahallen.
Scandinavian Sail and Motor Boat Show *(mid-Nov)*. Exhibition at Stockholm International Fairs with everything for large motor boats or yachts.
Det Goda Köket cookery exhibition *(mid-Nov)*. Food, wine, cooking equipment and master classes at Stockholm International Fairs.
Skating Premiere *(mid-Nov)*. Skating with music starts on a rink in Kungsträdgården.
Stockholm Film Festival *(mid-Nov)*. Ten-day event with public screenings and the presentation of awards.
Stockholm International Horse Show *(late Nov)*. World Cup competition in dressage and jumping plus entertainment at Globen.
Christmas displays *(late Nov)*. Shop windows and streets are seasonally decorated.

Profusion of autumn colours in Hagaparken

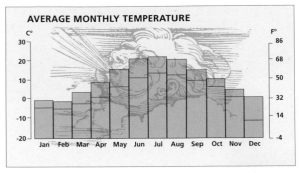

AVERAGE MONTHLY TEMPERATURE

Temperature Chart

Stockholm has a maritime climate and is much milder than might be expected. The summers are usually fairly cool, but sometimes there can be hot sunshine for several weeks running. Winter temperatures often fall below freezing, but it is rarely severely cold. The average maximum and minimum temperatures are shown.

WINTER

Winter can vary from temperatures a few degrees above freezing with slush on the streets to sparkling sunny days with the city under a dazzling white blanket of snow, ice-covered water and temperatures well below zero. Stockholmers get out their skis, skates, or toboggans, or go for long walks. There are also several cultural and sporting events.

DECEMBER

Sometimes the eagerly awaited Christmas season seems a long way off, but there is no shortage of activities in early December, when some of the year's most important events are staged.
Handicraft and Arts Exhibition *(early Dec)*. Popular arts and crafts show at Sollentuna Exhibition Centre.
Nobel Day *(10 Dec)*. The year's Nobel Prize laureates are honoured in a ceremony at Konserthuset (Concert Hall). In the evening the royal family attends a banquet at Stadshuset (City Hall).

Lucia, the "Queen of Light", with her attendants at Skansen

Lucia Celebrations *(13 Dec)*. Sweden's white-clad Lucia, the "Queen of Light", with her girl attendants and "star boys", serves the Nobel laureates early morning coffee with saffron buns and performs traditional songs. In the evening a Lucia procession winds through the city to celebrations and fireworks at Skansen. Many Swedish homes, schools and workplaces have their own Lucia.
Christmas Markets *(from early Dec)*. Christmas goods on sale at traditional markets at Skansen, Rosendals Slott, Stortorget in Gamla Stan and Drottningholms Slott.
Christmas *(24–26 Dec)*. Filled with traditions, Christmas is the most important Swedish holiday. The main event is Christmas Eve, when an abundant *smörgåsbord* is followed by gifts, often delivered by a family member disguised as Father Christmas.
Christmas Sales *(first weekday after Christmas)* Shops start their sales.
Ice Sculptures *(late Dec)*. If the weather permits, Djurgården is the centre for this unusual art form.
New Year *(31 Dec–1 Jan)*. A major festival when many Stockholmers go out on the town. Traditional celebrations at Skansen include a reading of Tennyson's *"Ring out wild bells…"* on the stroke of midnight. Churches ring their bells, and there is a spectacular fireworks display.

Christmas market at Stortorget in Gamla Stan, a traditional prelude to the festive season

JANUARY

Winter Games *(early Jan)*. This youth sports festival takes place at various venues around the city and features a selection of both indoor and outdoor sports.

FEBRUARY

Globen Gala *(early Feb)*. International athletics stars converge on the Globen arena for one of the world's best indoor competitions.
Antiques Fair *(mid-Feb)*. A highlight for antiques lovers, staged at Stockholm International Fairs, Älvsjö.

PUBLIC HOLIDAYS

New Year (1 Jan).
Epiphany (6 Jan)
Good Friday
Easter Monday
Ascension Day (6th Thu after Easter)
Labour Day (1 May)
Whit Monday (May/Jun)
Midsummer Eve (end Jun)
Christmas Day (25 Dec)
Boxing Day (26 Dec)

STOCKHOLM AT A GLANCE

The old conception of Stockholm as a small, rustic capital of a cold country far away to the north is no longer valid – the city has a rich cultural heritage and has become a dynamic Continental-style capital.

Stockholm is an unbelievably beautiful city, surrounded by clear water and unspoilt countryside which stretches right into the heart of the urban area. Stockholm's 750-year history has produced many beautiful buildings, as well as plenty of impressive cultural treasures which can be discovered in its fine museums.

To make your visit as rewarding as possible the following 10 pages give a quick guide to the best museums and palaces, the most distinguished architecture, and outstanding modern design. Activities along the city's quaysides and waterways are also described. Below is a selection of sights that should not be missed.

STOCKHOLM'S TOP TEN SIGHTS

Stadshuset
See pp114–15

Nordiska museet
See pp90–91

Skansen
See pp96–7

Drottningholm
See pp146–49

Historiska Museet
See pp104–105

Moderna Museet
See pp80–81

Stockholm's Archipelago
See pp150–51

Nationalmuseum
See pp82–3

Royal Palace and its Guard
See pp50–53

Vasamuseet
See pp92–4

◁ Gamla Stan, and its romantic streets like Österlånggatan, is one of Stockholm's leading attractions

Stockholm's Best: Museums

Stockholm has around 100 museums. Their remarkable collections cover every conceivable subject and interest. The "Top Ten" shown here are of particular note. Kungliga Slottet (the Royal Palace), for instance, is effectively four museums in one, while the most spectacular is the museum housing the *Vasa* warship, salvaged from the depths of Stockholm's harbour after 333 years and now an international attraction.

Hallwylska Palatset
Thanks to a methodical countess and her impeccable taste this lavishly decorated palace from the 1890s has become a magnificent museum with 67,000 exhibits displayed in an original setting.

VASASTADEN

Medeltidsmuseet
Parts of the city wall from the 1530s can be seen in this underground Museum of Medieval Stockholm, which focuses on the capital's origins. The wall's reconstruction shows medieval building techniques.

CITY

Nationalmuseum
The National Museum of Fine Arts, Sweden's largest art museum, has fine collections of 17th- and 18th-century Swedish paintings and handicrafts, 18th-century French and 17th-century Dutch art. Rubens's Bacchanal on Andros dates from the 1630s.

SÖDERMALM

The Royal Palace
In addition to its own attractions, the Royal Palace houses four specialist museums: the Treasury, featuring Erik XIV's State Orb (1561); the Royal Armoury; Gustav III's Museum of Antiquities; and the Tre Kronor Museum.

0 metres	500
0 yards	500

Historiska Museet

Behind the sculpted bronze gateways of the Museum of National Antiquities is a wealth of material, including a section on Viking life. The Gold Room shows priceless prehistoric finds, such as the Timbobolm Treasure (400–450 BC).

Moderna Museet

Paradise (1966) by Tinguely de Saint Phalle marks the way up to the Modern Museum with its superb collections of international and Swedish modern art.

Sjöhistoriska Museet

The stern of the royal flagship Amphion, *dating from the late 18th century, is one of the many treasures on display in the National Maritime Museum, designed by Ragnar Östberg.*

ÖSTERMALM

Nordiska museet

This colossal building from 1907 houses many different artifacts illustrating everyday Swedish life and customs, including this coat of Count Axel von Fersen (1780s).

SKEPPS-
HOLMEN

DJURGÅRDEN

Skansen

The world's first open-air museum, founded in 1891, shows the Sweden of bygone days with farms and manor houses, urban scenes and crafts people at work. Nordic fauna and flora are also on display.

Vasamuseet

A fatal capsizal in 1628 and a successful salvage operation 333 years later gave Stockholm its most popular museum. The warship Vasa *is now 95% intact after painstaking renovation.*

Exploring Stockholm's Museums

Stockholm's wide range of museums gives the visitor a chance to experience exhibitions covering a multitude of different interests. Many are housed in magnificent historic palaces or institutions with notable collections and the resources to bring each subject to life. In addition, there are numerous specialist museums, including the homes of highly regarded artists. Various important private collections are open to the public. This guide lists more than 50 of the best museums Stockholm has to offer.

Karl XII's uniform, 1718, on show at Livrustkammaren

PALACE MUSEUMS

The period when Sweden was a great power (1611–1718) resulted in a number of beautiful buildings many of which are now museums. Foremost among these are the royal palaces in and around the city. **Kungliga Slottet** (Royal Palace, pp50–53) is a museum in itself. It also houses **Skattkammaren** (the Treasury) with Sweden's royal regalia, crowns and a large silver font for the baptism of royal children.

Also in the Royal Palace are **Gustav III's Antikmuseum**, containing the antique marble sculptures that Gustav III brought home from his Italian travels, and **Livrust-kammaren** (Royal Armoury, p48) where visitors can see a variety of items used at the court through the centuries. **Museum Tre Kronor** reflects the history of the earlier castle.

Other royal museums include **Rosendals Slott** (p98) on Djurgården, a pre-

fabricated building from the 1820s in Karl Johan (Empire) style. **Gustav III's Paviljong** (pp122–3) in Hagaparken has furnishings and decorations which are fine examples of the late 18th-century Gustavian style. **Ulriksdals Slott** (p125) has some interesting interiors, including a living room for King Gustav VI Adolf and Queen Louise.

In a class of its own is **Drottningholms Slott** (pp146–49), a UNESCO heritage site, which includes a notable theatre museum.

HISTORICAL MUSEUMS

Several of Stockholm's museums focus on various historic aspects. **Historiska Museet** (Museum of National Antiquities, pp104–105) has treasures from prehistoric times in its magnificent Gold Room, as well as a superb section on the Vikings. **Nordiska museet** (pp90–91) and the open-air **Skansen** (pp96–7) show Swedish customs and traditions alongside traditional wooden homes. **Stockholms Stadsmuseum** (City Museum, p127) tells the story of Stockholm and its citizens. It also has a reference library.

The city's earliest history is highlighted at **Medeltidsmuseet** (Medieval Museum, p59). **Etnografiska Museet** (National Museum of Ethnography, p108) features anthropological

Amor and Psyche by J T Sergel, Nationalmuseum

Decorative Viking brooch, Historiska Museet

artifacts from all around the world.

The culture and history of the Jewish people is the theme of **Judiska Museet** (p118). **Medelhavsmuseet** (Museum of Mediterranean and Near Eastern Antiquities, p65) focuses on architecture and sculptures from the countries around the Mediterranean. **Östasiatiska Museet** (Museum of Far Eastern Antiquities, p78) contains large collections of arts and crafts from China, Japan, Korea and India.

ART MUSEUMS

The wide range of collections at the **National-museum** (National Museum of Fine Arts, pp82–3) cover European and Swedish paintings up to the early 20th century, as well as Swedish handicrafts and design. **Moderna Museet** (pp80–81) on Skeppsholmen has an outstanding collection of contemporary Swedish and international art. **Arkitektur-museet** (Museum of Architecture, p78), highlights Swedish building techniques over the last 1,000 years and provides an overview of the wider international picture.

Three magnificent art galleries are located in beautiful

buildings on Djurgården.
Liljevalchs Konsthall *(p95)*
focuses on 20th-century
Swedish and international art,
while **Waldemarsudde** *(p99)*
and **Thielska Galleriet** *(p99)*
both specialize in Swedish
and Nordic art from the late
19th to the early 20th century.

Spökslottet (the Haunted
Palace, *p116)* shows
Stockholm University's
collection of classic Swedish
paintings, as well as artistic
Swedish glass.

Millesgården *(p150)* on
Lidingö is where the sculptor
Carl Milles lived and worked,
and where he is now buried.
Some of his best works are on
show in a beautiful outdoor
setting with a panoramic view
of Stockholm.

MARINE MUSEUMS

A city located on water
offers plenty of interest for
anyone interested in ships
and the sea.

One of the city's biggest
attractions, **Vasamuseet**
(pp92–4), shows the
magnificent and almost intact
warship *Vasa*, which sank in
Stockholm harbour after a
maiden voyage of only
1,300 m (1,400 yd). In
addition to the painstakingly
restored hull, there are other
exhibits which give an insight
into life on board a 17th-
century warship.

Close to *Vasa* are
Museifartygen (Musum
Ships, *p89)*, including one of
the last Swedish lightships,
Finngrundet (1903), and the
powerful ice-breaker *St Erik*
(1915) featuring Europe's
largest marine steam engine.

Nearby is **Aquaria** *(p95)*,
where visitors can see a
variety of animals and plants
in a living ecological system
of tropical rainforest, sea
and Nordic waters.

Sjöhistoriska Museet
(National Maritime Museum,
p106) features a fine
collection of model ships.

A short boat trip takes visitors to the **Fjäderholmarna**
islands, where there are two
boat museums, an angling
museum and a Baltic
aquarium *(p150)*.

Drawing room in the lavishly decorated Hallwylska Palatset

MUSEUMS IN PRIVATE HOMES

One of the pearls among
Stockholm's museums,
Hallwylska Palatset *(p73)*, is
an opulent private residence
from the late 19th century,
complete with original
furnishings. The home of the
dramatist and author August
Strindberg, which became
**Strindbergsmuseet Blå
Tornet** (Strindberg's Blue
Tower Museum, *p69)*, gives
an insight into his life. A
statue of Strindberg by Carl
Eldh stands near **Carl Eldhs
Ateljémuseum** (Studio
Museum, *p121)*, the sculptor's
former residence.

MUSEUMS FOR SPECIAL INTERESTS

Stockholm has many
museums catering for special
interests. **Kungliga
Myntkabinettet** (Royal Coin
Cabinet, *p48)* shows coins

Stage costume from *Les Ballets
Suédois* (1920s), Dansmuseet

and other methods of pay-
ment dating back 1,000 years.

Junibacken *(p88)* is a
charming museum, bringing
to life the classic children's
books by Astrid Lindgren.

Leksaksmuseet (Toy
Museum, *p131)* is an
attraction for all ages with
its mechanical toys, models,
dolls and dolls' houses.

A traditional wine shop and
distillery can be seen at Vin-
& Sprithistoriska Museet
(Wine and Spirits Museum,
p120), housed in a former
wine warehouse. Another
human weakness, tobacco,
is documented at Skansen's
Tobaksmuseet (Museum of
Matches and Tobacco).

Postmuseum (Postal
Museum, *p55)* contains more
than 4 million stamps from
around the world.

Spårvägsmuseet (Transport
Museum, *p130)* has some
40 original trams and a large
collection of models. In the
same area is the delightful
**Almgrens Sidenväveri &
Museum** (Almgren's Silk-
weaving Mill & Museum,
p127).

The life of the 18th-century
troubadour Carl Michael Bellman *(p98)*, is portrayed at the
Bellmanmuseet *(p132)* on
Långholmen.

Dansmuseet (Dance
Museum, *p65)* reflects all
aspects of dance with a
superb international collection.

Musikmuseet (Music
Museum, *p72)* has some
6,000 instruments and the
country's biggest musical
archive, in which folk music
addicts can browse through
records covering 20,000
traditional ballads.

Stockholm's Best: Architecture

Sweden was spared the ravages of World War II, so Stockholm has preserved a rich variety of architectural treasures. Gamla Stan was the city's first built-up area. The surrounding districts known as Malmarna *(see p101)* remained mainly rural until an intensive period of building begun in the second half of the 19th century. From 1930 the city started to expand further and this period is reflected in a band of Functionalist-style buildings. Suburbs like Farsta and Vällingby were built after 1945. In the 1990s, new buildings began appearing in the inner city on former industrial sites.

Stadsbiblioteket
(Erik Gunnar Asplund, 1920–28). The City Library is Stockholm's most admired example of the 1920s Neo-Classicist style. The book hall has a fascinating cylindrical shape and many fine interior details. (See p117.)

VASASTADEN

Kungliga Dramatiska Teatern
(Fredrik Liljekvist, 1901–1908). The Royal Dramatic Theatre is one of Stockholm's few monumental buildings in Jugendstil. The façades are of white marble, and inside the staircase and foyer are embellished with lavish gold decorative work. (See p72.)

CITY

Nybrov

KUNGSHOLMEN

GAMLA STAN

Ström

SÖDERMALM

The Royal Palace
(Nicodemus Tessin the Younger 1690–1704; completed under Carl Hårleman). Work on the Royal Palace, based on plans by Tessin the Younger, started after the fire in 1697. The façade exhibits influences of Roman palaces; the magnificent interiors are of French and Swedish design. (See pp50–53.)

Wrangelska Palatset
(Nicodemus Tessin the Elder 1652–70). This is one of several majestic palaces built on Riddarholmen in the imposing style popular during the 17th century. Original details include the gateway and the courtyard arcade. (See p56.)

Tessinparken
(Arvid Stille, 1930 city plan by Sture Frölén). Functionalist style on a large scale was tested on the three-storey buildings on pillars at Tessinparken. (See p110.)

THE TESSIN TRIO

Nicodemus Tessin the Younger (1654–1728), who designed the Royal Palace *(see pp50–53)*, can be regarded as Sweden's leading architect because he influenced not only building design but also city planning, landscape gardening and handicrafts. His father, Nicodemus Tessin the Elder (1615–81), designed several country mansions, with Drott-ningholm Palace being his master work *(see pp146–49)*. The third-generation Tessin, Carl Gustaf (1695–1770), along with Carl Hårle-man, introduced the Rococo style to Sweden.

Etching of the Royal Palace, to which all three Tessins contributed

Nordiska museet
(Isak Gustaf Clason, 1889–1907). This museum was conceived as a national monument for Nordic culture. The impressive building in a Scandinavian version of Renaissance style is only one-third of its planned size. (See pp90–91.)

ÖSTERMALM

Moderna Museet
(Rafael Moneo, 1995–8). The spacious Modern Museum was designed to be novel yet not to disturb the historically sensitive surroundings of the island of Skeppsholmen. (See pp80–81.)

KEPPS-
OLMEN

DJURGÅRDEN

STOCKHOLM'S SURROUNDING AREAS

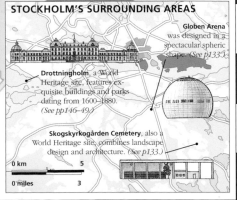

Globen Arena was designed in a spectacular spheric shape. *(See p133.)*

Drottningholm, a World Heritage site, features exquisite buildings and parks dating from 1600–1880. *(See pp146–49.)*

Skogskyrkogården Cemetery, also a World Heritage site, combines landscape design and architecture. *(See p133.)*

0 km   5

0 miles   3

Söder Cottages
Wooden cottages for port workers started to spring up from the early 18th century. Quite a few remain in the Söder area, for example at Åsöberget and on Fjällgatan. (See p129.)

metres   500

yards   500

Swedish Style

Swedish design first attracted international attention at the 1925 World Exhibition in Paris, when glassware in particular took the world by storm and the concept of "Swedish Grace" was launched. The nation's design tradition is characterized by its simplicity and functionality with an emphasis on natural materials. Swedish designers and architects are renowned for creating simple, attractive "human" objects for everyday use. The 1990s marked the beginning of a new golden age in which contemporary Swedish design once more won worldwide acclaim.

Stoneware, Hans Hedberg
Swedish stoneware from the 1940s, 1950s and 1960s attrac worldwide attention, and colle tors buy anything they can fine

Armchair (1969), Bruno Mathsson
Bruno Mathsson, one of Sweden's most famous 20th-century furniture designers, is one of the creators of what came to be known as the "Swedish Modern" style. He designed the first version of the Pernilla *armchair in 1942.*

Pale wood and simplicity is the concept most closely associated with Swedish style.

Bureau (1952), Josef Frank
Frank was born in Austria but worked in Sweden and was another disciple of the "Swedish Modern" style. He is best known for his printed textiles for Svenskt Tenn (see p184), but also designed furniture.

Rag mats are an old Swedish weaving tradition taken up by Karin Larsson, whose skill as a textile designer is now widely recognized.

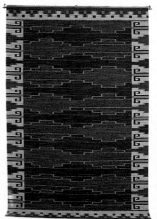

Carpet (1931), Märta Måås-Fjetterström
From 1919 Måås-Fjetterström wove her highly regarded carpets at her studio in southern Sweden. Her work was inspired by folklore and nature, and she created a design concept that was new but still deeply rooted in tradition.

Silver coffee pot (1953), Sigurd Persson
Persson had an unrivalled ability to handle metal. He made a big impact on the history of design with both his everyday industrial work and his exclusive artistic creations.

Flowers and plants along a windowsill and no curtains typify the Larssons' ideas on interior decoration.

Chair (1981), Jonas Bohlin
The Concrete chair became the most remarkable piece of Swedish furniture design in the 1980s. A graduation project, it represented a completely new approach to furniture design.

Bookshelf (1989), John Kandell
Books are placed flat on the Pilaster bookshelf instead of stacking them in the usual way. The lines are simple and typically Scandinavian. The maker, Källemo, is one of Sweden's most unconventional furniture manufacturers.

Gustavian late 18th-century style elements have remained a strong feature in Swedish design through the centuries, and made a particular comeback in the 1990s.

CARL LARSSON'S SUNDBORN

The home created by the artist Carl Larsson (1853–1919) and his wife Karin, became an inspiration to the world when it featured in his watercolour series *A Home*. The mixture of old and new, pure colours, plants and windows without curtains was an expression of the "Beauty for All" movement.

Vase (1998), Ann Wåhlström
Wåhlström is one of the new young glass designers at Kosta Boda. Her vase, Cyklon, is a good example of contemporary Swedish glass.

WHERE TO SEE SWEDISH DESIGN

Asplund
Sibyllegatan 31. **Map** 3 E3.
Contemporary Swedish and international design.
www.asplund.org

R.O.O.M.
Alströmergatan 20
Map 1 B2.
www.room.se

Svenskt Tenn
Strandvägen 5. **Map** 3 E4.
Josef Frank, etc.
www.svenskttenn.se

Klara
Svartmangatan 8.
Map 4 B3.
Contemporary Swedish and international design.
www.klaradesign.com

Bo
Östgötagatan 2. **Map** 9 D2.
Modern antiques.

Jacksons
Tyska Brinken 20. **Map** 4 B3.
Modern antiques.
www.jacksons.se

Stockholm, the City on the Water

The Swedish capital is often called "The Venice of the North", built as it is on 14 islands surrounded by the clear waters of Lake Mälaren and Saltsjön, an inlet from the Baltic Sea. For most visitors "the green city on the water" is a remarkable experience. Stockholm's quaysides and waterways offer a whole range of activities not normally associated with a capital city, which are made possible only because of the pollution-free environment. The waterside location is Stockholm's most beautiful feature.

Canoe Slalom on Strömmen
Spectacular canoe slalom competitions are held every year in the rushing water of the Strömmen channel below Gustav Adolfs Torg.

Sailing Race on Riddarfjärden
The waters of Stockholm are always busy with sailing boats. The Riddarfjärden Regatta takes place annually in early September in front of Stadshuset (City Hall).

CITY

KUNGSHOLMEN

GAMLA STAN

Strömmen

Riddarfjärden

Långholmen

SÖDERMALM

Swimming in the Heart of the City
During the summer months, swimmers bathe in the clean, warm water (about 20°C/68°F) in the city centre. Långholmen (see p132) has sandy beaches and smooth rocks offering an ideal setting for a refreshing dip.

Fishing for a Living
For 400 years fishermen have cast their nets from boats near Kungliga Slottet (Royal Palace). Today only four boats remain. Of the 30 species found here, smelt is the most commonly caught fish.

Vintage Mahogany Boat
Lovingly renovated vintage motor boats with shining mahogany and brass fittings are often seen on the waterways of Stockholm, as well as the more exclusive Riva racing boats.

Exploring on Your Own
Kayaks, pedalos, rowing boats, motor boats, and sometimes sailing dinghies, can be hired near the Djurgården Bridge by visitors who want to explore the waters of Stockholm on their own.

0 metres	500
0 yards	500

ÖSTERMALM

Djurgårdsbrunnsviken

DJURGÅRDEN

Saltsjön

Fishing for Perch
The clean waters of the inner city are rich in edible fish. Anglers spin for sea trout, and here on Djurgårdsbrunn Canal bait-fishing for perch is popular, and fly-fishing in autumn.

KEY

···· Paved walking path

≈ Open-air swimming

Cruise Ship Manoeuvres in Stockholm's Harbour
Cruise ships are an attractive sight when seen from the heights of Södermalm as they make their way through the narrow channel to their centrally located quay.

Central Stockholm with Gamla Stan and Kungliga Slottet (Royal Palace) in the foreground ▷

STOCKHOLM
AREA BY AREA

GAMLA STAN

Relics of Stockholm's early history as a town in the 13th century can still be found on Stadsholmen, Gamla Stan's (Old Town) largest island. The whole island is one huge area of historical heritage, with the many sights just a few metres apart.

The Royal Palace is the symbol of Sweden's era as a great power in the 17th and early 18th centuries *(see pp18–19)*, and its magnificent state rooms, apartments and artifacts are well matched to the Roman Baroque-style exterior. The historic buildings standing majestically

Anchor point on a palace façade

around Slottsbacken, underline Stockholm's role as a capital city.

This area has a special atmosphere with much to offer: from the bustling streets of souvenir shops, bookstores and antique shops to elegant palaces, churches and museums. Many medieval cellars are now restaurants and cafés, while the narrow streets recall a bygone era.

Bridges lead to Riddarholmen, with its 17th-century palaces and royal crypt, and to Helgeandsholmen for the newer splendours of Riksdagshuset (the Parliament building).

SIGHTS AT A GLANCE

Palaces and Museums
Kungliga
  Myntkabinettet ❸
Livrustkammaren ❷
Medeltidsmuseet ❹
Postmuseum ❿
The Royal Palace
  pp50–53 ❶

Public Buildings
Bondeska Palatset ⓱
Riddarhuset ⓰
Riksdagshuset ⓲
Stenbockska Palatset ⓯

Historic Buildings
Birger Jarls Torn ⓮

Tessinska Palatset ❹
Wrangelska Palatset ⓬

Streets and Squares
Evert Taubes Terrass ⓭
Mårten Trotzigs Gränd ❽
Stortorget ❻
Västerlånggatan ❾

Churches
Riddarholms-
  kyrkan ⓫
Storkyrkan ❺
Tyska Kyrkan ❼

KEY

- ▦ Street-by-Street map
  See pp46–7
- ⛴ Ferry landing point
- Ⓣ Tunnelbana station
- 🚌 Bus stop

| 0 metres | 250 |
| 0 yards | 250 |

◁ **Prästgatan in Gamla Stan with its yellow ochre plastering typical of the 18th century**

Street-by-Street: Slottsbacken

Slottsbacken is much more than just a steep hill linking Skeppsbron and the highest part of Gamla Stan (Old Town). It also provides the background for ceremonial processions and the daily changing-of-the-guard, and is the route for visiting heads of state and foreign ambassadors when they have an audience with the king at the Royal Palace. Alongside Slottsbacken the palace displays its most attractive façade, with the entrance to the Treasury (Skattkammaren), State Room (Rikssalen) and Palace Church (Slottskyrkan). Nicodemus Tessin the Younger's ambition to make Stockholm a leading European city in monumental terms was realized in 1799 with the addition of the Obelisk.

The Olaus Petri statue by Storkyrkan stands in front of a tablet telling the history of the cathedral since 1264.

Outer Courtyard

Axel Oxenstiernas Palats (1653) is, for Stockholm, an unusual example of the style known as Roman Mannerism. For 30 years, Axel Oxenstierna (1583–1654) himself was a dominant figure in Swedish power politics.

The Obelisk by Louis Jean Desprez was erected in 1799 to thank the citizens for their support of Gustav III's Russian war in 1788–90.

Stock Exchange *(See p54)*

TRÅNGSUND

STOR–TORGET

★ **Storkyrkan**
An impressive cathedral with a late Gothic interior, it is full of treasures from many different eras ❺

Stortorget
This square is the heart of the "city between the bridges", with a well dating from 1778. It was the scene of the Stockholm Bloodbath in 1520 ❻

STAR SIGHTS

★ The Royal Palace

★ Livrustkammaren

★ Storkyrkan

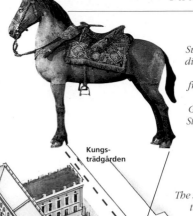

Kungs-
trädgården

LOCATOR MAP
See Street Finder map 4

★ **Livrustkammaren**
*Sweden's oldest museum
displays royal weaponry,
clothing and carriages
from over five centuries.
The picture shows
Gustaf II Adolf's stallion
Streiff, from the battle of
Lützen in 1632* ❷

★ **The Royal Palace**
*The southern façade has a
triumphal central arch
with four niches for
statues, created by
French artists
in the 18th
century* ❶

SKEPPSBRON

SLOTTSBACKEN

ÖSTERLÅNGGATAN

**Gustav III's
statue** was
sculpted by J T
Sergel in 1799 in
memory of the
"charming king"
who was mur-
dered in 1792.

↓ Slussen

KÖPMANGATAN

Köpmantorget with
statue of St George Slay-
ing the Dragon (1912).

Kungliga Myntkabinettet
*In a 16th-century setting, the Royal
Coin Cabinet has the world's largest
stamped coin, dating from 1644* ❸

Finska Kyrkan, Slottsbacken's oldest building,
dates from the 1640s. It
was originally a royal ball-
games court for the palace,
but since 1725 it has been
the religious centre for the
Finnish community.

Tessinska Palatset
*Built by and for Nicodemus Tessin
the Younger, architect of the Royal
Palace, in 1694–7, this palace has
been the residence of the Governor
of Stockholm County since 1968* ❹

| 0 metres | | 100 |
| 0 yards | | 100 |

KEY

– – – Suggested route

The Royal Palace ❶

See pp50–53.

Livrust-
kammaren ❷

Slottsbacken 3. **Map** 4 C2.
Tel 519 555 44. Ⓣ Gamla Stan.
🚌 2, 43, 55, 76. ◯ Jun–Aug:
10am–5pm daily; Sep–May: 11am–
5pm Tue–Sun (Thu also 5–8pm).
🎫 Eng: Jul–Aug. 🄰 ∅ 🄳 🄴
www.livrustkammaren.se

Sweden's oldest museum,
Livrustkammaren (the Royal
Armoury) was founded in
1628 and is full of *objets d'art*
and everyday items used by
the Royal Family over the
past five centuries. The oldest
exhibit is Gustav Vasa's
crested helmet dating from
1548. The museum also
houses a variety of royal
items which illustrate
events in Swedish
history. Among
them are Gustav II
Adolf's stuffed
stallion, Streiff,
which he rode at
the Battle of Lützen
in 1632; Gustav
III's costume from
the notorious
masked ball at
which he was murdered in
1792; and Karl XII's blue
uniform with the still muddy
boots he had on when he
died at the siege of
Frerikshald in Norway in 1718.

Coronation ceremonies are
illustrated by costumes such
as those worn by King Adolf
Fredrik and Queen Lovisa
Ulrika in 1751. The King's
attire alone was adorned with
some 2 kg (4 lb) of silver. The
coronation carriage, originally

**The coronation carriage of King Adolf Fredrik
and Queen Lovisa Ulrika in Livrustkammaren**

built in the 17th century, was
modernized for this event. Its
renovation in the 1970s took
eight years and cost 700,000
kronor. The cellar vault, once
used for firewood, is skilfully
lit, providing an imaginative
setting for the exhibits.

Kungliga
Myntkabinettet ❸

Slottsbacken 6. **Map** 4 C3.
Tel 519 553 04. Ⓣ Gamla Stan.
🚌 2, 43, 55, 59, 76. ◯ 10am–4pm
daily. 🎫 by arrangement. 🖼 🄳 🍴
🖥 🄴 **www**.myntkabinettet.se

The Royal Coin Cabinet is a
museum highlighting the
history of money from the
10th century to the present
day – from the little cowrie
shell via the drachma and
denarius to the cash card of
the 21st century. The
museum also gives an
insight into the art
of medal design
over the past 600
years and shows
both traditional
portrait medals and
more modern
examples like
those that have
been awarded to
Nobel laureates.

**Sweden's first coin,
struck in about AD 995**

Visitors can also see the first
Swedish coin, struck in the
late 10th century by King Olof
Skötkonung. Other rarities
include Queen Kristina's coin
from 1644, weighing 19.7 kg
(43 lb) and reckoned to be
the world's heaviest coin.
From the island of Yap in
Micronesia the museum has
acquired the world's largest
means of payment, a so-
called "rai-stone" which greets
visitors in the foyer.

The many
sections in the
museum include
"The World's
Money", "State
Finance" and
"Saving in a Piggy
Bank and Bank".
"Summa
Summarum" is a
section designed
for children and
illustrates the use
of money in play
and real life.

**The elegant Baroque garden in
Tessinska Palatset's courtyard**

Tessinska
Palatset ❹

Slottsbacken 4. **Map** 2 C3.
Ⓣ Gamla Stan. 🚌 2, 43, 55, 59, 76.
⬤ to the public.

The Tessin Palace at Slottsbacken is considered by
many to be the most beautiful
private residence north of
Paris. It is the best-preserved
palace from Sweden's era as a
great power in the 17th
century and was designed by
and for Tessin the Younger
(1654–1728), the nation's
most renowned architect.

Completed in 1697, the
building is located on a
narrow site which widens out
towards a courtyard with a
delightful Baroque garden.
The relatively discreet façade
with its beautiful porch was
inspired by the exterior
design of Roman palaces.
The decor and garden were
influenced by Tessin's time in
Paris and Versailles.

Tessin, who became a count
and State Councillor, spent
large sums on the building's
ornamentation. Sculptures and
paintings were provided by
the same French masters
whose work had graced the
Royal Palace. Later, however,
his son, Carl Gustaf, had to sell
the palace for financial reasons.

The building was acquired
by the City of Stockholm as a
residence for its Governor in
1773. In 1968 it became the
residence of the Governor of
the County of Stockholm.

Storkyrkan ⑤

Trångsund 1. **Map** 4 B3.
Tel 723 30 16. ⊤ Gamla Stan.
🚌 2, 43, 55, 59, 76. ☐ May–Aug:
9am–6pm daily; Sep–Apr: 9am–4pm
daily. ⬆ 11am Sat & Sun. ◪ Eng:
Jul–Aug: 1pm (tour of the tower 2pm).
♿ ⊘ (during services). ⊓

Stockholm's 700-year-old cathedral is of great national religious importance. It was from here that the Swedish reformer Olaus Petri (1493–1552) spread his Lutheran message around the kingdom. It is also used for royal ceremonies.

Originally, a small village church was built on this site in the 13th century, probably by the city's founder Birger Jarl. It was replaced in 1306 by a much bigger basilica, St Nicholas, which was altered over the centuries.

The Gothic character of the interior, acquired in the 15th century, was revealed in 1908 when, during restoration work, plaster was removed from the pillars, exposing the characteristic red tiling. The late Baroque period provided the so-called "royal chairs" and the pulpit, while the façade was adapted to bring it into keeping with the rest of the area around the Royal Palace. The 66-m (216-ft) high

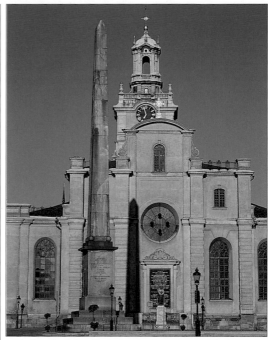

Storkyrkan's façade in Italian Baroque style, seen from Slottsbacken

tower, added in 1743, has four bells, the largest of which weighs about 6 tons.

The cathedral houses some priceless artistic treasures, including *St George and the Dragon*, regarded as one of the finest late Gothic works of art in Northern Europe. The sculpture, situated to the left of the altar, was carved from oak and elk horn by Lübeck sculptor Bernt Notke. Unveiled in 1489, it commemorates Sten Sture the Elder's victory over the Danes in 1471 (*see p15*).

The Last Judgment (1696) is a massive Baroque painting by David Klöcker von Ehrenstrahl. The 3.7-m (12-ft) high bronze candelabra before the altar, likely to be German, has adorned the cathedral for some 600 years. One of

the cathedral's most prized treasures is the silver altar, which gave the interior a completely new appearance in the 1650s. It was a gift from the diplomat Johan Adler Salvius.

The pews nearest to the chancel, the "royal chairs", were designed by Nicodemus Tessin the Younger in 1684 to be used by royalty on special occasions. In 1705, the pulpit was installed

Storkyrkan's silver altar (detail)

above the grave of Olaus Petri.

On 20 April 1535, a light phenomenon was observed over Stockholm – six rings with sparkling solar halos. *The Parhelion Painting*, recalling the event (*see p14*), hangs in Storkyrkan and is thought to be the oldest portrayal of the capital. It shows the modest skyline dominated by the cathedral, at that time still the basilica of St Nicholas.

The sculpture *St George and the Dragon* by Bernt Notke (1489) in Storkyrkan

The Royal Palace (Kungliga Slottet) ❶

Royal Sceptre

Defensive installations or castles have stood on the island of Stadsholmen ever since the 11th century. The Tre Kronor (Three Crowns) fortress was completed in the mid-13th century, but during the following century it became a royal residence. The Vasa kings turned the fortress into a Renaissance palace which burned to the ground in 1697. In its place the architect Nicodemus Tessin the Younger created a new palace in Roman style with an Italianate exterior and a French interior toned down by Swedish influences. The palace's 608 rooms were decorated by Europe's foremost artists and craftsmen. King Adolf Fredrik was the first king to move into the palace, in 1754. It is no longer the king's private residence, but remains one of the city's leading sights.

★ Changing of the Guard
Stockholm's most popular tourist event is the daily changing of the guard at midday in the Outer Courtyard.

Entrance to the State Apartments

The Western Staircase
Tessin was especially proud of the two stair-cases, made from Swedish marble and porphyry. On the western staircase stands a bust of the gifted architect.

★ The Hall of State
This opulent hall has an atmosphere of ceremonial splendour and forms an ideal setting for Queen Kristina's silver throne, probably the palace's most famous treasure.

The Guest Apartments

Entrance to Treasury and Royal Chapel

A ROYAL WORKPLACE

The king and queen have their offices at the palace, where they hold audiences with visiting dignitaries, and official ceremonies. They travel around the country attending special events, official openings and anniversaries, and they make regular State visits abroad. The king is well known for his interest in the environment while the queen is heavily involved with her work for children, especially the disabled.

King Carl XVI Gustav and Queen Silvia

The Royal Chapel
This delightful little church has a rich interior decorated by many different artists. The pulpit is the work of J P Bouchardon.

STAR FEATURES

★ Karl XI's Gallery

★ The Hall of State

★ Changing the Guard

VISITORS' CHECKLIST

Gamla Stan. **Map** 4 B2.
Tel *402 61 30.* 🚇 *Gamla Stan,
Kungsträdgården.* 🚌 *43, 46, 55,
59, 76.* **The Royal Apartments,
The Treasury, Gustav III's
Museum of Antiquities, Tre
Kronor Museum** ◯ *15 May–
Aug: 10am–4pm daily; Sep–14
May: noon–3pm Tue–Sun.* ⬤
*during official functions of the
Court.* 🎫 *for tours in English,
call 402 61 30 for details.* 📷
📷 ♿ 🚻 **The Royal Chapel**
◯ *Jun– Aug: noon–3pm Wed
& Fri; Mass 11am Sun.*
✝ *May–Aug: 11am Sun.* 📷 ♿
www.royalcourt.se

Gustav III's State Bedchamber

*Sergel's bust of Gustav III (1779)
stands in the room where the king
died after being shot at the Opera
House. The decor by J E Rehn
dates from the 1770s.*

The Bernadotte Apartments
are situated on the floor below
Karl XI's Gallery.

**Tre Kronor
Museum**
entrance from
Lejonbacken.

★ Karl XI's Gallery

*One of the most
magnificent rooms in
the palace, this fine
example of Swedish
Late Baroque is used
for banquets hosted by
the king and queen.
In the cabinet is this
priceless salt-cellar
dating from 1627–8.*

Carl Hårleman
played an
important role in
the design of the
palace. His bust
adorns this niche.

Logården
is the terrace
between the
palace's east
wings.

**Livrustkammaren
(see p48)**

Gustav III's Museum of Antiquities

*The museum's collection includes
antique statues brought home by
Gustav III from his journey to Rome.*

Exploring the Royal Palace

The public areas of the Royal Palace allow you to walk through grand rooms of sumptuous furnishings and priceless works of art and craftsmanship. The Hall of State and the Royal Chapel are both characterized by their magnificent lavish decor and Gustav III's Museum of Antiquities contains ancient marble sculptures from the king's journey to Italy. The palace also houses the Treasury with the State regalia; the new Tre Kronor Museum, which depicts the palace before the 1697 fire; and the Livrustkammaren *(see p48)*.

The Pillar Hall in the Bernadotte Apartments with original decor

Karl XI's Gallery, the finest example of the Late Baroque period in Sweden

THE STATE APARTMENTS

The royal family has lived at Drottningholm Palace *(see pp146–49)* since 1982, but official functions still take place in the State Apartments, including banquets hosted by the king during visits by foreign heads of state. Other official dinners are staged here, as well as the festivities held every year to honour the Nobel laureates.

These meals are served in Karl XI's Gallery, the finest example of Swedish Late Baroque, modelled on the Hall of Mirrors at Versailles. Each window is matched with a niche on the inner wall where some of the palace's priceless works of arts and crafts are exhibited. Most remarkable is the salt-cellar made from ivory and gilded silver designed by the Flemish painter Rubens (1577–1640). The room known as "The

King Karl XIV Johan's egg cup

White Sea" serves as a drawing room. Gustav III's State Bedchamber, where the king died after being shot at the Opera House in 1792 *(see pp22–3)*, is the height of Gustavian elegance. Along with Queen Sofia Magdalena's State Bedchamber, it was designed by the architect Jean Eric Rehn. The lintels on the doors to the Don Quixote Room, named after the theme of its tapestries, were made by François Boucher and are among the palace's most treasured pieces.

THE GUEST APARTMENTS

An imposing part of the palace, these apartments are where visiting heads of state stay. The beautiful rooms include the Meleager Salon, where official gifts and decorations are exchanged, and a large bedroom with a sculpted and gilded bed. Other impressive rooms are the Inner Salon, whose decor was inspired by the excavations in Pompeii, and the Margareta Room, named after the present king's grandmother, which displays some pictures painted by her.

The apartments contain remarkable works of craftsmanship by such 18th-century masters as Georg Haupt, Ephraim Ståhle and Jean Baptiste Masreliez.

THE BERNADOTTE APARTMENTS

This magnificent suite has earned its name from the gallery displaying portraits of the Bernadotte dynasty. The apartments have some notable ceiling paintings and mid-18th-century chandeliers, and are used for many a ceremonial occasion. The elegant Pillar Hall is the venue for investitures, and the East Octagonal Cabinet with probably the palace's best Rococo decor, is where the king receives foreign ambassadors. Along with the western cabinet, its interior has remained just as it was planned by Carl Hårleman more than 250 years ago.

Oscar II's very masculine Writing Room, dating from the 1870s, also still looks much as it did in his day. However, it is clear the palace was kept up to date with technical advances. Electricity was installed in 1883, and the telephone only one year later.

THE HALL OF STATE

Rococo and Classicism were brought together in perfect harmony by the architects Nicodemus Tessin the Younger and Carl Hårleman when they designed the two-storey Hall of State. It provides a worthy framework for Queen Kristina's silver throne, a gift for the coronation in 1650 and one of the most valuable treasures in the palace. The throne was given to the Queen by Magnus Gabriel de la Gardie and was made in Augsburg by the goldsmith Abraham Drentwett. The canopy was added 100 years later for the coronation of King Adolf Fredrik and was designed by Jean Eric Rehn.

The decor of the Hall of State is lavish. The throne is flanked by colossal sculptures of Karl XIV Johan and Gustav II Adolf, while those on the cornice symbolize Peace, Strength, Religion and Justice.

Until 1975 the Hall of State was the scene of the ceremonial opening of the Swedish Parliament (Riksdagen) which included a march past of the royal bodyguard in full regalia. It is now used more for other official occasions and, like the Royal Chapel, is a venue for summer concerts (see pp176–77).

The Hall of State, the most important ceremonial room in the palace

THE ROYAL CHAPEL

It took 50 years to build the Royal Palace, and a lot of effort went into the interior decoration of the Royal Chapel. The work was carried out largely by Carl Hårleman under the supervision of Tessin. As with the Hall of State, the co-operation between the two produced a magnificent result, enhanced by the contributions of several foreign artists.

A number of remarkable artifacts have been added over the centuries. The most recent was a group of six 17th-century-style bronze crowns, as well as two crystal crowns, given by the Court to King Carl XVI Gustaf and Queen Silvia to mark their marriage in 1976.

It also has some rare relics of the original Tre Kronor

fortress: new benches that had been ordered by Tessin. They had been rescued during the palace fire in 1697 and preserved but not put in the chapel until the 19th century. The benches were made by Georg Haupt, grandfather of the Georg Haupt who was to create some of the palace's most prized furnishings (see p82).

Erik XIV's crown, made by Cornelis ver Weiden in Stockholm in 1561

GUSTAV III'S MUSEUM OF ANTIQUITIES

Opened in 1794 in memory of the murdered king, the Museum of Antiquities initially housed more than 200 exhibits, mainly acquired during Gustav's Italian journey in 1783–4 and then supplemented with more purchases later.

In 1866 the museum's collection was moved to the city's National Museum (see pp82–3). During the 1950s the main gallery was renovated, followed by the smaller galleries 30 years later, which enabled the collection to be returned to its original setting.

The most prized exhibits are in the main gallery, the best known being the sculpture of Endymion, the eternally sleeping young shepherd and lover of the Moon Goddess Selene. The 18th-century sculptor Johan Tobias Sergel is represented by The Priestess, ranked as the collection's second most important piece. She is flanked by two large candelabras.

THE TREASURY

At the bottom of 56 well-worn steps, below the Hall of State on the south side of the palace, is the entrance to the Treasury (Skattkammaren) where the State regalia, the most potent symbols of the monarchy, are kept.

On the rare occasions that King Erik XIV's crown, sceptre, orb and the keys of the kingdom are taken out of their showcase, they are placed beside the uncrowned

King Carl XVI Gustaf. The 1-m (3-ft) high silver baptismal font, which took the French silversmith Jean François Cousinet 11 years to make, is 200 years old and is still used for royal baptisms. Hanging in the Treasury is the only undamaged tapestry among six dating from the 1560s, salvaged from the 1697 fire.

TRE KRONOR MUSEUM

The newest attraction at the Royal Palace is the Tre Kronor (Three Crowns) Museum, which is housed in the oldest parts of the ruined Tre Kronor fortress, preserved under the north side of the palace. About half of a massive 12th-century defensive wall and brick vaults from the 16th and 17th centuries provide a unique setting for the museum which illustrates the palace's history of almost 1,000 years.

Two models of the Tre Kronor fortress show changes made during the second half of the 17th century and how it looked by the time of the fire. Among items rescued from the ashes are a schnapps glass, amber pots and bowls made from mountain crystal.

A glass bowl in the Tre Kronor Museum, saved from the 1697 fire

The imposing Stock Exchange on the north side of Stortorget

Stortorget ❻

Map 4 B3. Ⓣ *Gamla Stan.* 🚌 *2, 3, 43, 53, 55, 59, 76.*

It was not until 1778, when the Stock Exchange (Börsen) was completed, that Stortorget, the square in the heart of the Old Town, acquired a more uniform appearance. Its northern side had previously been taken up by several buildings that served as a town hall. Since the early Middle Ages the square had been a natural meeting point with a well and marketplace, lined with wooden stalls on market days.

A pillory belonging to the jail, which was once sited on nearby Kåkbrinken, used to stand on the square. It is now in the Town Hall on Kungsholmen *(see p112)*.

The medieval layout is clear on Stortorget's west side, where the red Schantska Huset (No. 20) and the narrow Seyfridtska Huset were built in around 1650. The Schantzska Huset

remains unchanged and has a lovely limestone porch adorned with figures of recumbent Roman warriors. The artist Johan Wendelstam was responsible for most of the notable porches in the Old Town. The 17th-century gable on the Grilska Huset (No. 3) is also worth closer study. Today there are cafés and restaurants in some of the medieval vaulted cellars.

The decision to construct the Stock Exchange was taken in 1667 but the many wars delayed the start of building by 100 years. The architect was the young and talented Erik Palmstedt (1741–1803), who also created the decorative cover for the old well. However, 200 years of trading on the floor of the Stock Exchange came to an end in 1990. On the upper floor, the Swedish Academy still holds its ceremonial gatherings, a tradition maintained since Gustav III gave his famous inauguration speech here on 5 April 1786.

Radiating from Stortorget, the three main streets of Köpmangatan, Svartmangatan and Skomakargatan have been laid out with the prescribed wider measure of 8 ells (about 4.80 m/16 ft) wide to allow for the horse-drawn carts.

Tyska Kyrkan ❼

Svartmangatan 16. **Map** 4 B3.
Tel *411 11 88.* Ⓣ *Gamla Stan.*
🚌 *2, 3, 43, 53, 55, 59, 76.*
🕐 *May–Sep: noon–4pm daily;*
Oct–Apr: noon–4pm Sat & Sun. 🕐
11am Sun, German. 🔲 *by appt in Swedish & German.* ♿

The German church is an impressive reminder of the almost total influence that Germany had over Stockholm during the 18th century. The Hanseatic League trading organization was in control of the Baltic and its ports, which explains why the basic layout of Gamla Stan resembled that of Lübeck. Germany's political influence was only broken after the Stockholm Bloodbath and Gustav Vasa's accession to the throne in 1523 *(see p16)*, but its cultural and mercantile influence remained strong as German merchants and craftsmen settled in the city.

The church's parish assembly, which today has some 2,000 members, was founded in 1571. The present twin-nave church was built in 1638–42, as an extension of a smaller church which the parish had used since 1576.

In German Late Renaissance and Baroque style, the interior has a royal gallery, added in 1672 for German members of

---

THE STOCKHOLM BLOODBATH

Detail of a painting of the Bloodbath (1524)

Stortorget is intimately linked with the Stockholm Bloodbath of November 1520. The Danish King Kristian II besieged the Swedish Regent, Sten Sture the Younger, until he capitulated and the Swedes chose Kristian as their king. He promised an amnesty and ordered a three-day feast at Tre Kronor Fortress. Near the end of the festivities, the revellers were suddenly shut in and arrested for heresy. The next day more than 80 noblemen and Stockholm citizens were beheaded in the square.

The royal gallery in the 17th-century Tyska Kyrkan

the royal household. The pulpit (1660) in ebony and alabaster is unique in Sweden and the altar, from the 1640s, is covered with beautiful paintings surrounded by sculptures of the apostles and evangelists.

The sculptures on the south porch by Jobst Hennen date from 1643 and show Jesus, Moses and three figures portraying Faith, Hope and Love.

Mårten Trotzigs Gränd, the narrowest street in the city

Mårten Trotzigs Gränd ❽

Map 4 C4. Ⓣ *Gamla Stan.* 🚍 *2, 3, 43, 53, 55, 59, 76.*

At only 90 cm (3 ft) wide, Mårten Trotzigs Gränd is the city's narrowest street, and climbing up the 36 steps gives a good idea of how different parts of the Old Town vary so much in height and how tightly packed together the houses are.

Mårten Trotzigs Gränd is named after a German merchant called Traubzich, who owned two houses here at the end of the 16th century. After being fenced off at both ends for 100 years, the street was reopened in 1945.

Västerlånggatan ❾

Map 4 B3. Ⓣ *Gamla Stan.* 🚍 *2, 3, 43, 53, 55, 59, 76.*

Once a main road outside the city proper, built along parts of the original town wall, Västerlånggatan now runs through the heart of the Old

Town, and is usually thronging with people – tourists and locals – shopping or strolling. Starting at Mynttorget in the north, where the Chancery Office (Kanslihuset) and Lejonbacken are, the lively and atmospheric street finishes at Järntorget in the south, where the export of iron was once controlled. Alongside is Bancohuset, which served as the headquarters of the State Bank from 1680 to 1906.

The building at No. 7 has been used by the Swedish Parliament since the mid-1990s. Its late 19th-century façade has a distinctive southern European influence.

No. 27 was built by and for Erik Palmstedt, who also designed the Stock Exchange and the well at Stortorget. No. 29 is a really venerable building, dating from the early 15th century. The original pointed Gothic arches were revealed during restoration in the 1940s.

No. 33 is a good example of how new materials and techniques in the late 19th century made it possible to fit large shop windows into old houses. The cast-iron columns which can be seen in many other places also date from this period.

No. 68, Von der Lindeska House, has a majestic 17th-century façade and a beautiful porch with sculptures of Neptune and Mercury.

Postmuseum ❿

Lilla Nygatan 6. **Map** 4 B3. *Tel* 781 17 55. Ⓣ *Gamla Stan.* 🚍 *3, 53.* ⬜ *11am–4pm Tue–Sun, Sep–Apr also Wed 4pm–7pm.* 🏷 *by arrangement.* ♿ 🍴 📷 📼 📺 **www**.posten.se/museum

An attraction in itself, the Postmuseum building takes up a whole area bought by the Swedish Post Office in 1720. About 100 years later

Västerlånggatan, Gamla Stan's most popular shopping street

the majestic-looking Post Office was built, incorporating parts of the 17th-century buildings already there. Stockholm's only Post Office until 1869, it was turned into the Postal Museum in 1906.

Letters have been sent in Sweden since 1636, and the museum's permanent exhibits

Mauritian stamp in the Postmuseum

include a portrayal of early "peasant postmen" fighting the angry Åland Sea in their boat *Simpan*. Also on display is the first post bus which ran in northern Sweden in the early 1920s and a stagecoach used in eastern Sweden.

The collection includes Sweden's first stamp-printing press and no less than four million stamps among which are the first Swedish stamps, produced in 1855. Also on display is the "Penny Black", the world's first stamp dating from 1840, and some stamps issued by Mauritius in 1847.

The reference section has a philatelic library holding 51,000 volumes and stamp collections, as well as computers and multimedia equipment for research purposes.

There is a special exhibition for children in the basement.

Riddarholms-kyrkan ⓫

Birger Jarls Torg. **Map** 4 A3.
Tel 402 61 30. T *Gamla Stan.* 3,
53. ◯ *May–Aug: 10am–4pm daily;*
Sep–Apr: noon–3pm Sat & Sun. ♿ *Eng:*
11am, 1pm, 2pm & 3pm. 🎫 ∅ ♿

Wrangelska Palatset, a royal residence after the Tre Kronor fire of 1697

This church on the island of Riddarholmen is best known as a place for royal burials. Its interior is full of ornate sarcophagi and worn grave-stones, and in front of the altar are the tombs of the medieval kings Karl Knutsson and Magnus Ladulås.

Built on the site of the late 13th-century Greyfriars abbey, founded by Magnus Ladulås, the majestic brick church was gradually enlarged over the centuries. After a serious fire in 1835, the church acquired its present lattice-work, cast-iron tower.

The church is surrounded by ornate burial vaults which date back as far as the 16th century. The coffins rest on a lower level with space for a memorial above. The most recent was built in 1858–60 for the Bernadotte dynasty.

The vaults contain the remains of all the Swedish monarchs from Gustav II Adolf in the 17th century to the present day with two exceptions: Queen Kristina was buried at St Peter's in Rome in 1689 and Gustav VI Adolf, who died in 1973, was interred at Haga (*see pp122–3*). The most magni-ficent sarcophagus is that of the 19th-century king, Karl XIV Johan, which had to be towed here by sledge from his porphyry work-

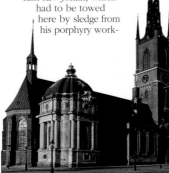

Riddarholmskyrkan with the external burial vault by Tessin and Hårleman

shops in the Älvdalen region in northern Sweden.

Particularly moving are the graves of royal children who met an early death, including the many small tin coffins that surround the last resting place of Gustav II Adolf and his queen, Maria Eleonora.

Wrangelska Palatset ⓬

Birger Jarls Torg 16. **Map** 4 A3.
T *Gamla Stan.* 3, 53. ◯ *to the public.*

Only two parts of the fortification work which Gustav Vasa undertook around 1530 still remain – Birger Jarl's Tower and the southernmost tower of what became the Wrangel Palace. Built as a residence for the nobleman Lars Sparre in 1629, it was extensively rebuilt only a few decades later. The owner by then was Carl Gustaf Wrangel, a field marshal during the Thirty Years War, who chose Nicodemus Tessin the Elder as his architect. The result was Stockholm's largest palace in private hands.

In 1693 Wrangel lost many valuable posses-sions in a major fire, and four years later his palace became a royal residence when the Royal Family moved to Riddarholmen after the Tre Kronor fortress (*see pp50–53*) was ravaged by another fire. The palace then became

known as the King's House, and it was here in 1697 that the 15-year-old Karl XII took the oath of office after the death of his father. Three years later the young king left his palace to go to war; he would never return to Stock-holm. Gustav III was born here, ten years before the Royal Family moved back to the new Royal Palace in 1756.

The Court of Appeal now uses the whole building, where in 1792 the assassin of Gustav III was manacled in the dungeons during his trial.

The court also rents the Rosenhane Palace (Birger Jarls Torg 10) and the Hessenstein House (Birger Jarls Torg 2), which was built in 1630 by Bengt Bengtsson Oxenstierna. It was named after Fredrik Wilhelm von Hessenstein, the son of Fredrik I and his lover Hedvig Taube. Later it was occupied by Carl Gustav Tessin, son of the Royal Palace architect and a leading personality in the world of culture.

The city founder Birger Jarl's statue on the square that bears his name

Evert Taubes Terrass ⓭

Norra Riddarholmshamnen. **Map** 4
A3. Ⓣ *Gamla Stan.* 🚌 *3, 53.*

A statue of Evert Taube
(1890–1976), the much-loved
troubadour and ballad writer,
stands on the terrace below
Wrangelska Palatset looking
out over the waters of
Riddarfjärden. In an ideal
position, given the poet's
close links to the sea, the
bronze sculpture was created
by Willy Gordon
in 1990. Close
by, Christer
Berg's
Solbåten (the
Sun Boat), an
elegant sculp-
ture in granite,
was unveiled in
1966. Inspired by
the shape of a
shell, from
some angles it
looks like a sail.

**Evert Taube
(1890–1976)**

Birger Jarls Torn ⓮

Norra Riddarholmshamnen. **Map** 4
A3 Ⓣ *Gamla Stan.* 🚌 *3, 53.* ◔ *to
the public.*

When the St Klara convent
on Norrmalm was pulled
down in 1527 following the
Reformation, Gustav Vasa
used some of its stonework to
build a defensive installation
on Riddarholmen. The north-
ernmost of the two towers
came to be known as Birger
Jarls Torn in the 19th century
when some thought it had
been erected 600 years earlier.
The tower has been linked
with one of the legends that

surround the founding
of Stockholm by Birger
Jarl. The story goes that
the inhabitants of the
town of Sigtuna floated
a log on Lake Mälaren
after a fire in 1187. It
drifted on to the shore
where the tower now
stands, and it was this
log – or "stock" in
Swedish – that gave
the capital its name.
A famous picture in
Storkyrkan *(see p14)*,
dating from 1535,
shows the waves break-
ing over the rocks
beneath the tower.

The 16th-century Birger Jarls Torn

Stenbockska Palatset ⓯

Birger Jarls Torg 4. **Map** 4 A3.
Ⓣ *Gamla Stan.* 🚌 *3, 53.* ◔ *to the
public.*

Both externally and internally
the Stenbock Palace is the
best-preserved building on
Riddarholmen. Built in the
1640s by the State Councillor

**Stenbockska Palatset, the best-preserved
nobleman's residence on Riddarholmen**

Fredrik Stenbock and his wife
Katarina de la Gardie, the
family's coat of arms can be
seen above the porch. The
palace underwent major
extension work in 1863 when
it was taken over by the State
Archives. Then in 1969–71 it
was restored as the head-
quarters of the Supreme Court.

Many leading Swedish and
foreign architects and artists
have all played their part in
enhancing the
palace's outstanding
appearance. The
roof beams and
flooring are from
the Stenbock period,
and the staircase
was designed by
Nicodemus Tessin
the Elder.

Several beautiful
ceilings are the
work of the master
of stucco, Carlo
Carove from Italy
(d. 1697), and there
is a cabinet created
by Rococo architect
Carl Hårleman.

TIMELINE: RIDDARHOLMEN

1250s The island, then called Kidskär, is a cattle-grazing area outside the settlement		**1527** Following the Reformation, the monks are evicted from the island	**Late 17th century** The prosperity of the nobility starts to diminish. Palaces are replaced by government offices	**1697–1754** The royal family takes over Wrangelska Palatset after Tre Kronor fortress is destroyed by fire	**1865–66** The Parliament building and Hebbe House are rebuilt for new two-chamber Parliament
1200	**1300**	**1400**	**1500**	**1600**	**1700**	**1800**	**1900**
	1270–85 The Greyfriars' abbey is founded. Kidskär is renamed Gråmunke-holmen. The abbey church is used for royal burials		**1625–35** Land is do-nated to noblemen and distinguished officers. The name is changed to Riddarholmen *Wrangelska Palatset*			**1830s** Fleming House used for Parliament by priests, burghers and peasants. Noblemen stay in Riddarhuset	**1905** Parliament moves to new build-ing on Helgeands-holmen

Riddarhuset in lavish Dutch Baroque style, built in the 17th century

Riddarhuset ⑯

Riddarhustorget 10. **Map** 4 A3.
Tel 723 39 90. Ⓣ *Gamla Stan.*
🚌 *3, 53.* ◯ *11:30am–12:30pm
Mon–Fri.* 📷 ✔ *by arrangement.*
www.riddarhuset.se

Often regarded as one of
Stockholm's most beautiful
buildings, Riddarhuset (House
of Nobility) stands on
Riddarhustorget, which as late
as the mid-19th century was
still the city's centre.

Built in 1641–7 on the
initiative of the State
Chancellor, it was designed
by the architects Simon and
Jean de la Vallée, Heinrich
Wilhelm and Justus
Vingboons. The nobility,
whose privileges were
granted in 1280, then
had a base for meet-
ings and events.

The building is a
supreme example
of Dutch Baroque
design and colouring.
Over the entrance on
the northern façade is
the nobility's motto *Arte et
Marte* (Art and War) with
Minerva, Goddess of Art and
Science, and Mars, God of
War, on either side.

The sculptures on the
vaulted roof symbolize the
knightly virtues. On the south
side is *Nobilitas* (Nobility) holding a small Minerva and spear.
She is flanked by *Studium*
(Diligence) and *Valor*
(Bravery). Facing the north is
the male equivalent, *Honor*,
flanked by *Prudentia* (Prud-
ence) and *Fortitudo* (Strength).

The interior is equally
impressive. The lower hall is
dominated by a magnificent
double staircase which leads

**The motto at
Riddarhuset**

up to the Knights' Room. This
has a masterly ceiling painting
by David Klöcker Ehrenstrahl
(1628–98) and Riddarhuset's
foremost treasure, a sculpted
ebony chair that dates from
1623. The walls are covered
by some 2,320 coats of arms.

Bondeska Palatset ⑰

Riddarhustorget 8. **Map** 4 B3.
Ⓣ *Gamla Stan.* 🚌 *3, 53.* ◉ *to the
public.*

The seat of the Supreme
Court since 1949, the Bonde
Palace was created in 1662–73
by popular architect
Nicodemus Tessin the
Elder in the style of a
French town house.
The year previously,
the State Treasurer
Gustav Bonde had
bought the site
opposite Riddarhuset
to build a palace with
the idea of renting out
most of it.

Since then the Bonde Palace
has had several owners and
was damaged by fires in 1710

**Bondeska Palatset, now the seat of
the Supreme Court**

and 1753. In 1730 the building became the property of
the city and served as the City
Hall until 1915. After that,
there was little interest taken
in the palace until renovation
planned by the architect Ivar
Tengbom was begun in the
late 1940s. It had even been
suggested that the building
should be destroyed, but
public opinion ensured that it
remained intact.

Riksdagshuset ⑱

Riksgatan 3 A. **Map** 4 B2. **Tel** *786
54 63.* Ⓣ *Kungsträdgården.* 🚌 *3,
43, 53, 62.* ◯ *tours & meetings in
the Chamber.* ✔ *ring for details on
tours of the building & art works.* ♿
📷 www.riksdagen.se

The Parliament Building
(Riksdagshuset) and State
Bank (Riksbank) on Helge-
andsholmen were inaugurated
in 1905 and 1906 respectively.
Since 1983, when Parliament
returned after 12 years at
Sergels Torg, the two buildings
have been combined and enlarged. Parliament also occupies five premises in Gamla
Stan, as well as an information
office at Västerlånggatan 1. All
the buildings are connected by
underground passages and together amount to 130,000 sq m
(1,400,000 sq ft), with a staff
force of about 600, plus 250 in
the political parties' offices.

Parliamentary debates can
be watched from the public
gallery, which holds up to 500
visitors. There are guided tours
of the buildings every day
during the summer and only
at weekends in winter. Visitors
should use the public entrance
at Riksgatan 3A.

From the gallery level is a
striking view from as far as
Gustav Adolfs Torg to Riddarholmen. The main chamber
has benches of Swedish birch
and wall panelling in Finnish
birch, carved in Norway. A
large tapestry, *Memory of a
Landscape* (1983), by Elisabeth
Hasselberg-Olsson, covers 54
sq m (581 sq ft) of wall,
weighs 100 kg (220 lb) and
took 3,500 hours to make.

The old two-chamber Parliament's beautifully renovated
rooms are now used for

meetings of the majority party. The former Upper House has three paintings by Otte Sköld (1894–1958), and in the other chamber there are works by Axel Törneman and Georg Pauli, who realized Törneman's sketches after his death. Between the chambers is a 45-m (148-ft) long hall with an elegant display of coats of arms, paintings and chandeliers. The Finance Committee meets in the old oak-panelled library surrounded by old prints and Jugendstil lamps.

Facing the old entrance at Norrbro, the magnificent stairwell still retains its colouring from 1905. Other impressive survivors from opulent days include eight columns, a floor, steps and balusters all in various types of marble. The

The chamber where the 349 Members of Parliament meet

present entrance was the State Bank's main hall until 1976. It has magnificent columns, too, made from polished granite, and some outstanding paintings from the Parliamentary collection of 3,000 works.

Medeltids-museet ⑲

Strömparterren, Norrbro. **Map** 4 B2. **Tel** 508 317 90. ⓣ Kungsträdgården. 🚌 43, 62. ◯ Jul & Aug: 11am–4pm Mon–Tue Thu–Sun, 11am–6pm Wed; Sep–Jun: 11am–4pm Tue & Thu–Sun, 4–6pm Wed. 🅿 ♿ 📷 ⊘ 🎞 **www**.medeltidsmuseet.stockholm.se

This fascinating museum of medieval Stockholm is built around the capital's archaeological remains, mainly parts of the city wall that date from the 1530s. They were found during intensive archaeological research in 1978–80 which unearthed a number of remarkable finds from Stockholm's medieval history.

Completely underground, the museum also includes artifacts from other parts of the city. Among them is the 22-m (72-ft) long Riddarholm ship which was discovered off Riddarholmen in 1930 and dates from the 1520s.

The museum provides a good picture of Stockholm's early days. From the entrance, a 350-year-old tunnel leads into a reconstructed medieval world. There is a pillory in the square and the gallows hill with the tools of the executioner's grisly trade. The old harbour has been rebuilt, complete with quayside, jetties, boathouses and warehouses, as well as authentic nautical smells. The spruce wreath hanging outside the wine cellar shows that supplies of wine and beer have arrived from the Continent. The large house is built from 6,000 original bricks.

The new Parliament building, with the older building behind

PARLIAMENTARY WANDERINGS

Sweden's first Parliament was opened in the 1860s on Riddarholmen in the combined properties of Fleming House and Hebbe House. From 1835–65, commoners – priests, burghers and farmers – met in Fleming House, which became known as the "House of Commons", while the noblemen sat in nearby Riddarhuset. Situated behind Riddarholmskyrkan at Birger Jarls Torg 5, Fleming House was constructed on the site of the Greyfriars abbey after the monks were forced to flee due to the Reformation in the 17th century *(see p57),*

and remains of the huge abbey can still be seen in the cellar.

A new base for Parliament, adapted for the needs of a two-chamber legislature, was inaugurated on Helgeandsholmen in 1905. When a single chamber was established in 1971, a lack of space meant that Parliament had to move to the newly built Kulturhuset *(see p67)* on Sergels Torg. It returned to Helgeandsholmen in 1983 into an extended and reconstructed Parliament building.

"Mother Svea" above the old Parliament building

Medieval carved stone head of Birger Jarl at Medeltidsmuseet

CITY

The area known as City today was where, in the mid-18th century, the first stone-built houses and palaces outside Gamla Stan started to appear for the burghers and nobility. After World War II, the run-down buildings around Hötorget were demolished to form what is now Sergels Torg; many homes were replaced by rather dreary office blocks.

In recent years, though, the area has been livening up after dark and become the true heart and commercial

Street light near Kungliga Operan

centre of Stockholm. A hub for public transport and banking, City is the place for the best department stores and shopping malls, exclusive boutiques and nightspots.

The centre also has some beautiful parks and pleasant squares serving as popular meeting places. The unique landscape surrounding Stockholm permeates even City – here and there appear unexpected glimpses of the water with its bustling boat life and a string of anglers along the embankments.

SIGHTS AT A GLANCE

Museums
Armémuseum **25**
Dansmuseet **5**
Hallwylska Palatset **29**
Medelhavsmuseet **6**
Musikmuseet **26**
Strindbergsmuseet **18**

Squares
Hötorget **13**
Kungsträdgården **2**
Sergels Torg **12**
Stureplan **21**

Public Buildings
Arvfurstens Palats **7**
Centralbadet **16**
Hovstallet **27**
Konstakademien **9**
Kulturhuset and Stadsteatern **11**
Kungstornen **15**
Kungliga Biblioteket **20**
Rosenbad **8**
Sweden House **1**

Theatres and Musical Stages
Dansens Hus **17**
Konserthuset **14**
Kungliga Dramatiska Teatern **28**
Kungliga Operan **4**

Churches
Adolf Fredriks Kyrka **19**
Hedvig Eleonora Kyrka **24**

Jacobs Kyrka **3**
Klara Kyrka **10**

Markets & Malls
Sturegallerian and Sturebadet **22**
Östermalmshallen **23**

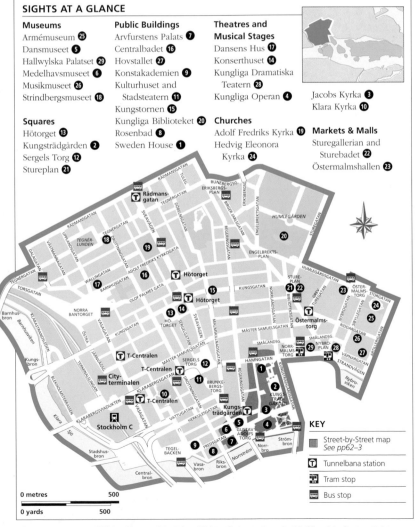

KEY

⬛ Street-by-Street map
   See pp62–3

🚇 Tunnelbana station

🚋 Tram stop

🚌 Bus stop

0 metres — 500
0 yards — 500

◁ **Sagerska Palatset, official residence of the Prime Minister, between Rosenbad (left) and Arvfurstens Palats**

Street-by-Street: Around Kungsträdgården

With a history going back to the 15th century, the King's Garden (Kungsträdgården) has long been the city's most popular meeting place and recreational centre. Both visitors and Stockholmers gather here for summer concerts and festivals, or just to enjoy a stroll among the lime trees. Close by is Sweden House where the tourist office is based, and around the park is a wealth of shops, boutiques, churches, museums and restaurants. A short walk takes you to Gustav Adolfs Torg, flanked by the Royal Opera House and other stately buildings, including the Swedish Foreign Office.

Dansmuseet
Anything connected with dance such as costumes, stage set sketches and posters for the famous Les Ballets Suédois, can be seen here ❺

★ Medelhavsmuseet
This museum near Gustav Adolfs Torg has vast collections from prehistoric cultures around the Mediterranean ❻

Gustav II Adolf's equestrian statue, designed by L'Archevêques, was unveiled in 1796.

FREDSGATAN

Sagerska Palatset

STRÖMGATAN

GUSTAV ADOLFS TORG

REGERINGSGATAN

NORRBRO

NORRSTRÖM

STRÖMGATAN

Opera-källaren
(see p160)

SOPHIA·ALBERTINA ÆDIFICAVIT·

Arvfurstens Palats
The Swedish Foreign Office is based in this palace, built for Gustav III's sister Sofia Albertina in 1794 ❼

★ Kungliga Operan
Built in 1898 with a magnificently ornate auditorium, the Royal Opera House replaced an earlier one from the time of Gustav III ❹

KEY

— — — Suggested route

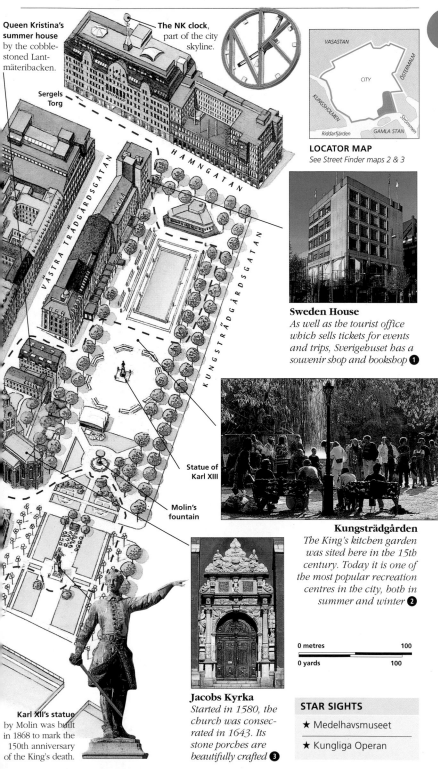

Queen Kristina's summer house by the cobblestoned Lantmäteribacken.

The NK clock, part of the city skyline.

Sergels Torg

HAMNGATAN

VÄSTRA TRÄDGÅRDSGATAN

KUNGSTRÄDGÅRDSGATAN

Statue of Karl XIII

Molin's fountain

Karl XII's statue by Molin was built in 1868 to mark the 150th anniversary of the King's death.

LOCATOR MAP
See Street Finder maps 2 & 3

VASASTAN
CITY
ÖSTERMALM
KUNGSHOLMEN
Strömmen
Riddarfjärden
GAMLA STAN

Sweden House
As well as the tourist office which sells tickets for events and trips, Sverigehuset has a souvenir shop and bookshop ❶

Kungsträdgården
The King's kitchen garden was sited here in the 15th century. Today it is one of the most popular recreation centres in the city, both in summer and winter ❷

0 metres	100
0 yards	100

Jacobs Kyrka
Started in 1580, the church was consecrated in 1643. Its stone porches are beautifully crafted ❸

STAR SIGHTS

★ Medelhavsmuseet

★ Kungliga Operan

Sweden House ❶

Hamngatan 27. **Map** 3 D4.
Tel 789 24 00. Ⓣ Kungsträdgården.
🚌 2, 47, 55, 59, 62, 76. **Tourist
Office** ◯ 9am–7pm Mon–Fri, 9am–
5pm Sat, 10am–4pm Sun. ● 24 &
25 Dec, 1 Jan. 🚻 🅿
www.stockholmtown.com

Sweden House (Sverigehuset)
is strategically placed on
Hamngatan, close to the
hustle and bustle of
Kungsträdgården and
opposite the NK
department store.
It is the home of the
Swedish Institute, which
promotes cultural
exchanges with other
countries and provides
information
on Sweden from its
offices abroad.
Also based here on
the ground floor is the
Stockholm Visitors Board, run
by the City and County
Councils and visited by about
700,000 people a year.
Information on the capital and
region is available in several
languages, along with more
limited information on the
rest of the country. There is
an accommodation booking
centre, and tickets can be
bought for excursions and
events. The shop sells high-
quality Swedish souvenirs.

Kungsträdgården ❷

Map 4 B1. Ⓣ Kungsträdgården.
🚌 2, 47, 55, 59, 62, 65, 76.

Once the royal kitchen
garden in the 15th century, the
"King's Garden" today is a
popular meeting place for
Stockholmers where there is
something going on for
everyone all year round. The
park, encircled by avenues, is
the city's oldest and at the
Strömgatan end has a square:
Karl XII's Torg with J P Molin's
statue of the warrior king,
unveiled in 1868, in the centre.
In Kungsträdgården itself there
is a statue of Karl XIII
(1809–18) by Erik Göthe.
During the summer concerts
of all kinds, food festivals,
dancing and live street theatre
take place here. In winter, the
central skating rink attracts
children and grown-
ups alike. Also
here is Molin's famous
fountain, made from gyp-
sum in 1866 and cast in
bronze seven years later.
During Erik XIV's reign
in the 16th century, the
kitchen garden was
transformed into a
formal Renaissance
garden and Queen
Kristina had a stone summer
house built in it. The beautiful
17th-century house still stands
at Västra Trädgårdsgatan 2
next to the cobble-stoned
Lantmäteribacken.

**Molin's
fountain**

Jacobs Kyrka ❸

Jakobs Torg 5. **Map** 4 B1.
Tel 723 30 38. Ⓣ Kungsträdgården.
🚌 2, 55, 59, 62, 65, 76. ◯ 11am–
9pm Mon–Sat, 9am–9pm Sun. 🅿
12:10pm Mon–Fri, 11am, 2pm & 6pm
(in English) Sun. **Concerts** 3pm Sat.
🎫 by arrangement. 🚻

Even in medieval times there
was a small chapel where
Kungsträdgården now lies.
Dedicated to St Jacob, the
patron saint of wayfarers, the
chapel and another modest-
sized church in the area were
destroyed by King Gustav Vasa
in the 16th century. Johan III
wanted to provide two new
churches in Norra Malmen,
as the area was then called,
and work to build the
churches of St Jacob and St
Klara (see p66) started in 1580.
St Jacob's was consecrated
first, in 1643. It has been
restored several times since
then, in some cases rather
clumsily. However, several
valuable items have been
preserved, including a baptismal font from 1634 and some
church silver, as well as
porches by stonemasons
Henrik Blom and Hans Hebel.
The organ's façade was
created by the architect Carl
Hårleman and the large painting on the west wall of the
southern nave is by Fredrik
Westin, Sweden's most distinguished historical painter in
the early 19th century.

**Altar in Jacobs Kyrka, partly
dating from the 17th century**

Kungliga Operan ❹

Gustav Adolfs Torg. **Map** 4 B1.
Tel 791 43 00. Ⓣ Kungsträdgården.
🚌 43, 62, 65. **Ticket Office**
◯ 12–6pm Mon–Fri, 12–3pm Sat.
🎫 by arrangement. 🚻 ▢ 🅿
www.operan.se

Opera has been performed in
Sweden since 18 January
1773, when a performance
took place at Bollhuset at
Slottsbacken. Kungliga
Operan (The Royal Opera
House) on Gustav Adolfs
Torg was inaugurated on 30
September 1782, but by the
late 19th century it had
become a fire hazard. The
architect Axel Anderberg was
commissioned to design a
new opera house which was

View of Kungsträdgården, towards Hamngatan

The 28-m (92-ft) long gold foyer at Kungliga Operan

transferred to the State in 1898 from a consortium founded by the financier K A Wallenberg.

The colouring of the building in late Renaissance style is in keeping with the Royal Palace and Parliament building, and some details of the architecture are common to all three. The beautiful staircase with ceiling paintings by Axel Jungstedt was inspired by the Paris Opera. The same artist's portrait of Oscar II hangs in the 28-m (92-ft) long gold foyer, where Carl Larsson was responsible for the decorative paintings. The wings at either side of the stage have been kept, as has the width of the proscenium arch (11.4 m/37 ft). Also saved was J T Sergel's group of angels, holding the national coat of arms, above the stage. An angel in Vicke Andrén's ceiling painting is holding a sketch of the Opera House.

Gold ceiling in Kungliga Operan

Dansmuseet ❺

Gustav Adolfs Torg 22–24.
Map 4 B1.**Tel** 441 76 50. ⊤
Kungsträdgården. 🚌 2, 53, 55, 59, 62, 65, 76. ◯ 11am–4pm Tue–Fri, 12am–4pm Sat & Sun. 🛇 ♿ ▣
🖻 www.dansmuseet.se

In 1999 the Dance Museum moved into new premises on Gustav Adolfs Torg, in the former bank building opposite the Norrbro bridge. The museum was originally founded in Paris in 1953 by the Swedish aristocrat Rolf de Maré (1888–1964). He was a noted art collector who founded the world-renowned Les Ballets Suédois.

The museum reflects all aspects of dance – costumes and masks, scenery sketches, art and posters, books and documents – and includes an archive on popular dance. Apart from the exhibition hall, there is also a data bank in the form of the Rolf de Maré Study Centre, with video facilities, a library and archives. The museum shop has Sweden's largest collection of dance videos for sale.

Medelhavs-museet ❻

Fredsgatan 2. **Map** 4 B1.
Tel 519 553 80. ⊤ Kungsträdgården. 🚌 2, 43, 53, 62, 65. ◯ 11am–8pm Tue–Wed, 11am–4pm Thu–Fri, 12–5pm Sat & Sun. 🛇 ♿ ▣ 🖻
www.medelhavsmuseet.se

Gods and people from prehistoric cultures around the Mediterranean rub shoulders in Medelhavsmuseet (Museum of Mediterranean and Near East Antiquities). Its many treasures include a large group of terracotta figures discovered by archaeologists on Cyprus in the 1930s. Models made of unusual materials like cork show how houses were once constructed, and the museum also has a fascinating gold room. The Islamic collections are complemented by temporary exhibitions.

The museum is housed in a former bank, originally built in the 17th century for Gustav Horn, a general in the Thirty Years War. The stairwell, dating from 1905, and the peristyles and colonnade around the upper part of the hall are worth a visit in themselves.

Arvfurstens Palats ❼

Gustav Adolfs Torg 1. **Map** 4 B1.
⊤ Kungsträdgården. 🚌 43, 62, 65.
⬤ to the public.

Opposite the Royal Opera House, on the other side of Gustav Adolfs Torg, stands Arvfurstens Palats (Prince's Palace), built for Gustav III's sister Sofia Albertina and inaugurated in 1794. She commissioned the architect Erik Palmstedt to carry out the work. He was a pupil of Carl Fredrik Adelcrantz, designer of the original opera house.

The palace and its decor are shining examples of the Gustavian style, thanks to the contributions of artists and craftsmen like Louis Masreliez and Georg Haupt and their pupils Gustaf Adolf Ditzinger, Johan Tobias Sergel and Gottlieb Iwersson. In 1906 the building was taken over by the Swedish Foreign Office.

Nearby is the elegant Sagerska Palatset (1894) in French Renaissance style, which is used by the Prime Minister as an official residence.

Arvfurstens Palats (1794), now the Swedish Foreign Office

Rosenbad, home of the Government and City Council committees

had a vision of this area as an extension of his work.

Traces of the older buildings can still be seen. The interior of the small meeting room was designed by Carl Fredrik Adelcrantz around 1780 and two tiled stoves from the same period have been preserved, along with the main porch facing Jakobsgatan. The four allegorical female figures which were once at the entrance have been recast in cement and placed on the roof.

Interior of Klara Kyrka with decor by Olle Hjortzberg

Rosenbad ❽

Rosenbad 4. **Map** 4 A2.
🅣 *Kungsträdgården.* 🚌 *3, 53, 62, 65.*
⬤ *to the public.*

Since 1981, the Rosenbad complex – a collection of palatial buildings overlooking the Strömmen channel – has housed the Swedish Government and the Prime Minister's private office in three internally linked sites.

Three of the late 19th century's most notable architects were commissioned to design these buildings. The Venetian-style palace along Strömgatan was the last one to be added, in 1904. Designed by Ferdinand Boberg (1860–1916), it used to house private apartments, a bank and a popular restaurant, traces of which survive in the ornamentation of the open loggia facing the water.

Gustav Wickman (1858–1916) designed the pink sandstone house on the corner of Fredsgatan and Drottninggatan in exuberant, almost baroque, Jugendstil. The Skåne Bank moved into this building in 1900.

The Florentine-style house on Fredsgatan facing Rödbod-torget is three years older. It was designed by Aron Johansson (1860–1936), architect of the old Parliament building on Helgeandsholmen.

Rosenbad got its name from a former 17th-century bath-house which offered bathers a choice of a lily bath, a chamomile bath or a rose bath – *rosenbad* in Swedish.

Konstakademien ❾

Fredsgatan 12. **Map** 4 A2.
Tel *23 29 45.* 🅣 *T-centralen.* 🚌 *3, 53, 62, 65.* ◐ *11am–5pm Tue–Fri , 12–4pm Sat & Sun.* ♿ *entrance Jakobsgatan 27.* ▢

The art collections of Konstakademien (Royal Academy of the Arts) reflect more than 250 years of paintings and sculptures, mostly by past and present members. Today the Royal Academy has around 120 members.

Between Fredsgatan and Jakobsgatan, the imposing corner house was designed by Tessin the Elder in the early 1670s. The Royal Academy moved in while under the patronage of Gustav III in the late 18th century. It has been rebuilt several times, the latest in 1897 by the architect Erik Lallerstedt. Its present look ties in with the Royal Opera House *(see p62)* and the Royal Palace *(see pp50–53)*, whose architect Tessin the Younger

The Fredsgatan entrance of Konstakademien

Klara Kyrka ❿

Klara Östra Kyrkogata. **Map** 2 C4.
Tel *723 30 31.* 🅣 *T-centralen* 🚌 *47, 52, 59, 65.* ◐ *10am–5pm daily.* ✝ *10:30am Tue, 8am Thu, 11am, 2pm (Swahili) Sun.* ♿ ▢

The convent of St Klara stood on the site of the present church and cemetery until 1527, when it was pulled down on the orders of Gustav Vasa. Later, his son Johan III commissioned a new church, completed in 1590.

The church was ravaged by fire in 1751 and its reconstruction was planned by the period's two outstanding architects, first Carl Hårleman and later C F Adelcrantz. The pulpit was made in 1753 to Hårleman's design, and J T Sergel *(see p83)* created the angelic figures in the northern gallery. A pair of identical angels adorn the exquisite chancel, based on the sculptor's gypsum originals.

In the 1880s, the 116-m (380-ft) tower was added and for many years could be seen from all over the city. The 20th-century church artist, Olle Hjortzberg, created the vault paintings, dating from 1904.

Edvin Öhrström's glass obelisk in Sergels Torg, with Kulturhuset behind to the left

Kulturhuset and Stadsteatern ⓫

Sergels Torg 3. **Map** 2 C4. **Kulturhuset Tel** *508 315 08*. **Stadsteatern Tel** *506 202 00*. Ⓣ *T-centralen.* 🚌 *47, 52, 56, 59, 69.* ⭘ *10am–7pm Tue–Fri, 10am–5pm Sat–Sun.* 🖼 *some areas.* ♿ 🍴 💻 📷 www.kulturhuset.stockholm.se

A quarter of a century after it was opened in 1974, Kulturhuset (Cultural Centre) was renovated to meet the needs of the new millennium. Typical of its era, the creation of the architect Peter Celsing blends well with surrounding Sergels Torg and has become a symbol of Swedish Modernism. The building, which was the winner of a Nordic design competition, has a façade of glass all along the southern side of the square.

Kulturhuset offers something for everybody: three galleries hold regularly changing exhibitions suitable for all tastes, and the auditorium presents varied programmes of music, dance, drama and lectures. "Kilen" is the centre for an artform which is a cross between drama, stand-up, installations and dance.

The Children's Room gives youngsters an opportunity to read books, draw pictures, listen to stories or watch a film. "Lava" is a meeting place for young people and for nationwide youth culture.

The centre is also home to Sweden's only library for fans of strip cartoons, along with reading rooms which provide international newspapers and magazines, as well as newly published Swedish literature. Visitors can borrow anything from books to CD-ROMs.

Café Panorama offers food for mind and body, and Café Access is for surfing the Internet. Several shops sell items of Swedish design.

Kulturhuset also houses Stadsteatern (City Theatre), whose main auditorium was finally inaugurated in 1990. This section had been occupied by Parliament while its usual meeting place on Helgeandsholmen was being rebuilt (*see p59*).

The ambitions of the theatre's architects Lars Fahlsten and Per Ahrbom were eventually realized when the six stages of varying size and style were all united under one roof; from the main auditorium seating 700 to the tiny Dolls' Theatre with space for about 70. Every year the theatre holds around 1,400 performances for audiences totalling about 225,000.

Sergels Torg ⓬

Map 2 C4. Ⓣ *T-centralen.* 🚌 *47, 52, 59, 65, 69.*

As part of the city centre's transformation, around 1930 there was a strong lobby in favour of extending Sveavägen through to Gustav Adolfs Torg. But in 1945 it was decided to end the road at the junction with Klarabergsgatan and Hamngatan to form a new square, Sveaplan. In 1957 a two-level square was proposed – a lower level for pedestrians and an upper level for traffic. The plan was finalized in 1960 and the name changed to Sergels Torg.

In 1972 the sculptor Edvin Öhrström's glass obelisk, *Crystal Vertical Accent in Glass and Steel* was erected in the centre and now shimmers at night due to improved lighting.

CITY'S TRANSFORMATION

During the 20th century Stockholm's population grew from 250,000 to more than 1.6 million. By the 1920s it was obvious that the old heart of the city did not meet the future needs of business, public administration and the growth in traffic. In 1951 a controversial 30-year programme to transform the lower Norrmalm city centre was launched. Slums on 335 of the 600 sites were pulled down and 78 new houses were built. Two-thirds of the area's buildings were added during this period.

The first steps towards a new Hötorg City, 1958

Fresh produce on sale at Hötorget, a marketplace since the 17th century

Hötorget ⑬

Map 2 C4. ⑦ *Hötorget.* 🚌 *1, 52, 56.* 🛒 *7:30am–6pm Mon–Fri, 7:30am–4pm Sat, 10am–5pm Sun.*

Tradition is still going strong on Hötorget (Hay Market). Formerly belonging to St Klara convent, in the 1640s the square evolved into an important place for trading in animal fodder, milk, vegetables and meat. Today it is still a lively market for fresh produce.

The buildings around the square are relatively new. The most recent is the glass-fronted cinema complex opened in 1995, while the PUB department store was added in 1916 and Konserthuset in 1926. On nearby Sergelgatan, where the five high-rises of Hötorgs City were constructed in 1952–6, there is a reminder of the old

city centre. A tablet marks where the renowned sculptor Johan Tobias Sergel (1740–1814) had his studio. A later sculptor, Carl Milles *(see p150)*, created the well-noted fountain, *Orpheus*, that stands in front of Konserthuset.

Konserthuset ⑭

Hötorget. **Map** 2 C4. **Tel** *786 02 00.* ⑦ *Hötorget.* 🚌 *1, 3, 52, 56.* **Ticket Office** 🕐 *11am–6pm Mon–Fri, 11am–3pm Sat, and 2 hours before a concert.* 📷 🛗 🖥 🌐 www.konserthuset.se

A Nordic version of a Greek temple, Konserthuset (the Concert Hall) is a masterpiece of the architect Ivar Tengbom (1878–1968) and is an outstanding example of the 1920s' Neo-Classical style. Tengbom's tradition has been carried on by his son Anders (b. 1911), who was in charge of its renovation in 1970–71, and his grandson Svante

(b. 1942), who had a similar task in 1993–6.

Constructed in 1923–6, the main hall at the outset matched Ivar Tengbom's original concept. However, acoustical problems led to major reconstruction work and modernization. Its internal decor is rather frugal, but the Grünewald Hall, by the artist Isaac Grünewald (1889–1946), is more lavish in the style of an Italian Renaissance palace.

The four marble statues in the main foyer are by Carl Milles, creator of the *Orpheus* sculpture group outside. Other artists who have contributed to the decor are Einar Forseth, Simon Gate, Edward Hald and Carl Malmsten.

The Concert Hall has been the home of the Swedish Royal Philharmonic Orchestra since it opened. The orchestra gives some 70 concerts every year and international star soloists perform here regularly. It is also the venue for the Nobel Prize presentations.

Kungstornen ⑮

Kungsgatan 30 and 33. **Map** 3 D4. ⑦ *Hötorget.* 🚌 *1, 43, 56.* ⛔ *to the public.*

In 1915 the young architect Sven Wallander submitted a sketch showing how Stockholm could be given a modern, USA-inspired main street. His plans were accepted during the 1920s, when a

---

THE NOBEL PRIZES

Alfred Nobel (1833–96) was an outstanding chemist and inventor, and the prestigious Nobel Prizes – consisting of a monetary award and a medal – have been presented every year since 1901 on 10 December, the date of his death. The ceremony takes place in Konserthuset, where prizes are presented for physics, chemistry, physiology or medicine, and literature. Since 1969 the Bank of Sweden has also given a prize for economic sciences in Nobel's memory. The Nobel Peace Prize is presented in Oslo's City Hall on the same day. In 1901 each prize was worth 150,000 kr, while in 1999 it had increased to 7.9 million kr.

The Nobel Medal, awarded annually

The *Orpheus* sculpture group by Carl Milles at Konserthuset

new road was excavated through the Brunkeberg hill linking Hötorget with Stureplan. A bridge was built over what is now Kungsgatan, and a few years later the twin Kungstornen (King's Towers) were added.

Designed in Neo-Classical style by Wallander, the northern tower was originally owned by the sugar company Sockerbolaget. The southern tower was designed by Ivar Callmander and owned by L M Ericsson. Apart from a period when restaurants occupied the top of each one, the towers have been used only as offices. Both 16 floors high, the northern tower, covering an area of 7,000 sq m (75,320 sq ft), is referred to as the "male", with his more graceful, slightly larger twin, as the "female". At the entrance of the northern tower are some beautiful granite sculptures created by Eric Grate.

The "male" and "female" Kungstornen on Kungsgatan

Centralbadet **⑯**

Drottninggatan 88. **Map** 4 C4. *Tel* 545 213 13. 🚇 Hötorget. 🚌 52. ⏱ 6am–8pm Mon–Fri, 8am–8pm Sat, 8am–5pm Sun. 🌙 Sun in Jul. 📷 💻 🍴 🛍 www.centralbadet.se

Designed by the architect Wilhelm Klemming in Jugendstil, Centralbadet swimming and fitness centre was completed in 1904. Since then, it has been rebuilt and extended but the façade remains the same, while the Jugendstil influence continues into the main pool and restaurant.

A protected cultural heritage building, the classic swimming centre has a 23-m (25-yd) long

Centralbadet's characteristic Jugenstil façade

pool, bubble and treatment pools, three saunas and skincare and massage departments.

The garden situated between Drottninggatan and Centralbadet was originally designed by the prolific 18th-century architect Carl Hårleman. A few of the trees growing there today are thought to date from his era, while the rest are from more recent plantings. The garden is a delightful oasis set round an ornamental pool and fountain, and there is also a sculpture showing a Triton riding a dolphin, created by Greta Klemming in the 1920s.

Dansens Hus **⑰**

Barnhusgatan 12–14. **Map** 2 C3. *Tel* 508 990 90. 🚇 T-centralen. 🚌 1, 47, 53. **Ticket Office** ⏱ noon–6pm Mon–Sat. 📷 🛗 💻 🛍 www.dansenshus.se

The "House of Dance" has been Stockholm's main permanent stage for modern dance since 1991 when it took over this site from the City Theatre which moved to Kulturhuset in 1990 *(see p67)*. Dansens Hus has two auditoriums: one for audiences of more than 800, and Blå Lådan (the Blue Box) for experimental performances seating 150.

The theatre does not have a resident ensemble but during the season it presents a dozen national and international guest performances, usually staying for three to five days. Exhibitions are staged in the foyer,

designed by Sven Markelius (1889–1972). Seminars and lectures are also held here and it is the base for the Dance Production Service (DPS), a choreographers' organization.

Strindbergsmuseet Blå Tornet **⑱**

Drottninggatan 85. **Map** 2 C3. *Tel* 411 53 54. 🚇 Rådmansgatan. 🚌 52, 69. ⏱ noon–7pm Tue, noon–4pm Wed–Sun; Jun–Aug: noon–4pm Tue–Sun. 📷 when booked in advance. 🛗 📷 🛍 www.strindbergsmuseet.se

The world-famous dramatist August Strindberg (1849–1912) had 24 different addresses in Stockholm over the years. He moved to the last of these in 1908, and gave it the name Blå Tornet (The Blue Tower). By then he had gained international recognition.

The house, now the Strindbergsmuseet, was newly built with central heating, toilet and lift, but lacked a kitchen. Instead he relied on Falkner's Pension, in the same building, for food and other services. On his last few birthdays the great man would stand on his balcony and watch his admirers stage a torchlight procession in his honour.

Opened in 1973, the museum includes reconstructions of the author's home with his bedroom, dining room and study, as well as 3,000 books and archives for photographs, press cuttings and posters. In the adjoining premises, a permanent exhibition portrays Strindberg as author, theatrical director, artist and photographer. Temporary exhibitions and other activities are often held here.

Strindberg's desk and writing materials in his study

Adolf Fredriks Kyrka ⑲

Holländargatan. **Map** 2 C3.
Tel 20 70 76. Ⓣ Hötorget. 🚌 52.
◻ 1–7pm Mon, 10am–4pm Tue–Sat,
10am–4pm Sun; later in summer. 🔔
7pm Mon, 12:15pm Wed & Thu, 8am
Fri, 11am Sun. 📷 by appointment.
🚹 ▢ 🏠

King Adolf Frederik laid the
foundation stone of this
church in 1768 on the site of
an earlier chapel dedicated to
St Olof. Designed by Carl
Fredrik Adelcrantz, in Neo-
Classical style with traces of
Rococo, the church has been
built in the shape of a Greek
cross and has a central dome.

The interior has undergone
a number of changes, but
both the altar and
pulpit have remained
intact. The sculptor
Johan Tobias Sergel
created the altarpiece,
which is probably
his most important
religious work. The
memorial to French
philosopher
Descartes (see
p17) is also
Sergel's work.
The paintings
on the dome
were added in
1899–1900 by
Julius Kron-
berg. More
recent items
of value include altar silverware by Sigurd Persson.

**Memorial to
Descartes**

The cemetery is the resting
place of the assassinated Prime
Minister Olof Palme, as well
as the politician Hjalmar
Branting, a key figure of the
Social Democratic movement.
J T Sergel is also buried here.

The "Devil's Bible" from the early 13th century,
one of Kungliga Biblioteket's foremost rarities

Kungliga Biblioteket ⑳

Humlegården. **Map** 3 D3.
Tel 463 40 00. Ⓣ Östermalmstorg.
🚌 1, 2, 55, 56, 91, 96. ◻ 9am–
8pm Mon–Thu, 9am–7pm Fri, 10am–
5pm Sat; 21 Jun–8 Aug: 9am–6pm
Mon–Thu, 9am–5pm Fri, 11am–3pm
Sat. 📷 by appointment. 🚹 ▢
www.kb.se

This is Sweden's national
library and an autonomous
Government department in its
own right. Ever since 1661,
when there were only nine
printing presses in Sweden,
copies of every piece of
printed matter have had to
be lodged with Kungliga
Biblioteket (Royal Library).
Since 1993 this requirement
has also applied to electronic
documents. As there are now
some 3,000 printers and publishers in Sweden the volume
of material is expanding
rapidly. The stock of books is
increasing at the rate of 35,000
volumes a year, not to mention
40,000 magazine issues.

The library's shelving space
is increasing by 1,300 m
(4,265 ft) per year and the
collection now covers more
than 3 million books and
magazines, more than 500,000
posters, 300,000 maps, 750,000
portraits and 500,000 pictures
of varying types.
The imposing orig-
inal building, dating
from 1865–78, had
to be expanded in
the 1920s, and
again in the 1990s.
This major
extension provided
an auditorium for
120 people, an
exhibition area and,
most importantly, two
underground book storage
areas covering an area in total
of 18,000 sq m (193,680 sq ft).
The first of these is already
fully utilized despite its 843
mobile shelves. Altogether the
library's shelves cover 137 km
(85 miles).

The library is in a beautiful
setting in Humlegården,
created by Gustav II Adolf in
1619 to grow hops for the
royal household. Ever since
the 18th century, the park has
been a favourite recreation
area for Stockholmers.

Stureplan ㉑

Map 3 D4. Ⓣ Östermalmstorg.
🚌 1, 2, 55, 56, 91.

A new town plan for Stockholm towards the end of the
19th century recommended
that the Stureplan area should
become the capital's new
centre. The proposal was
accepted and the area around
Svampen (The Mushroom)

Stureplan and Svampen, one of the
city's most popular meeting places

THE MURDERED PRIME MINISTER

**Olof Palme
(1927–86)**

On 28 February 1986 the Swedish Prime
Minister Olof Palme was killed in a
Stockholm street on his way home from
a cinema without a bodyguard. The murder happened at the corner of Sveavägen
and Tunnelgatan, whose western section
was renamed Olof Palmes Gata. A
memorial tablet has been placed there.
The murder provoked strong reactions
but was still unsolved at the beginning
of the new millennium. His grave is in
the nearby Adolf Fredrik cemetery.

rain shelter became a popular meeting place, as more and more shops and restaurants opened. However, a new street layout after the introduction of right-hand driving in Sweden in 1967 brought its halcyon days to a close.

But now Stureplan has staged a phoenix-like comeback out of the ashes of a major fire at the Sturebadet swimming pool in 1985. Plans to revamp the area were made: the pool was modernized and the Sturegallerian shopping mall was built, revitalizing the whole eastern part of the city. Once again Stureplan became one of the capital's most popular meeting places.

Sturegallerian and Sturebadet ㉒

Stureplan 4. **Map** 3 D4.
Ⓣ *Östermalmstorg.* 🚌 *1, 2, 55, 56, 91.* **Shopping mall** ⏲ *10am–7pm Mon–Fri, 10am–5pm Sat, noon–5pm Sun.* **Pool Tel** *545 015 00.* ⏲ *6:30am–10pm Mon–Fri, 9am–4pm Sat; other times by appointment & members only.* 🖥 🍴

The original Sturebadet swimming pool, opened in 1885, was sited within the present-day StureCompagniet complex. Rebuilt on its present site in 1902, it was ahead of its time – even in the 1930s it was offering exercise facilities.

After a disastrous fire in 1985 some 600 million kr was invested, partly on reconstructing the pool according to its original design and partly on developing Sturegallerian, a world-class shopping mall. The architects managed to link the late 19th-century exterior with interiors of modern design using marble, granite, steel, copper, cedar and mahogany.

Indoor streets and squares with some 50 retail outlets have been created, including restaurants, cafés and various services. Today's swimming pool is now the most traditional part of the complex, which also includes offices.

Opened in 1989, the development won an international award in 1990 for its excellent design.

Painstakingly restored Jugendstil decor at Sturebadet

Östermalms- hallen ㉓

Humlegårdsgatan 1–3. **Map** 3 E4.
Ⓣ *Östermalmstorg.* 🚌 *56, 62.* ⏲ *9:30am–6pm Mon–Thu, 9:30am–6:30pm Fri, 9:30am–4pm Sat, 9:30am–2pm Sat in Summer.* 🔌 🍴

The temple of gastronomy, this market hall on Östermalmstorg is as far removed from a fast-food outlet as you could imagine. Nowhere else in the city is there such a range of high quality delicacies under one roof. But it was certainly an example of fast building. Taking only eight months to erect, the hall was opened by King Oscar II in 1888. It is regarded as a fine example of the city's late 19th-century architectural heritage. Construction of a brick building around a cast-iron shell was a novelty in Sweden, and the architects Gustaf Clason and Kasper Sahlin won acclaim for their design, inspired by the arcades of Mediterranean markets. Renovation in 1999 has preserved the delightful atmosphere. In the early days there were 153 stalls, and today there are 13 larger specialist shops and some popular lunch spots.

Hedvig Eleonora Kyrka ㉔

Storgatan 2. **Map** 3 E4.
Tel *663 04 30.* Ⓣ *Östermalmstorg.* 🚌 *62.* ⏲ *11am–6pm daily.* ✝ *12:15pm Tue & Thu, 7pm Wed, 11am Sun.* 🔑 *by appt.* 🔌 🈁

Founded in 1669 to give the Swedish Navy its own place for religious services, the church was not officially opened until 1737. The first plans were drawn up by Jean de la Vallée, but the work was completed with Göran Josuae Adelcrantz as architect. The dome was added in 1866–8. The main bell was cast in Helsingør, Denmark, in 1639 and hung in Kronborg Castle before being seized as a war trophy by General Carl Gustaf Wrangel (*see p56*).

The church has many valuable artifacts. The altarpiece *Jesus on the Cross* was painted in 1738 by Engelhard Schröder. The designer of the majestic pulpit in Neo-Classical style was Jean Eric Rehn, who saw his work unveiled on Christmas Day in 1784.

The new organ was built in the mid-1970s, but Carl Fredrik Adelcrantz's 1762 organ façade is still in its original state. Included in the silverware is a Baroque chalice from 1650 and a christening bowl dated 1685. The 1678 font is now housed in the baptismal chapel which was added at the time of the church's restoration in 1944.

Östermalmshallen, a culinary temple inspired by markets in southern Europe

Armémuseum, with the dome of Hedvig Eleonora Kyrka in the background

Armémuseum ㉕

Riddargatan 13. **Map** 3 E4.
Tel *519 56 300.* T *Östermalmstorg.*
▥ *47, 62.* ◯ *11am–8pm Tue,*
11am–4pm Wed–Sun. ▨ ▨ ▨ ⚠
▯ ▯ ▯

The old armoury on
Artillerigården has been the
home of the Armémuseum
(Royal Army Museum) since
1879. During the 1990s the
250-year-old building and its
exhibits underwent extensive
renovation. It is now one of
the capital's best-planned and
most interesting museums.

It puts Sweden's history in a
1,000-year perspective, present-
ing exciting information in a
more comprehensive way.
The march of history is
illustrated by life-size settings,
and visitors can see many
unique objects from the
collection of 80,000 exhibits.

Processions for royal visits
in the city start from the
museum, and during the
summer guardsmen march
from here to the Royal Palace
at 11.45am every day for the
changing of the guard.

Musikmuseet ㉖

Riddargatan/Sibyllegatan. **Map** 3 E4.
Tel *519 554 90.* T *Östermalmstorg.*
▥ *2, 47, 55, 62, 69, 76.* ◯ *noon–*
5pm Tue–Sun. ▨ ▨ ⚠ ▯ ▯
www.stockholm.music.museum

After being housed on nine
different sites, the Museum of
Music finally moved into this
former royal bakery in 1979.
It is the capital's oldest
preserved industrial building,
right in the city centre. Bread
was baked here for military
personnel in Stockholm from
1640 right up to 1958. Today
the museum's collection

includes about 6,000 instruments, and it also holds
Sweden's national musical
archive. With some 20,000
manuscripts, it is a gold
mine for anyone
interested in Swedish
folk music. The archive
is open to visitors by
arrangement, and
there is a regular
programme of
temporary
exhibitions.

A so-called *hummel*
instrument once
owned by the troub-
adour C M Bellman

Hovstallet ㉗

Väpnargatan 1. **Map** 3 E4. **Tel** *402*
60 00. T *Östermalmstorg.* ▥ *47,*
62, 69, 76. ◯ *for guided tours.* ◖
public hols. ▨ *2pm Sat & Sun;*
Jul–Aug: 2pm Mon–Fri. ▨ ▯

Formerly on Helgeands-
holmen, Hovstallet (the Royal
Mews) was moved here in
1893 when the new Parlia-
ment building was being
constructed. Together with
the Museum of Music, it now
occupies a large site next to
the Royal Dramatic Theatre.

The Mews arranges the transport for the Royal Family and

Coach and four, with riders on the
left-hand horses, at Hovstallet

the Royal Household. It
maintains about 40 carriages,
a dozen cars and carriage
horses, and a few horses used
for riding. The royal horses
are Swedish half-breeds.

There are many treasures
among the carriages, such as
the State coach with glass
panelling known as a
"Berliner" made in Sweden at
the Adolf Freyschuss carriage
works. It was first seen at
Oscar II's silver jubilee in
1897 and is still used on
ceremonial occasions.

Incoming foreign ambassa-
dors travel to the Royal Palace
for their formal audience with
the monarch in Karl XV's
coupé. Open carriages from
the mid-19th century drawn
by two horses are normally
used for processions.

Kungliga Drama-
tiska Teatern ㉘

Nybroplan. **Map** 3 E4. **Tel** *667 06 80.*
T *Östermalmstorg.* ▥ *47, 62, 69,*
76. **Ticket Office** ◯ *noon–7pm*
Tue–Sat, noon–4pm Sun. ▨ ▨ ⚠
▯ **www**.dramaten.se

When plans were drawn up
in the early 20th century to
build the present Kungliga
Dramatiska Teatern (Royal
Dramatic Theatre) at Nybroplan, the State refused to give
financial aid, so it was funded
by lotteries instead. The results
exceeded all expectations,
giving the architect Fredrik
Lilljekvist generous resources
which he used to the full.

The new theatre, known as
Dramaten, was opened in 1908
after six years' construction
work, and its fittings and decor
were remarkable for their era.

The Jugendstil façade
inspired by Viennese architecture is in costly white

marble. Christian Ericsson provided the powerful relief frieze, Carl Milles the centre section and John Börjesson the bronze statues *Poetry* and *Drama*. These are complemented in the foyer by *Tragedy* and *Comedy* by Börjesson and Theodor Lundberg respectively.

The lavish design continues inside, both in the choice of materials and in the contributions by leading Swedish artists. The ceiling in the foyer is by Carl Larsson, while the upper lobby's back wall was painted by Oscar Björk, and the auditorium's ceiling and stage lintel by Julius Kronberg. Gustav Cederström provided the central painting in the marble foyer, which also has some fantastic sculptures and busts.

Georg Pauli gave his name to a café where visitors can see his paintings and enjoy a meal without necessarily attending a performance.

The 805-seat auditorium and revolving stage with a diameter of 15 m (49 ft) have a classic beauty. When Gustav III founded the Royal Dramatic Theatre in 1788 it performed in a building on Slottsbacken. The probable colour scheme there – blue, white and gold – was chosen for the new national stage but was changed to the traditional "theatre red" in the 1930s. The auditorium was returned to its original colouring during renovation in 1988.

About 100 contracted actors give some 1,200 performances every year on the theatre's five stages to audiences totalling about 300,000.

The Hallwylska Palatset courtyard, seen through the gateway arch

Hallwylska Palatset ❷

Hamngatan 4. **Map** 3 D4. **Tel** *519 555 99.* Ⓣ *Östermalmstorg.* 🚌 *2, 47, 55, 62, 69, 76.* 📷 *noon–3pm every hour Tue–Sun, also 6pm Wed, 1pm Sun (Eng). 26 Jun–15 Aug: 11am–4pm daily every hour.* 📷 📷 📷 www.hallwylskamuseet.se

The impressive façade of Hamngatan 4 is nothing in comparison with what is concealed by the heavy gates. The Hallwyl Palace was built from 1892–7 as a residence for the immeasurably rich Count and Countess Walther and Wilhelmina von Hallwyl. They decided quite early that the house should eventually become a museum. When the Countess died in 1930 the State was left a fantastic gift: an

The Steinway grand piano in Hallwylska Palatset

unbelievably lavish private palace whose chatelaine had amassed a priceless collection of *objets d'art* over many decades. Eight years later the doors opened on a new museum with 67,000 catalogued items.

Wilhelmina left nothing to chance. The architect Isac Gustav Clason (1856–1930) had no worries about cost and nor did Julius Kronberg, who was a decorative painter and artistic adviser. Everything had to be perfect down to the smallest detail. A typical example is the billiards room which has gilt-leather wallpaper and walnut panelling, with billiard balls sculpted into the marble fireplace.

The paintings in the gallery, mostly 16th- and 17th-century Flemish, were bought over a period of only two years. Adjoining the gallery, the family skittles alley has become a showcase for top-class glazed earthenware. Visitors can also see a rich variety of household objects which could well form a separate exhibition.

Various styles were chosen for the different rooms. The main salon in late Baroque style is built around four grandiose Gobelin tapestries and is finished in 24-carat gold leaf, clearly influenced by Hårleman's work at the Royal Palace *(see pp50–53)*. It is difficult to believe that this was once a room in a private residence.

The most remarkable artifact is a Steinway grand piano, dating from 1896, adapted to fit into its majestic setting with a "casing" of hardwood and inlaid wood. In 1990 it was flown to New York in two sections, weighing a total of 900 kg (1,980 lb), for a renovation lasting several months. Visitors strolling through the salon can listen to a recording of music played on this magnificent piano.

Kungliga Dramatiska Teatern's Jugendstil façade in white marble

BLASIEHOLMEN & SKEPPSHOLMEN

Porthole in wooden boat

Opposite the Royal Palace on the eastern side of the Strömmen channel lies Blasieholmen, a natural springboard to the islands of Skeppsholmen and Kastellholmen.

Several elegant palaces were built at Blasieholmen during Sweden's era as a great power in the 17th and early 18th centuries. But the area's present appearance was acquired in the period between the mid-19th century, when buildings like Nationalmuseum were erected, until just before World War I. In the early 1900s, stately residences such as Bååtska Palatset became overshadowed by prestigious hotels, lavish banks and entertainment venues. Blasieholmen is also the place for auction houses, art galleries, antique shops and second-hand bookshops. And the quayside is the departure point for sightseeing and archipelago boats.

Skeppsholmen is reached by a wrought-iron bridge with old wooden boats moored next to it. In the middle of the 17th century the island became the base for the Swedish Navy and many of its old buildings were designed as barracks and stores. Today they house some of the city's major museums and cultural institutions, juxtaposed with the avant-garde construction of the Moderna Museet.

SIGHTS AT A GLANCE

Museums
Arkitekturmuseet ❸
Moderna Museet pp80–81 ❷
Nationalmuseum pp82–3 ❼
Östasiatiska Museet ❶

Public Buildings
Konsthögskolan ❺

Islands and Squares
Blasieholmstorg ❾
Kastellholmen ❻
Raoul Wallenbergs Torg ⓬

Synagogues
Synagogan ❿

Hotels and Restaurants
af Chapman ❹
Berns' Salonger ⓫
Grand Hôtel ❽

Concert Halls
Nybrokajen 11 ⓭

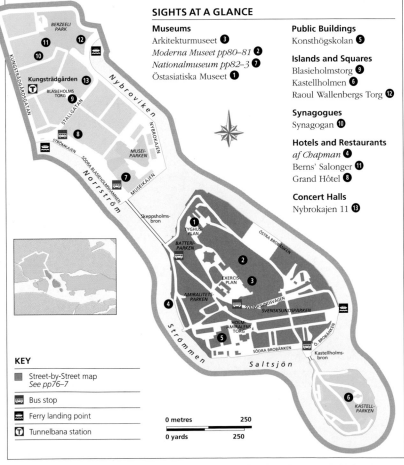

KEY

	Street-by-Street map *See pp76–7*
🚌	Bus stop
⛴	Ferry landing point
Ⓣ	Tunnelbana station

0 metres 250
0 yards 250

◁ **Skeppsholmsbron linking Blasieholmen and Skeppsholmen, with the ship *af Chapman* in the background**

Street-by-Street: Skeppsholmen

Skeppsholmen has long since lost its importance as a
naval base and has been transformed into a centre for
culture. Many of the naval buildings have been restored
and traditional wooden boats are moored here, but pride
of place now goes to the exciting new Moderna Museet.

The island is ideal for a full-day visit, with its location
between the waters of Strömmen and Nybroviken acting
as a breathing space in the centre of Stockholm. The
attractive buildings, the richly wooded English-style park
and the view towards Skeppsbron and Strandvägen also
make Skeppsholmen an ideal place for those who
would just prefer to have a quiet stroll.

Teater Galeasen is
Stockholm's avant-garde
theatre for new Swedish
and international drama.

Skepps-
holmsbron

Blasie-
holmen

★ Östasiatiska Museet
*This belt plaquette in Ordos style
from the 1st or 2nd century BC
is included in a remarkable collection of arts and crafts from
China, Japan, Korea and India,
covering the period from the
Stone Age to the 19th century* ❶

**Skeppsholmen
Church**
(1824–42) in
well-preserved
Empire style.

**Salute
battery**

Admiralty House

Paradise (1963), a
sculpture group by
Jean Tinguelys and
Niki de Saint Phalles
for Montreal's World
Exposition, has stood
outside the site of
the Moderna Museet
since 1972.

SVENSKSUNDSVÄGEN

VÄSTRA BROBÄNKEN

Youth Hostel

**Swedish
Society of
Crafts & Design**

af Chapman
*Built in 1888, the full-rigged former freighter
and school ship has served as a popular youth
hostel since 1949. Skeppsholmen Church (left)
and the Admiralty House (1647–50, rebuilt
1844–6) are in the background* ❹

Kungliga Konsthögskolan
*The first part of the Royal College
of Fine Arts was completed in
the 1770s, but it acquired its
present appearance in
the mid-1990s. This
cast-iron boar
stands at the
entrance* ❺

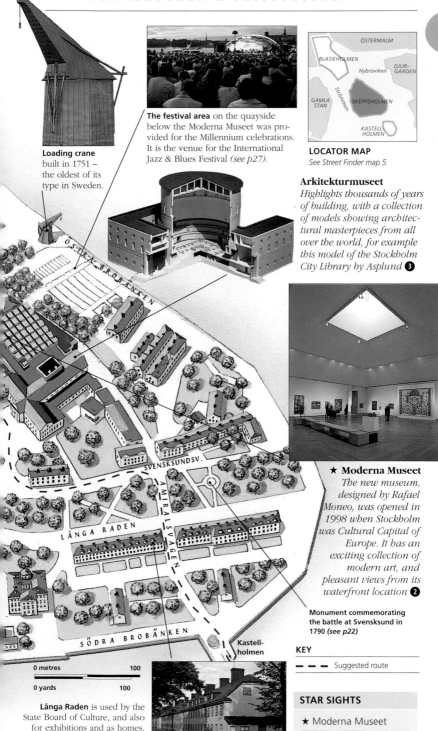

Loading crane
built in 1751 –
the oldest of its
type in Sweden.

The festival area on the quayside
below the Moderna Museet was provided for the Millennium celebrations.
It is the venue for the International
Jazz & Blues Festival *(see p27)*.

ÖSTERMALM

BLASIEHOLMEN

Nybroviken

DJUR-
GARDEN

Strömmen

GAMLA
STAN

SKEPPSHOLMEN

KASTELL-
HOLMEN

LOCATOR MAP
See Street Finder map 5

Arkitekturmuseet
*Highlights thousands of years
of building, with a collection
of models showing architectural masterpieces from all
over the world, for example
this model of the Stockholm
City Library by Asplund* ❸

ÖSTRA BROBÄNKEN

SVENSKSUNDSV.

AMIRALSVÄGEN

LÅNGA RADEN

SÖDRA BROBÄNKEN

Kastell-
holmen

★ **Moderna Museet**
*The new museum,
designed by Rafael
Moneo, was opened in
1998 when Stockholm
was Cultural Capital of
Europe. It has an
exciting collection of
modern art, and
pleasant views from its
waterfront location* ❷

**Monument commemorating
the battle at Svensksund in
1790** *(see p22)*

KEY

— — — Suggested route

| 0 metres | 100 |
| 0 yards | 100 |

Långa Raden is used by the
State Board of Culture, and also
for exhibitions and as homes.
The buildings, dating from about
1700, originally accommodated
King Karl XII's bodyguard.

STAR SIGHTS

★ Moderna Museet

★ Östasiatiska Museet

Arkitekturmuseet, housed in the Neo-Classical former naval drill hall

Östasiatiska Museet **❶**

Tyghusplan. **Map** 5 D2. *Tel* 519 557 70. Ⓣ *Kungsträdgården.* 🚌 65. 🚢 *Djurgårdsfärja.* ◯ *11am–8pm Tue, 11am–5pm Wed–Sun.* 🗓 🛇 ♿ 🏛 www.ostasiatiska.se

It is not unusual for Western capitals to have a museum devoted to art and archaeology from China, Japan, Korea and India. But it is not every Museum of Far Eastern Antiquities that, like Östasiatiska Museet, can claim one of the world's foremost collections of Chinese art outside Asia.

On a visit to the Yellow River valley in China in the early 1920s, the Swedish geologist Johan Gunnar Andersson discovered hitherto unknown dwellings and graves containing objects dating from the New Stone Age.

He was allowed by the Chinese to take a rich selection of finds back to Sweden, and these formed the basis for the museum, founded in 1926. A key figure in its development was the then Crown Prince, later to become King Gustaf VI Adolf, who was both

Chinese Bodhisattva in limestone from about AD 530

interested in and knowledgeable about archaeology. He eventually bequeathed to the museum his own large collection of ancient Chinese arts and crafts.

The museum has been on Skeppsholmen since 1963, when it was moved into a restored house which had been built in 1699–1700 as a depot for Karl XII's bodyguard.

Moderna Museet **❷**

See pp80–81.

Arkitektur- museet **❸**

Exercisplan. **Map** 5 E3. *Tel* 587 270 00. Ⓣ *Kungsträd-gården.* 🚌 65. 🚢 *Djurgårdsfärja.* ◯ *10am–8pm Tue–Wed, 10am–6pm Thu–Sun.* 🗓 *by arrangement (for a fee).* 🛇 ♿ 🍴 🖥 🏛 🎧 www.arkitekturmuseet.se

The Swedish Museum of Architecture shares an entrance hall and restaurant with the new Moderna Museet. It has also taken over

its earlier home, the one-time naval drill hall.

In the permanent exhibition, over a hundred models guide visitors through a thousand years of building. These cover categories from the oldest and simplest of wooden houses to the highly varied building techniques and architectural styles of the present day.

It is fascinating to switch from an almost 2,000-year-old longhouse to a Konsum supermarket, in between encountering examples of architecture in Gothenburg dating from the 17th century to the 1930s and the new Årsta bridge situated to the south of Stockholm.

Models of historic architectural works worldwide, from 2000 BC up to the present day, are also on show.

The museum offers an ambitious programme – albeit only in Swedish – alongside the permanent and temporary exhibitions, including lectures, study days, walks around the city, guided tours, school visits and family events on Sunday afternoons.

THE SKEPPSHOLMEN CANNONS

A salute battery of four 57-mm rapid-fire cannons is sited on Skeppsholmen and are still in use. Salutes are fired to mark national and royal special occasions at 12 noon on weekdays and 1pm at weekends: 28 January – the King's name day; 30 April – the King's birthday; 6 June – Sweden's National Day; 14 July – Crown Princess Victoria's birthday; 8 August – the Queen's name day; 23 December – the Queen's birthday.

The salute battery on Skeppsholmen

af Chapman ④

Västra Brobänken. **Map** 5 D3.
Tel 463 22 66 Ⓣ Kungsträdgården.
🚌 65. 🚢 Djurgårdsfärja. 🖵 See
Where to stay p149.

The sailing ship af Chapman
is one of Sweden's most
attractive and unusual youth
hostels and has 136 beds. The
hostel also includes the 152-
bed building facing the ship's
gangway.

Visitors staying in more
conventional accommodation
can still go on board and
enjoy af Chapman's special
atmosphere. The three-masted
ship was built in 1888 at the
English port of Whitehaven
and used as a freight vessel.
She came to Sweden in 1915
and saw service as a school
ship until 1934. The City of
Stockholm bought the ship
after World War II and she
has been berthed here since
1949. She is named after
Fredrik Henrik af Chapman, a
master shipbuilder who was
born in Gothenburg in 1721.

Kungliga Konst-
högskolan ⑤

Flaggmansvägen 1. **Map** 5 E3.
Tel 614 40 00. Ⓣ Kungsträdgården.
🚌 65. 🚢 Djurgårdsfärja. ⬭ to the
public for special events. ♿ 🖵

A stroll around Skeppsholmen
provides an opportunity to
have a closer look at the
beautifully restored 18th-
century naval barracks which
now houses Kungliga
Konsthögskolan (the Royal
College of Fine Arts). At the
entrance there are two statues
depicting a lion and a boar.
"In like a lion and out like a
pig" is an old saying among
the lecturers and the 200 or so
students at this college, rich in
tradition.

The college started out in
1735 as an academy for
painting and sculpture for the
decorators working on Tessin's
new Royal Palace. Gustaf III
granted it a royal charter in
1773. Before it moved here in
1995, the college was located
on Fredsgatan as part of
Konstakademien (see p66),
although since 1978 it had

been run independently with
departments for painting,
sculpture, graphics, computing
and video, as well as offering
courses for architects.

The college is not normally
open to the public, apart from
an "open house" once a year.
Then visitors can enjoy the
beautiful interiors, especially
the vaulted 18th-century cellars.

**The medieval-style castle on
Kastellholmen, built in 1846–8**

Kastellholmen ⑥

Map 5 F4. Ⓣ Kungsträdgården.
🚌 65. 🚢 Djurgårdsfärja.

Right in the middle of
Stockholm, Kastellholmen is a
typical archipelago island with
granite rocks and steep cliffs.
From Skeppsholmen it is
reached by a bridge built in
1880. Every morning since
1640 a sailor has hoisted the
three-tailed Swedish war flag
at the castle. Whenever a
visiting naval vessel arrives,
the battery's four cannons

fire a welcoming salute from
the castle terrace.

The charming brick pavilion
by the bridge was built in 1882
for the Royal Skating Club,
which used the water between
the two islands when it froze.

Nationalmuseum ⑦

See pp80–81.

Grand Hôtel ⑧

Södra Blasieholmshamnen 8. **Map** 4
C1. **Tel** 679 35 00. Ⓣ Kungsträdgården. 🚌 55, 59, 62, 65, 76. See
Where to stay p151 and **Where
to eat** p161.

Oscar II's head chef, Régis
Cadier, founded the Grand
Hôtel, Sweden's leading five-
star hotel, in 1874. And since
1901, the hotel has
accommodated the Nobel
Prize winners every year.

Traditional Swedish
delicacies are served in an
abundant smörgåsbord in
the elegant Grands Veranda,
while Franska Matsalen is a
stylish gourmet restaurant.
The Cadier Bar is named after
the hotel's founder.

The hotel has 19 banquet-
ing and meeting suites, the
best known of which is the
Vinterträdgården (Winter
Garden) with a ceiling height
of 20 m (66 ft) and space for
more than 700 people. The
Spegelsalen (Hall of Mirrors) is
a copy of the one at Versailles
and was where the Nobel Prize
banquet was held until 1929,
when the event became
too big and was moved to
the City Hall (see p114).

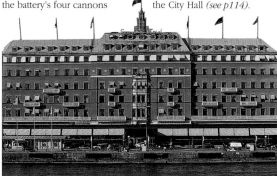

Grand Hôtel on Blasieholmen, Sweden's only five-star hotel

Moderna Museet ❸

The Museum of Modern Art is an airy new building, designed by the Catalan architect Rafael Moneo, in 1998. The museum has a top-class collection of international and Swedish modern art, as well as photography and film. Built partly underground, the museum includes a cinema and auditorium; the photographic library is the most comprehensive collection of its type in northern Europe and there is also a collection of video art and art documentaries. A wide choice of books on art, photography, film and architecture can be found in the bookshop and the Restaurant MM Mat has attractive views over the water.

★ **Iván by the Armchair**
(1915) *Isaac Grünewald painted this portrait of his son after studying under Henri Matisse in Paris.*

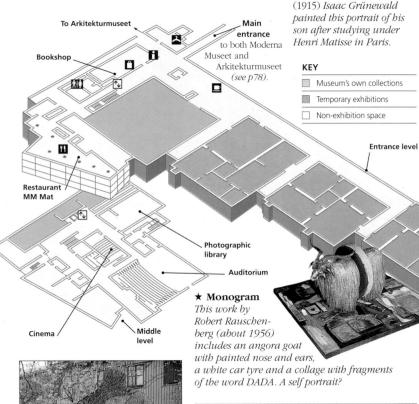

To Arkitekturmuseet

Bookshop

Main entrance
to both Moderna Museet and Arkitekturmuseet *(see p78).*

KEY

▢	Museum's own collections
▢	Temporary exhibitions
▢	Non-exhibition space

Entrance level

Restaurant MM Mat

Photographic library

Auditorium

Cinema

Middle level

★ **Monogram**
This work by Robert Rauschenberg (about 1956) includes an angora goat with painted nose and ears, a white car tyre and a collage with fragments of the word DADA. A self portrait?

Breakfast Outdoors (1962)
This sculpture group by Picasso, executed in sandblasted concrete by Carl Nesjar, stands in the museum garden near the entrance.

RAFAEL MONEO

Rafael Moneo (b. 1937) is one of the leading contemporary architects. As a young architect Moneo took part in the project to build the Sydney Opera House. His flair for adapting building design to sensitive surroundings was recognized in 1989 when he was chosen out of 211 entries as the winner of the competition to design the new Moderna Museet.

Moderna Museet's northern façade

VISITORS' CHECKLIST

Exercisplan. **Map** 5 E3.
Tel 519 552 82. ⊤ Kungsträdgården. 🚌 65. ⛴ Djurgårdsfärja. ◯ 10am–8pm Tue–Wed,
10am–6pm Thu–Sun. ● 24–25,
31 Dec, 1 Jan, Easter Mon, Whit
Mon, midsummer eve. 🗓 Eng:
summer. 📷 some temporary
exhibitions. 🚫 ♿ 🍴 🎧 🖥
🔲 www.modernamuseet.se

GALLERY GUIDE

*The large room on the entrance
level is used for temporary
exhibitions. Three rooms on
the same level have an alternat-
ing selection of collections
from three eras: 1900–45,
1946–70, and 1971 to the
present day. The middle level
has an auditorium, cinema
and photographic library. The
lowest level has an entrance.*

★ **The Child's Brain** (1914)
*The surrealist Giorgio de
Chirico gave his work the
title* The Ghost *but Louis
Aragon renamed it in a
pamphlet about the artist's
1927 retrospective exhibition.*

STAR EXHIBITS

★ Iván by the Armchair
 by Grünewald

★ Monogram
 by Rauschenberg

★ The Child's Brain
 by de Chirico

Blasieholmstorg ❾

Map 4 C1. ⊤ Kungsträdgården.
🚌 2, 55, 59, 62, 65, 76.

Two of the city's oldest
palaces are located in this
square, flanked by two bronze
horses. The palace at No. 8
was built in the mid-17th
century by Field Marshal
Gustaf Horn. It was rebuilt
100 years later, when it
acquired the character of an
18th-century French palace.
Foreign ambassadors and
ministers started to lodge here
when they visited
the capital, so it
became known
as the Ministers'
Palace. Later it
became a base for
overseas admin-
istration and soon
earned its present
name of Utrikes-
ministerhotellet
(Foreign Ministry
Hotel). Parts of the
building are now used as
offices by the Musical Academy
and the Swedish Institute.

Bååtska Palatset stands
nearby at No. 6. Its newly
restored exterior dates from
1669 and was designed by
Tessin the Elder. In 1876–7 it
was partly rebuilt by F W
Scholander for the Free-
masons, who still have their
lodge here.

Another interesting complex
of buildings can be found on
the square at No. 10. The
façade which faces on to
Nybrokajen, along the water's
edge, is an attractive example
of the Neo-Renaissance style
of the 1870s and 1880s.

**Bronze horse on
Blasieholmstorg**

Synagogan ❿

Warendorfsgatan 3. **Map** 4 C1.
Tel 587 858 00. ⊤ Kungsträdgården.
🚌 46, 55, 59, 62, 65, 76. ⚡
5:30pm Mon, Thu, Fri; 9:15 Sat;
Hebrew, partly Swedish. 🗓 Summer
and on request. ♿

It took most of the 1860s
to build the Conservative
Jewish community's syna-
gogue on what was once the
seabed. When it was inaugurated in 1870, the synagogue
was standing on 1,300 piles

**Monument to the victims of the
Holocaust during World War II**

which had been driven down
to a depth of 15 m (50 ft). It
is built in what the architect,
F W Scholander, called
"ancient Eastern style".

Alongside this synagogue,
which can be visited
on guided tours
during the summer,
is the
congregation's
assembly room and
library. Outside is a
monument erected
in 1998 to the mem-
ory of 8,000 victims
of the Holocaust whose
relations had been rescued
and taken to Sweden during
World War II.

There is also an Orthodox
synagogue in the city centre,
reached through the Jewish
Centre (Judiska Centret) on
Nybrogatan at No. 19.

Berns' Salonger ⓫

Berzeli Park. **Map** 3 D4. **Tel** 566 322
00. ⊤ Kungsträdgården,
Östermalmstorg. 🚌 2, 55, 59, 62,
65, 76. ♿ **Where to eat** p160.

This has been one of Stockholm's most legendary
restaurants and entertainment
venues since 1863. Both
salons, with their stately
galleries, magnificent crystal
chandeliers and elegant
mirrors, have recently been
restored to their original
splendour by the British
designer Terence Conran to
mark the new millennium.

The new-look Berns' is one
of Stockholm's biggest
restaurants with seating for
400 diners. The gallery level,
with its beautifully decorated
dining rooms, was made
famous by August Strindberg's
novel *The Red Room* (1879).

Nationalmuseum ❼

The National Museum is a landmark on the southern side of Blasieholmen. The location by the Strömmen channel inspired the 19th-century German architect August Stüler to design a building in the Venetian and Florentine Renaissance styles.

Completed in 1866, the museum houses Sweden's largest art collection, with some 16,000 classic paintings and sculptures. Drawings and graphics from the 15th century up to the early 20th century bring the total up to 500,000. The applied art and design section has 30,000 works spanning five centuries, including a 500-year-old tapestry, Scandinavia's largest collection of porcelain, as well as examples of work by master furnishers, such as Georg Haupt, and of modern Swedish design.

The Love Lesson (1716–17)
Antoine Watteau's speciality was the so-called fêtes galantes, depicting young couples in playful mood.

★ The Conspiracy of the Batavians under Claudius Civilis (1661–62)
Originally intended for Amsterdam, Rembrandt depicts the Batavians' conspiracy against the Romans, symbolizing the Dutch liberation campaign against Spain.

Level 2

Chest of Drawers (1780)
This impressive piece of furniture was created by Georg Haupt, who was one of the foremost Swedish cabinet-makers of the 18th century.

Atrium through levels 1 and 2

Gravure gallery

Entrance

Entry for wheelchairs

David and Bathsheba (1490)
This tapestry from Brussels is created in the decorative medieval style, with pomegranates, faces and hands forming an exquisite work.

STAR PAINTINGS

★ The Lady with the Veil by Roslin

★ The Conspiracy of the Batavians by Rembrandt

★ **The Lady with the Veil**
*Alexander Roslin's elegant
portrait (1769) is often
considered a symbol for
18th-century Sweden.*

The Upper Staircase
*At the back is Carl Larsson's
monumental mural* The Entry
of King Gustav Vasa of
Sweden in Stockholm 1523.
On the opposite wall is his
Midwinter Sacrifice.

The Faun (1774)
*Johan Tobias Sergel was the
foremost sculptor of the Gustavian
era. This piece is regarded as his
most triumphant work.*

Level 1

Auditorium

Entrance
level

KEY

▢ Painting and sculpture

▢ Applied art and design

▢ Temporary exhibitions

▢ Non-exhibition space

▢ No admission

GALLERY GUIDE

*Level 2 is devoted to painting
and sculpture. The accent is
on Swedish 18th- to early
20th-century art, but the 17th-
century Dutch and Flemish,
and 18th-century French
schools are also represented.
Exhibits may change. Level 1
shows mainly Swedish applied
art and design, particularly
furniture, porcelain, silver
and glass from the 15th
century up to modern Swedish design. To the left of the
main entrance is the Gravure
Gallery with temporary
exhibitions of graphics etc.*

Raoul Wallenbergs Torg ⑫

Map 3 E4. 🚇 Östermalmstorg.
🚌 2, 55, 59, 62, 65, 76.

This square is dedicated to
Raoul Wallenberg (1912–
unknown), who during World
War II worked as a diplomat
at the Swedish Embassy in
Budapest. By using Swedish
"protective passports" he
helped a large number of
Hungarian Jews to escape
deportation to the Nazi
concentration camps.

In 1945, when Budapest
was liberated, he was impris-
oned by the Soviets and
according to Soviet sources
he died in Moscow's Lubianka
prison in 1947. His fate,
however, has never been
satisfactorily explained.

The small square adjoins
Berzelii Park and Nybroplan
and faces the Nybrokajen
waterfront. The definitive
design of the square has been
hotly debated because it is
set in a sensitive architectural
environment, but great efforts
have been made to ensure
that it remains a worthy
memorial to Raoul Wallenberg.

Nybrokajen 11 ⑬

Nybrokajen 11. **Map** 4 C1.
Tel 401 17 00. 🚇 Kungsträdgården,
Östermalmstorg. 🚌 47, 62, 69, 76.
🚢 Djurgårdsfärja. 🕐 for concerts
(phone for details). ♿
www.nybrokajen11.rikskonserter.se

Constructed in the 1870s,
this building facing the waters
of Nybroviken once housed
the Musical Academy. Its concert hall, opened in 1878, was
the first in the country, and
was used for the first
presentations of the Nobel
Prize in 1901. Designed in
Neo-Renaissance style with
cast-iron pillars, the hall has a
royal box and galleries, and
can seat up to 600 people.

After extensive restoration,
it is now run by the state
musical organization
Rikskonserter which has
provided a much-needed concert stage for chamber, choral,
jazz and folk music (see p177).

DJURGÅRDEN

Once a royal hunting ground, Djurgården is an island right in the centre of Stockholm covered by a natural park. It has very few buildings with only around 800 permanent residents and forms part of the Stockholm National City Park, the only one of its type in the world *(see p121)*.

Museum tram

From 1580 parts of Djurgården were a royal animal reserve where Johan III kept reindeer, red deer and elk. A century later the area was fenced off by Karl XI to be used for hunting. It developed into a popular recreational park during the 18th century, and in the time of troubador Carl Bellman *(see p98)* many inns appeared. The Gröna Lund funfair was established just a few decades before Artur Hazelius founded the fascinating outdoor museum of Skansen and Nordiska Museet in around 1900. Today, there is a wealth of museums on Djurgården offering a mixture of nature, culture and entertainment. A royal connection survives in the beautiful Rosendal Palace which has magnificent Empire-style decor.

SIGHTS AT A GLANCE

Museums
Aquaria **8**
Biologiska Museet **7**
Junibacken **2**
Liljevalchs Konsthall **9**
Museifartygen **6**
Nordiska museet pp90–91 **3**
Waldemarsudde **14**
Skansen pp96–7 **12**
Thielska Galleriet **15**
Vasamuseet pp92–3 **5**

Historic Areas
Djurgårdsstaden & Beckholmen **11**
Rosendals Slott & Trädgårdar **13**

Memorials
Estoniaminnesvården **4**

Bridges
Djurgårds-bron **1**

Amusement Parks
Gröna Lund **10**

KEY

- Street-by-Street map See pp86–7
- Bus stop
- Tram stop
- Ferry landing point

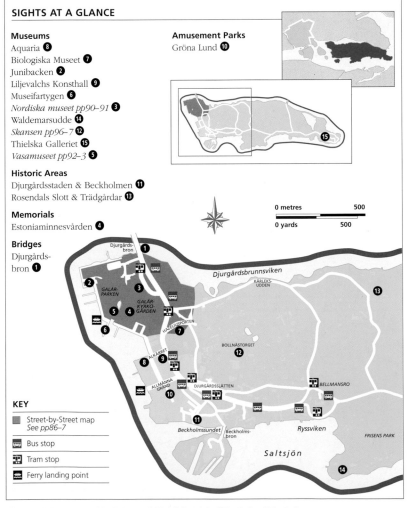

◁ **Some of the 300-year-old oaks in Royal Djurgården, part of the National City Park**

Street-by-Street: Around Lejonslätten

Lions were kept for animal-baiting up to 1792 on the spot where Nordiska Museet now stands, hence the name of this area – Lejonslätten (The Lion Plain). Today visitors can safely stroll along the waterfront, look at the boats, and take in the panorama across to Nybroviken, Skeppsholmen and the heights of Södermalm.

This area also offers several sights of cultural interest. The majestic Nordiska Museet, built in Neo-Renaissance style, reflects Swedish cultural history over almost 500 years. In Vasamuseet lies the beautifully restored 17th-century warship and two more vintage ships are moored outside. Nearby, Junibacken brings Pippi Longstocking and other favourite children's book characters imaginatively to life.

Junibacken
A fun place for children, dedicated to the author Astrid Lindgren. It also features characters from stories by other authors ❷

LADUGÅRDSLANDSVIKEN

GALÄRPARKEN

★ Vasamuseet
The royal warship Vasa *was salvaged after 300 years in the depths of Stockholm's harbour. It is now housed in Stockholm's most popular museum* ❺

Museifartygen
Alongside Vasamuseet are two faithful vessels: the icebreaker Sankt Erik and the lightship Finngrundet ❻

| 0 metres | | 100 |
| 0 yards | | 100 |

STAR SIGHTS

★ Vasamuseet

★ Nordiska Museet

Estoniaminnesvården
Near the Galär cemetery, a national memorial has been erected to the 852 people who lost their lives in the Estonia *ferry disaster on the night of 27–28 September 1994. The ferry sank on its way from Tallinn to Stockholm* ❹

Djurgårdsbron
There has been a bridge to Djurgården since 1661. The current bridge was built in 1896 to mark the Stockholm Exhibition the following year ❶

LOCATOR MAP
See Street Finder maps 5, 6 & 7

Blå Porten is a copy of one of the many blue-painted gateways once set in a 20-km (12-mile) fence around the former royal hunting reserve.

Strand-vägen

DJURGÅRDSBRUNNSVIKEN

Villa Lusthusporten was built in the Italian style during the 1880s.

Kaptens-udden

Lejon-slätten

DJURGÅRDSVÄGEN

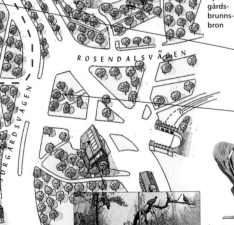

Djur-gårds-brunns-bron

★ **Nordiska museet**
Artur Hazelius, creator of Skansen, also founded Nordiska museet, which portrays Swedish cultural history from the 1520s to the present day ❸

ROSENDALSVÄGEN

DJURGÅRDSVÄGEN

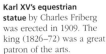

Karl XV's equestrian statue by Charles Friberg was erected in 1909. The king (1826–72) was a great patron of the arts.

Galärkyrkogården (cemetery)

Biologiska Museet
Swedish fauna is shown in realistic natural settings in this charming old museum ❼

KEY

 Suggested route

One of the beautifully decorated pillars supporting Djurgårdsbron

Djurgårdsbron ❶

Map 3 F4. 🚌 *44, 47, 69, 76.* 🚋 *7.* 🚢 *Djurgårdsfärja.*

The Djurgården bridge came into use a few days before the major Art and Industrial Exhibition opened in Stockholm in May 1897. Made at the Bergsund plant in Södermalm, the bridge is richly ornamented with cast-iron railings in the form of stylized water plants. At that time Sweden was in union with Norway, and King Oscar II's monogram and motto "The sister nations' wellbeing" can be seen on the central span. The capital's patron saint, St Erik, is depicted on the pillar supports among sea gods and water lilies.

Wrought-iron lamps and sculptures portraying mythological gods, created by Rolf Adlersparre, adorn the four granite pillars at either end. On the Strandvägen side, the pillars show Heimdal, the watchman, and Frigga, the wife of Oden. On the opposite side is Thor, with his hammer, and Freja, goddess of love and fertility.

The gate of Blå Porten, just to the left on the Djurgården side, recalls the time when the island was a royal hunting ground during the 17th century, and the surrounding fence was punctuated by blue-painted wooden gateways. This gate, decorated with Oscar I's monogram, was made from cast iron in 1849.

Junibacken ❷

Galärvarvsvägen. **Map** 5 F1. **Tel** 587 230 00. 🚌 *44, 47.* 🚋 *7.* 🚢 *Djurgårdsfärja.* ◯ *Jun & Aug: 10am–5pm daily; Jul: 9am–7pm daily; Sep–May: 10am–5pm Tue–Fri, 9am–6pm Sat & Sun.* 🗺 ♿ 🍴 🛍 🏪 **www.**junibacken.se

You can find them all here – Pippi Longstocking, Mardie, Karlsson on the Roof, Emil, Nils Karlsson Pyssling, Ronja the robber's daughter, the Lionheart Brothers and many more characters from Astrid Lindgren's children's books. In accordance with the popular novelist's wishes, visitors can also meet the creations of other Swedish children's authors. When she heard about Staffan Götesam's project for a children's cultural centre she was adamant it should not be just an Astrid Lindgren museum.

Nevertheless Junibacken is still something of a tribute to the much-loved author. It was officially opened by the Royal Family in the summer of 1996 and has become one of the city's most popular tourist attractions. A mini-train takes

A colourful scene from one of Astrid Lindgren's stories seen from the mini-train

visitors from a mock-up of the station at Vimmerby (the author's home town) to meet some of her characters, finishing with a visit to Pippi's home in Villekulla Cottage, where children can play in the different rooms. There is also a well-stocked children's bookshop and a restaurant.

Nordiska Museet ❸

See pp90–91.

Estoniaminnes-vården ❹

Galärkyrkogården. **Map** 5 F2. 🚌 *44, 47.* 🚢 *Djurgårdsfärja.*

On the night of 27–28 September 1994 the ferry MS *Estonia* sank in the Baltic on its journey from Tallinn to Stockholm with the loss of 852 lives. They came from many countries including Sweden, Estonia, Latvia, Russia, Finland, Norway, Denmark, Germany, Lithuania, Morocco, the Netherlands, France, the United Kingdom, Canada, Belarus, Ukraine and Nigeria. Their names and their fate will never be forgotten.

So reads the inscription on the national memorial to the victims of the *Estonia* disaster adjoining the cemetery of Galärkyrkogården. It was designed by the Polish artist Miroslaw Balka (b. 1958), who created it together

ASTRID LINDGREN AND PIPPI LONGSTOCKING

Astrid Lindgren wrote around 100 children's books which have been translated into 74 languages, making her one of the world's most-read children's authors. Publishers turned down her first book about Pippi Longstocking, but she went on to win a children's book competition two years later with it, in 1945. Her headstrong and tough character Pippi soon won the hearts of children worldwide.

Following her death in 2002, the Swedish government created the world's largest prize for children's literature in her name.

Astrid Lindgren

Museifartygen: the lightship *Finngrundet* and ice-breaker *Sankt Erik* outside Vasamuseet

with the two landscape architects Anders Jönsson and Thomas Andersson.

Unveiled on 28 September 1997, the memorial is made of blasted granite and forms a roofless, triangular room with 11-m (36-ft) long sides and a height of 2.5 m (just over 8 ft). The exact position of where the ferry sank is given on a metal ring around a tree in the triangle. With relatives' consent, the names of most of the dead have been carved in the walls.

Vasamuseet ❺

See pp92–4.

Museifartygen ❻

Galärvarvet. **Map** 5 F2.
Tel 519 548 91. 🚌 44, 47. 🚋 7 🚢 Djurgårdsfärja. ◗ 10 Jun–20 Aug: noon–5pm daily; also during various public holidays, ring for details. 🎫 ♿ 🚻
www.vasamuseet.se/museifartygen

The two vintage ships moored alongside Vasamuseet are both fine examples of the ships built to handle various tasks in Swedish waters during the early 20th century. The lightship *Finngrundet*, built in 1903, used to be anchored during the ice-free season on the Finngrund banks in the southern Gulf of Bothnia. In the 1960s lightships started to be replaced by permanent automatic lighthouses, so *Finngrundet* was withdrawn from service and became a museum ship. At 31 m (102

ft) long and 6.85 m (22 ft 6 in) wide, with a draught of 3.1 m (10 ft 3 in), she was designed for a crew of eight. The light had a range of 11 nautical miles.

Built in 1915, *Sankt Erik* was Sweden's first seagoing ice-breaker. This classic Baltic model slides up over the ice and crushes it. She also has a system that enables the ship to be rocked sideways to loosen the ice and widen the channel. One of the two three-cylinder engines is Sweden's largest working marine steam engine. The ice-breaker is 60 m (197 ft) long and 17 m (56 ft) wide and needs a crew of 30.

Biologiska Museet ❼

Lejonslätten. **Map** 6 A3. **Tel** 442 82 15. 🚌 44, 47. 🚋 7. ◗ Apr–Sep: 11am–4pm daily, Oct–Mar: noon–3pm Tue–Fri, 10am–3pm Sat & Sun. 🎫 by arrangement. ♿ 🚻
www.biologiskamuseet.com

The national romantic influences of the late 19th century inspired the architect Agi Lindegren when he was commissioned to design Biologiska Museet (Museum of Biology) in the 1890s. He based his plans on the simple lines of the medieval Norwegian stave churches.

The man behind the museum was the zoologist, hunter and conservationist Gustaf Kolthoff (1845–1913). In 1892, he persuaded

the industrialist C F Liljevalch – who later financed the nearby art gallery – to form a company whose aim was "to develop and maintain a biological museum to include all the Scandinavian mammals and birds as stuffed specimens in natural surroundings". The result was the world's first museum of its type. Within a few months of opening in autumn 1893, Gustaf Kolthoff had delivered a couple of thousand stuffed animals, as well as birds' nests, young and eggs. Many of the creatures are shown against a diorama background, with about 300 species of Scandinavian birds and land mammals in their respective biotypes. Kolthoff's friend, the artist Bruno Liljefors, painted the backgrounds.

Since 1970 the Museum of Biology has belonged to the Skansen Foundation. During the 1990s it underwent extensive renovation and was reopened on 13 November 1993 – exactly 100 years after its original inauguration.

Biologiska Museet's wooden façade, inspired by Nordic medieval design

Nordiska museet ❸

Resembling an extravagant Renaissance castle, Nordiska museet portrays everyday life in Sweden from the 1520s to the present day. It was created by Artur Hazelius (1833–1901), who was also the founder of Skansen (see pp96–7). In 1872, he started to collect objects which would remind future generations of the old Nordic farming culture.

The present museum, designed by Isak Gustaf Clason, was opened in 1907. Today it has more than 1.5 million exhibits, with everything from luxury clothing and priceless jewellery to everyday items, furniture and children's toys, and replicas of period homes.

Dolls' Houses
The dolls' houses show typical homes from the 17th century to modern times. This example illustrates one from 1860.

Level 3

Corridor to staircase

Level 2 (Main Hall)

Ground floor

State Bedchamber from Ulvsunda Castle
At the end of the 17th century, the lord of the manor at Ulvsunda accommodated prominent guests in this prestigious bedchamber.

STAR FEATURES

★ Main Hall

★ Strindberg Collection

★ Table Settings

GALLERY GUIDE

The museum has four floors. From the entrance, stairs lead up to the temporary exhibitions in the Main Hall. On the ground level is a section covering the Sami People and Culture. Floor 3 has the Strindberg Collection, Dolls' Houses, Table Settings, Traditions and the Fashion and Textile Galleries. On the fourth floor are sections on Folk Art, Interiors, Swedish Homes, and Small Objects.

Obelisk with an inscription meaning: "The day may dawn when not even all our gold is enough to form a picture of a bygone era".

Main entrance

★ Table Settings
In the mid-17th century, table settings were a feast for the eyes. A swan is the centrepiece at this meal.

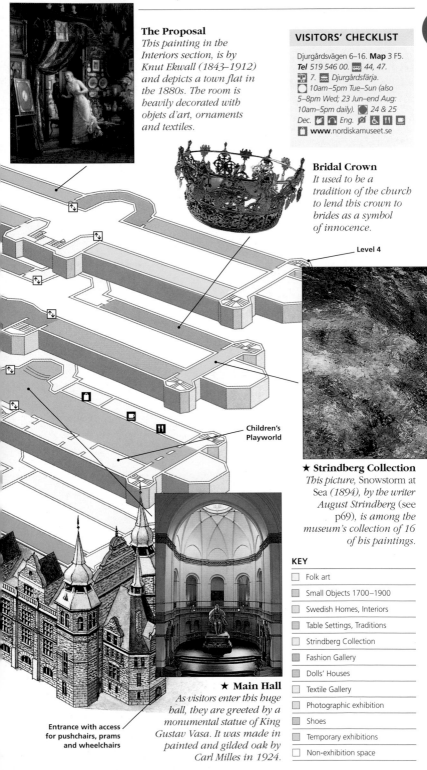

The Proposal
This painting in the Interiors section, is by Knut Ekwall (1843–1912) and depicts a town flat in the 1880s. The room is heavily decorated with objets d'art, ornaments and textiles.

VISITORS' CHECKLIST

Djurgårdsvägen 6–16. **Map** 3 F5.
Tel 519 546 00. 44, 47.
7. Djurgårdsfärja.
10am–5pm Tue–Sun (also
5–8pm Wed; 23 Jun–end Aug:
10am–5pm daily). 24 & 25
Dec. Eng.
www.nordiskamuseet.se

Bridal Crown
It used to be a tradition of the church to lend this crown to brides as a symbol of innocence.

Level 4

Children's Playworld

★ **Strindberg Collection**
This picture, Snowstorm at Sea *(1894), by the writer August Strindberg (see p69), is among the museum's collection of 16 of his paintings.*

KEY

☐	Folk art
☐	Small Objects 1700–1900
☐	Swedish Homes, Interiors
☐	Table Settings, Traditions
☐	Strindberg Collection
☐	Fashion Gallery
☐	Dolls' Houses
☐	Textile Gallery
☐	Photographic exhibition
☐	Shoes
☐	Temporary exhibitions
☐	Non-exhibition space

★ **Main Hall**
As visitors enter this huge hall, they are greeted by a monumental statue of King Gustav Vasa. It was made in painted and gilded oak by Carl Milles in 1924.

Entrance with access for pushchairs, prams and wheelchairs

Vasamuseet ❺

After a maiden voyage of just 1,300 m (4,265 ft) in calm
weather, the royal warship *Vasa* capsized in Stockholm's harbour on 10 August 1628. About 50 people
went down with what was supposed to be the pride of
the Navy, only 100 m (330 ft) off the southernmost point
of Djurgården. Guns were all that were salvaged from
the vessel in the 17th century and it was not until 1956
that a marine archaeologist's persistent search led to the
rediscovery of *Vasa*. After a complex salvage operation
followed by a 17-year conservation programme, the city's
most popular museum was opened in June 1990, less
than a nautical mile from the scene of the disaster.

Gun-port Lion
*More than 200 carved
ornaments and 500 sculp-
ted figures decorate* Vasa.

To the
restaurant

Museum
shop

★ Lion Figurehead
*King Gustav II Adolf, who com-
missioned Vasa, was known as
the Lion of the North. So a
springing lion was the obvious
choice for the figurehead.
It is 4 m (13 ft) long and
weighs 450 kg (990 lb).*

Information
desk

Entrance

Emperor Titus
*Carvings of 20
Roman emp-
erors stand on
parade on* Vasa.

Bronze Cannon
More than 50 of Vasa's
*64 original cannons were
salvaged already in the
17th century. Three 11-kg
(24-lb) bronze cannons are
on display in the museum.*

★ Stern
Vasa's stern was badly damaged but has been painstakingly restored to reveal the ship's magnificent ornamentation.

VISITORS' CHECKLIST

Galärvarvet. **Map** 5 F2.
Tel 519 548 00. 🚌 44, 47, 69.
🚢 Djurgårdsfärja. 🚃 7.
🕐 10am–5pm daily (Wed until 8pm); 10 Jun–20 Aug: 8:30am–6pm daily. 🔴 23–25 Dec, 31 Dec, 1 Jan. 🎧 English. **Films** with English subtitles are shown every hour. 🎦 ♿ 🍴 📷 🛍
www.vasamuseet.se

The main mast was originally 52 m (170 ft) high.

Exit to Museifartygen *(see p89)*

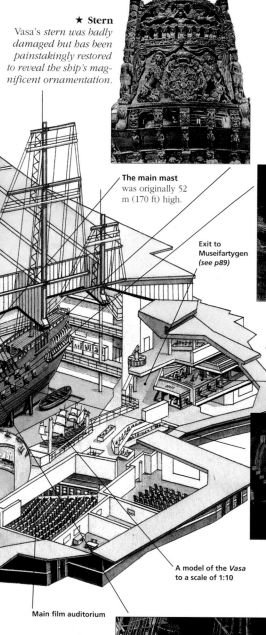

The Gun Ports
Vasa carried more heavy cannons on its two gun-decks than earlier ships of the same size. This contributed to its capsizing.

Reconstruction of the upper gun deck

A model of the Vasa to a scale of 1:10

Main film auditorium

Gun Deck
Visitors cannot board the ship, but there is a full-size copy of the upper gun deck with carved wooden dummies of sailors, which gives a good idea of conditions on board.

Upper Deck
The entrance to the cabins was towards the stern. This area was the grandest part of the ship, reserved for senior officers. Part of the original mainmast can be seen on the right.

STAR FEATURES

★ Stern

★ Lion Figurehead

Exploring the Vasa Museum

The Royal Warship *Vasa* has been restored to 95 per cent of its original appearance. The low salt content of the water saved the ship's timber – which came from more than 1,000 oaks – from attacks by ship worms. The hull was all present, but fitting the 13,500 loose pieces together was like doing a jigsaw puzzle without a picture, as there were no detailed designs to follow. The salvage operation produced more than 700 sculpted figures and carved ornaments, as well as many everyday items.

A sailor's simple belongings found on *Vasa*

Carved soldiers on Vasa's stern

THE SHIP

In 1628 *Vasa* was potentially the world's mightiest ship, able to carry 64 cannons and 300 soldiers (out of a total 450 men on board). *Vasa* was equipped for both traditional close combat and for artillery battles. From its high stern it would have been possible to fire down on smaller ships. The musketeers had shooting galleries for training, and on the upper deck were so-called "storm pieces", erected as protection against musketry fire.

All this may appear very impressive, but it is uncertain exactly what the ship's role would have been if it had survived. The main task of the Swedish navy at that time had been to transport weapons and soldiers as well as to protect shipping or block harbours. It seems doubtful that *Vasa* would have been suitable for these roles.

THE IMAGERY OF POWER

The Warship's many figures and carved ornaments formed an important part of that era's language of power and were designed as a type of war

propaganda. Most of the sculptors who worked in the shipyard that built *Vasa* came from Germany and Holland, and their work was typical of the late Renaissance and early Baroque eras. The German wood-carver Mårten Redtmer made most of the larger sculptures. Created out of oak, pine and lime wood, the figures were inspired mainly by Greek mythology, as well as the Bible and 17th-century Swedish royal personalities.

Despite the multitude of finds, some mysteries remain. It is, for example, known that the figures were brightly painted but not exactly how.

LIFE ON BOARD

Vasa's destination on its maiden voyage, with about 150 people on board, was intended to be the Älvsnabben naval base in the southern Stockholm archipelago, where 300 soldiers were to embark. The ship was fully equipped, and the divers were able to recover many everyday items, including food and drink. But when the chief diver, Per Edvin Fälting, tasted the 333-year-old butter from a tub made of wood and tin, sores erupted around his mouth.

The museum has full-scale models of *Vasa's* upper gun deck and the Admiral's cabin. The sailors and soldiers had to eat and sleep on deck among the cannons. No wonder that in the 17th century more died from illness than in battle.

In a fascinating exhibition of original artifacts, you can see the medical equipment that was used, an officer's backgammon game, some of the sailors' wooden spoons and plates and the officers' dinner service in pewter and earthenware. The divers also found about 4,000 coins, made mainly from copper, and a chest still neatly packed with hats, clothing and other personal belongings.

Replicas of some of these artifacts are on sale in the museum shop.

THE SALVAGE OPERATION

The marine archaeologist Anders Franzén had been looking for *Vasa* for many years. On 25 August 1956 his patience was rewarded when he brought up a piece of blackened oak on his plumb line. From the autumn of 1957, it took divers two years to clear tunnels under the hull for the lifting cables. The first lift with six cables was a success, after which *Vasa* was lifted in 16 stages into shallower water. Thousands of plugs were then inserted into holes left by rusted iron bolts. The final lift started on 24 April 1961, and on 4 May *Vasa* was finally towed into dry dock.

Vasa in dry dock after being salvaged in 1961

Aquaria ❽

Falkenbergsgatan 2. **Map** 6 A3.
Tel 660 49 40. 🚌 44, 47. 🚢 Djurgårdsfärja. 🚋 7. ◯ 10am–4:30pm
Tue–Sun; 15 Jun–15 Aug: 10am–6pm
daily. 🎟 by arrangement. 📷 📱 ♿
www.aquaria.se

For many years Göran Flodin
ran an aquarium shop but
always wanted to open his
own water museum one day.
His dreams were realized
towards the end of the 1980s
when he took over a waterfront site which had been
used to restore the *Vasa* after
its salvage. The resulting
privately owned water
museum was opened in June
1990 and now attracts 250,000
visitors a year.
  Aquaria illustrates many
habitats, from tropical rain-
forests to white-water salmon
rivers. The
South American
rainforest is
portrayed by
thunderstorms
and cloudbursts
and you can
see giant
moths, cicadas,
stingrays and
piranhas. From
the rainforest it
is only a short step to a scene
depicting a northern mountain
lake full of Arctic char, alongside a waterfall with trout.
Most popular are the free-
swimming sharks which you
can watch at close quarters.
  Some 100,000 litres (22,000
gallons) of water are pumped
in every hour from nearby Nybroviken. The water runs back
into the system via a small
lake and a salmon ladder.

**Free-swimming sharks in the
Aquaria water museum**

Liljevalchs
Konsthall ❾

Djurgårdsvägen 60. **Map** 6 A3.
Tel 508 313 30. 🚌 44, 47. 🚋 7.
🚢 Djurgårdsfärja. ◯ 11am–8pm
Tue & Thu, 11am–5pm Wed & Fri–
Sun. 🎟 2:15pm Mon–Fri. 📷 ♿
🍴 📱 ♿ www.liljevalchs.com

Originally constructed
thanks to a donation from the
industrialist Carl Fredrik
Liljevalch, this heritage building is regarded as one of

northern Europe's
most attractive art
galleries. It was
designed by the
architect Carl G
Bergsten and built
in 1913–16 in a Neo-
Classical style which
was typical of its
era, particularly
in Stockholm.
  Liljevalch's portrait
bust, sculpted in
granite by Christian
Eriksson, is set in the
northern wall of this
heritage building.
On a high column
outside the entrance
is Carl Milles' sculp-
ture *The Archer*.
  The city of
Stockholm owns and admin-
isters the gallery, which
features Liljevalch's collections
of Swedish, Nordic and international art
over the 20th
century, as well
as handicrafts
dating from the
same period.
  Every year
four or five
major exhibi-
tions are staged,
including the
Spring Salon
which is always a major
attraction for Stockholm art-
lovers. The exhibitions are
complemented by daily
guided tours, lectures,
debates and concerts.
  Children and young people
have a special section where
they can create their own
works of art from various
different types of materials.

Gröna Lund funfair seen from Kastellholmen

Gröna Lund ❿

Lilla Allmänna gränd 9. **Map** 6 A4.
Tel 587 502 00. 🚌 44, 47. 🚋 7.
🚢 Djurgårdsfärja. ◯ mid-Apr–11
Sep opening hours vary. 📷 ♿ 🍴
📱 www.gronalund.com

A tavern called Gröna Lund
(Green Grove) existed on this
site in the 18th century, and it
was one of the haunts of the
renowned troubadour Carl
Michael Bellman *(see p98)*.
Jakob Schultheis used the
tavern's name for the modest-
sized funfair which he
opened here in 1883 with a
two-level horse-drawn round-
about as the main attraction.
Today Gröna Lund is Sweden's
oldest amusement park.
  The 130-day season, starting
on 1 May, is short but hectic.
However, Gröna Lund draws
about 10,000 visitors per day
to its exciting attractions that
include a thrilling roller-
coaster, ferris wheel and
haunted house. The latest
addition is the free-fall "Power
Tower", an 80-m (262-ft) high
tower from which visitors
drop at a frightening speed.
  The park also has 13
restaurants and cafés, three
stages, a cabaret restaurant
with space for 600 guests, and
a theatre with 200 seats. The
main stage has hosted world
stars such as Bob Marley
who, in 1980, played to a
record audience of 32,000.
  Gröna Lund's beautiful
gardens include 30,000 pansies
and 25,000 summer flowers.

**Liljevalchs Konsthall's spacious
main exhibition hall**

Skansen ⑫

The world's first open-air museum, Skansen opened in 1891 to show an increasingly industrialized society how people once lived. About 150 houses and farm buildings were assembled from all over Sweden, portraying the life of both peasants and landed gentry, as well as Lapp *(Same)* culture. The Town Quarter has wooden urban dwellings and crafts like glass-blowing and printing. Nordic flora and fauna feature everywhere, with bears, wolves and elks in natural habitat enclosures and more exotic creatures in the Aquarium. Many festivals are celebrated in Skansen *(see pp26–9)*.

★ **Älvros Farmstead**
The living room in this 500-year-old wooden cottage from Härjedalen shows the tools for daily tasks.

A cable car runs from the Hazelius Gate entrance.

Tingsvallen/ Bollnästorget is the venue for the Christmas market and Midsummer celebrations.

Swedenborg's Pavilion
Set in the rose garden is the pavilion which used to belong to the philosopher and scientist Emanuel Swedenborg (1688–1772).

Hazelius Gate

Skogaholm Manor
The main building in this Carlovingian manor estate (1680) comes from the Skogaholm ironworks village in central Sweden.

★ **Town Quarter**
Original Stockholm wooden town houses replicate a medium-size 19th-century town. Glass-blowers, shoemakers and other craftsmen demonstrate their traditional skills in restored workshops.

Solliden stage

Main entrance

Skansen Aquarium

Vastveit Storehouse
This storehouse from eastern Norway was built in the 14th century and is Skansen's oldest building.

VISITOR'S CHECKLIST

Djurgårdsslätten 49. **Map** 6 B3.
Tel 442 80 00. 🚌 44, 47. 🚋
7. 🚢 Djurgårdsfärja. ⭕ daily:
Jan–Apr: 10am–4pm; May:
10am–8pm; Jun–Aug:
10am–10pm; Sep: 10am–5pm;
Oct–Dec: 10am–4pm. 🎫
Jun–Aug. ⬤ 24 Dec. 🍴 ♿
🍴 🛍 🛈 **Seglora Church** 🛈
11am Sun. **www**.skansen.se

★ Bear Pit
Skansen's brown bears are firm favourites, not least in April, when the new cubs emerge.

Wolves

Bredablick is a 30-m (98-ft) high viewing tower.

Skåne farmstead

0 metres   100
0 yards   100

Seglora Church
This shingle-roofed wooden church was built in 1729–30 in western Sweden and has an interesting interior decor with a pulpit which is even older than the church itself. It is popular for weddings.

Hornborga Cottage
A timber cottage with a straw and peat roof from western Sweden shows how poorer people lived in the 19th century.

STAR FEATURES

★ Älvros Farmstead

★ Town Quarter

★ Bear Pit

Djurgårdsstaden & Beckholmen ⓫

Map 6 A4. 🚌 *44, 47.* 🚋 *7.*
⛴ *Djurgårdsfärja.*

Behind Gröna Lund amusement park lies Djurgårdsstaden, a tranquil oasis of wooden houses, providing flats for about 200 people. The area was originally developed from a town plan drawn up around the Admiralty churchyard in 1736, to house workmen at the nearby Johan Lampas shipyards.

When the Djurgården shipyard took over in 1768 the carpenters were given the opportunity to buy their homes. The company then erected the majestic two-storey stone building at Lilla Allmänna Gränd 15–17 with offices, employees' homes and a chapel. Other buildings on this street also date from the 18th century such as Apotekshuset, the shipyard manager's residence, and Mjölnargården, now belonging to the amusement park. Several two-storey wooden houses were built on the churchyard, which had fallen into disuse, in the 19th century.

At the junction of Östra Varvsgränd and Breda Gatan is the house of the ship's carpenter Sven Månsson. Enlarged in 1749, the building still looks much as it did then, with original tiled stoves and wood fires. It is now used by the Djurgården Local Culture Society and has undergone extensive renovation.

Lying just to the south of Djurgårdsstaden is the island

The Karl Johan-style Rosendals Slott on Djurgården

of Beckholmen which, during the 17th century, was used as a warehouse for commercial goods. It was also used to store tar and pitch. The fire hazard meant that such dangerous items could not be stored any closer to the city centre.

In 1848 the Wholesalers' Society decided to build a shipping repair yard on the island and two docks were blasted out of the solid rock on the southern side. They were later widened to accommodate more wharves. In 1917 another large dock was opened, named after King Gustaf V and they were used by the Navy and the Finnboda shipbuilding firm. The fleet moved to the island of Muskö in 1969 and Finnboda remained until 1982. The docks and houses form an unusual industrial setting. The 18th-century tar inspector's residence, the dock-master's 19th-century home, and workmen's cottages from the 1890s are well preserved.

Door lintel, Rosendals Slott's Gold Room

Skansen ⓬

See pp96–7.

Rosendals Slott & Trädgårdar ⓭

Rosendalsvägen. **Map** 6 C3. 🚌 *47, then 5 min walk.* **Palace Tel** *402 61 30.* ⭘ *for guided tours Jun–Aug: Tue–Sun, Sep: Sat & Sun.* 🎧 *every hour noon–3pm.* 📷 ♿ **Gardens** ⭘ *all year.* 🏪 🏛 *summer.*

What was considered elsewhere as Empire style was named Karl Johan style in Sweden after King Karl XIV Johan (1818–44). One of the best examples is Rosendal Palace, built as a summer retreat for the king. Constructed in the 1820s and designed by Fredrik Blom, a prolific architect of the era, the palace was one of Sweden's first prefabricated homes. In 1913, it was opened to the public as a museum devoted to the life and times of Karl XIV Johan and represents a pioneering work of historic restoration.

The decor is magnificent, with Swedish-made furniture and lavish textiles in wonderful colours. The carpeting and curtains are worth a visit in themselves. The dining room

---

AN IMMORTAL TROUBADOUR

Carl Michael Bellman (1740–95) was a much-loved troubadour. Gustav III gave him a job as secretary of a lottery, but he was best known around Stockholm's many taverns – particularly on Djurgården. His works about the drunken watchmaker Jean Fredman and his contemporaries (*Fredman's Epistles and Fredman's Songs*) have never lost their popularity and form part of Sweden's musical heritage. A bust of Bellman was unveiled on Djurgården in 1829 in the presence of Queen Desideria.

Bust of Bellman by J N Byström (1829)

Well-preserved wooden homes in Djurgårdsstaden

is fitted out in heavily woven fabric to create the impression of being in a tent. Tiled stoves are everywhere, along with some grandiose artifacts and delightful details. In front of the palace is a large bowl made in porphyry from Karl XIV's own workshops at Älvdalen in central Sweden.

Close to the palace is Rosendals Trädgårdar, a biodynamic market garden managed by a foundation since 1984. Its aim is not just to use biodynamic cultivation methods but also to run courses, lectures and exhibitions. Plants are available to buy at the shop and there is a café.

Waldemarsudde ⑭

Prins Eugens Väg 6. **Map** 6 C4.
Tel 545 837 00. 🚌 47. 🚋 7. ◯ 11am–5pm Tue–Sun. 🎨 📷 ♿ 🍽 💻 📷 **www**.waldemarsudde.com

Prince Eugen's Waldemarsudde, which passed into State ownership after his death in 1947, is one of Sweden's most visited art museums. The prince was trained as a military officer but became a successful artist and was one of the leading landscape painters of his generation. He produced monumental paintings for Kungliga Operan, Kungliga Dramatiska Teatern and Rådhuset. Among his own works hanging in Waldemarsudde, his former home, are three of his most prized

paintings: *Spring* (1891), *The Old Castle* (1893) and *The Cloud* (1896).

Based on works by his contemporaries, the collection represents early 20th-century Swedish art with names like Oscar Björck, Carl Fredrik Hill, Richard Bergh, Nils Kreuger, Eugène Jansson, Bruno Liljefors and Anders Zorn.

Prince Eugen was a generous patron to the next generation – for example, the group known as "The Young Ones" – so works by younger artists like Isaac Grünewald, Einar Jolin, Sigrid Hjertén and Leander Engström are also in the collection. Sculptors of the same era are well represented, particularly works by Per Hasselberg which can be seen in the gallery and the park.

Along with the architect Ferdinand Boberg, Prince Eugen drew up the sketches for the house, completed in 1905. The same architect was called in later to plan the gallery, which was finished in 1913. This now includes parts of the collection of some 2,000 works, as well as the Prince's own paintings.

The guest apartments remain largely unchanged to this day, and the two upper floors with the Prince's studio at the top are used for temporary exhibitions.

Hornsgatan (1902) by Eugène Jansson, in Thielska Galleriet

Thielska Galleriet ⑮

Sjötullsbacken 6–8. **Map** 7 F4.
Tel 662 58 84. 🚌 69. ◯ noon–4pm Mon–Sat, 1–4pm Sun. 📷 by appt. 📷 💻 **www**.thielska-galleriet.a.se

When the magnificent apartments of the banker Ernest Thiel (1860–1947) on Strandvägen started to overflow with his excellent collection of contemporary paintings, he commissioned the well-known architect Ferdinand Boberg to design a dignified villa on Djurgården.

However, during World War I Thiel lost most of his fortune. In 1924, the State bought his collection, mostly covering Nordic art from the late 19th and early 20th centuries, and opened Thielska Galleriet in his villa two years later.

Thiel was regarded as something of a rebel in the banking world and he was particularly fond of works by painters in the Artists' Union, which had been formed in 1886 to counter the influence of the traditionalist Konstakademien *(see p66)*.

There are paintings by all the major Swedish artists who formed an artists' colony at Grèz-sur-Loing, south of Paris, such as Carl Larsson, Bruno Liljefors, Karl Nordström and August Strindberg. And there are paintings by Eugène Jansson, Anders Zorn and Prince Eugen, as well as wooden figures by Axel Petersson and sculptures by Christian Eriksson. Thiel also acquired works by foreign artists, not least his good friend Edvard Munch.

Prince Eugen's Waldemarsudde, seen from the water

MALMARNA & FURTHER AFIELD

As Stockholm started to grow, the heart of the city, Gamla Stan, became cramped and building spread out to the surrounding areas, known as "Malmarna" (the "ore hills"). Parts of these now make up present-day Stockholm.

Window on Vikingagatan

Södermalm came into the ownership of the city in 1436. Much of Stockholm's old charm can still be found in the areas around Fjällgatan, Mosebacke and Mariaberget. To the north, the Norrmalm area expanded rapidly and became known as Stockholm's northern suburb in the 17th century. Much of Vasastan is a residential area, but in recent years it has become popular because of its wide choice of restaurants. The once-rural Östermalm was transformed in the late 19th century into an affluent residential area with grand, wide boulevards, contrasting with the 1930s Functionalist style of the adjoining Gärdet district. This is the location of some of Stockholm's most important museums, including Historiska Museet with its impressive Gold Room, and Folkens Museum Etnografiska.

To the west is Kungsholmen, the centre for local government, with distinguished buildings like Stadshuset (the City Hall) and Rådhuset (the Law Court). Ekoparken (the National City Park), the first of its kind in the world, is a green area of ecological and cultural interest surrounding the city and reaching into its central districts.

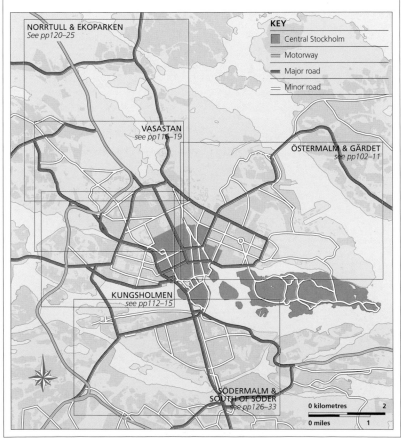

KEY

	Central Stockholm
	Motorway
	Major road
	Minor road

NORRTULL & EKOPARKEN
See pp120–25

VASASTAN
see pp116–19

ÖSTERMALM & GÄRDET
see pp102–11

KUNGSHOLMEN
see pp112–15

SÖDERMALM & SOUTH OF SÖDER
see pp126–33

0 kilometres 2
0 miles 1

◁ **Stadshuset with Norr Mälarstrand on Kungsholmen and the Västerbron bridge in the background**

Östermalm & Gärdet

The four wide boulevards, Strandvägen, Karlavägen, Narvavägen and Valhallavägen, were created around 1870–80 as part of the development of Östermalm into one of the city's most affluent residential districts, adjoining the extensive green area of Ladugårdsgärde. Apart from embassies and the headquarters of Swedish Radio and TV, four leading museums are located in this green oasis, as well as Kaknästornet. The area between Östermalm and the former military exercise grounds was developed in the 1930s with housing in the clean lines of the Functionalist style typical of the period.

Housing at Karlaplan, built in the late 19th century

SIGHTS AT A GLANCE

Berwaldhallen **5**
Diplomatstaden **6**
Engelbrektskyrkan **18**
Filmhuset **13**
Etnografiska Museet **10**
Försvarshögskolan **15**

Gärdet **9**
Historiska Museet (see pp104–105) **2**
Kaknästornet **11**
Karlavägen **3**
Ladugårdsgärde **12**
Sjöhistoriska Museet **7**

Stadion **16**
Strandvägen **1**
Sveriges Radio och TV **4**
Tekniska Högskolan **17**
Tekniska Museet **8**
Tessinparken **14**

KEY

▓	Central Stockholm
▬	Major street
═	Other street
Ⓣ	Tunnelbana station

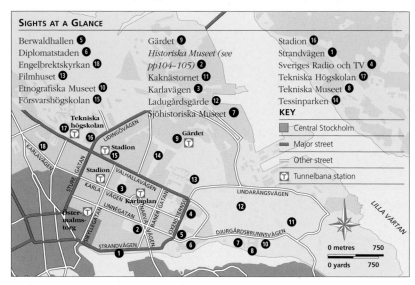

Strandvägen ❶

Map 5 E1. 🚌 *47, 69, 76.*
Ⓣ *Östermalmstorg, Karlaplan.* 🚊 *7.*

In the early 1900s Stockholm's 10 richest citizens lived in palatial new houses along Strandvägen. Seven of them were wholesale merchants. Up to 1897's major exhibition on Djurgården, the hilly and muddy former Ladugårdslands Strandgata had been moving towards the goal of becoming "a street, the like of which will not be found anywhere else in Europe". It was a long process. Even after all the stately buildings had been completed the wooden quay erected in the 1860s was something of an eyesore. It was still used up to the 1940s by boats bringing fire wood from the archipelago islands.

All the same, Strandvägen and its three rows of lime trees soon became the elegant boulevard envisaged and, then as now, it was a popular place for admiring the elegant façades, watching the boats and to see and be seen.

The financiers behind the housing projects of the early 1900s were wealthy and could call on the best architects, including I G Clason (1856–1930). Clason was influenced by Italian and French Renaissance styles for his work on No. 19–21 (Thaveniuska Huset) and No. 29–35 (Bünsowska Huset), where he designed gateways made of ship's timbers. No. 55 (Von Rosenska Palatset) was also created by him.

Historiska Museet ❷

See pp104–105.

Strandvägen with stately houses and boats along the quayside

Karlavägen ❸

Map 3 E3. 🚇 *Karlaplan, Stadion.*
🚌 *1, 42, 44.*

Until 1885 Karlavägen was
known as Esplanaden, a 42-m
(138-ft) wide avenue planted
with lime trees and flower
beds. Towards the end of the
19th century several
impressive houses were built
there, many in Neo-Renaissance style. The street has
retained its character as a
grand boulevard despite a lot
of new building and the
arrival of shops and offices.

A major development was
undertaken in the 1960s when
the central section of the road
was gradually converted into
an open-air sculpture gallery.
At the crossroads with Engel-
brektsgatan is *The City* by
Lars Erik Husberg; at Villa-
gatan a female figure by the
French sculptor Paul Cornet;
at Floragatan Gunnar Nilsson's *Mimi*, which can also be
seen at other places in the
city; at Sturegatan *Living Iron*
by Willy Gordon, a gift from
the LKAB mining company,
whose head office at No. 45
acquired a façade relief by
Eric Grate in 1970. Also
situated at this crossroads is
Scatola by the Italian sculptor
Arnoldo Pomodoro.

At Nybroplan is *Man –
Horse – Carriage* by Asmund
Arle; at Sibyllegatan *Woman
with Hand Mirror* by Ebba
Ahlmark-Hughes; in front of
Östra Real a bust of the
author August Blanche (1811–
68) by Aron Sandberg; the

secondary school
building designed
by Ragnar Östberg
with sculptures by
Carl Eldh; at Grev-
gatan *Incoming Sea*
by Håkan Bonds; at
Karlaplan a marble
sculpture by Gert
Marcus; at Tysta
Gatan *Jeanette* by
Curt Thorsjö; and
at Banérgatan Urn
by Hedy Jolly-
Dahlström. Finally
at No. 100 is the long
Garrison administration building with a sculpture group at
the entrance, a work in glazed
stoneware by Gustav Kraitz.

The fountain and round
pond at Karlaplan were
added in 1929. *The Aviator*
is by Carl Milles and was
unveiled two years later.

**Fountain on Karlaplan at the end
of the tree-lined Karlavägen**

**Swedish Television's main building at Gärdet,
next to Swedish Radio's headquarters**

Radio- och TV-
husen ❹

Oxenstiernsgatan 20 & 34. **Map** 6 A1.
🚇 *Karlaplan.* 🚌 *4, 56, 76.*
SR Tel *784 50 00.* 📷 *by appt.* ♿
www.sr.se **SVT Tel** *784 00 00.* 📷
by appt. ♿ **www**.svt.se

The headquarters of
Swedish Radio (SR) and
Swedish Television (SVT) take
up a 12 ha (29.6 acres) site
alongside Ladugårdsgärde. The
area's long history as a military training depot is reflected
by several old buildings once
used for stores. Now it is the
site not just of the modern
radio and TV buildings designed by the architects Erik
Ahnborg and Sune Lindström
but also of three old buildings
with military connections: the
gunpowder cellar from 1717,
the old stone coach-house
from 1750, and the Karl Johan
storehouses from 1820. Both
architects also designed
Berwaldhallen *(see p106)*, the
concert hall which is linked to
SR and SVT by a tunnel.

Swedish Radio started its
transmissions from Malm-
skillnadsgatan on 1 January
1925. It moved to No. 8
Kungsgatan in 1928 and into
its new premises in 1961.

SVT started transmissions
from the Svea Artillery
Regiment's old premises on
24 October 1954. In 1969 it
moved into the new TV
building in the former
barracks area, where an office
block was added four years
later. Additions in 1983–7
included a building for news
broadcasts. SVT now covers
an area of 51,600 sq m
(555,220 sq ft) with eight
studios, three of which are
used for news programmes.

BOATS ALONG STRANDVÅGEN

Until the 1940s sailing vessels used to carry firewood from
Roslagen on the Baltic coast to the quayside at Strandvägen.
This trade had lost its importance by the 1950s, and boating
enthusiasts started buying up these old vessels. Some were
renovated and sailed to the
Caribbean, others became
illegal drinking or gambling
clubs on Strandvägen. New
harbour regulations led to the
formation of two associations
to administer the boats. About
40 have survived and are
owned by people who want to
preserve a piece of cultural
heritage. By every boat there is
a sign describing its history.

**Old wood-carrying boats
along the Strandvägen quay**

Historiska Museet ❷

Sweden's Historiska Museet (Museum of National Antiquities) was opened in 1943. It was designed by Bengt Romare and Georg Sherman. Bror Marklund (1907–77) was responsible for the decoration around the entrance and the richly detailed bronze gateways depicting events in early Swedish history. The museum originally made its name with its exhibits from the Viking era, as well as its outstanding collections from the early Middle Ages. Contemporary church textiles are also on show. Many of Historiska Museet's gold treasures have been gathered together to form one of Stockholm's most remarkable sights, Guldrummet (the Gold Room).

Exhibitions showing the mass migrations and the Wendic era.

Upper floor

Bronze Age Find
This Bronze Age artifact, thought to be a percussion instrument, was discovered in a bog in southern Sweden in 1847.

Courtyard

★ The Alunda Elk
This 21-cm (8-inch) stone axe, discovered in 1920 at Alunda in central Sweden, resembles an elk's head. It is a ceremonial axe, probably made in Finland or Karelia in around 2000 BC.

Ground floor

Rosen-gården

The Bäckaskog Woman
The 155-cm (5-ft) long Bäcka-skog woman lived around 5000 BC. She died at the age of 40–50 and was buried sitting in a cramped pit.

STAR EXHIBITS

★ The Gold Room

★ Maria from Viklau

★ The Alunda Elk

The Viking Era
This eventful era is reflected in a department, whose exhibits include a Viking sword with artistic embellishments, and ornaments in the shape of Nordic animals.

The Skog Tapestry
This once hung in the wooden church at Skog in northern Sweden. It is one of the museum's oldest textile treasures.

VISITOR'S CHECKLIST

Narvavägen 13–17. **Map** 3 F4.
Tel 51 95 56 00. 🚌 44, 56.
🚇 Karlaplan. ⏰ Oct–Apr:
11am–5pm Mon–Wed &
Fri–Sun, 11am–8pm Thu;
May–Sep: 10am–5pm daily. 🚫
24, 25 & 31 Dec. 📷 ♿ ⃠
The Gold Room. ☐ 🏛
www.historiska.se

Baroque Hall

GALLERY GUIDE
The exhibitions are divided chronologically on two floors with the prehistoric section on the ground floor and the Middle Ages on the upper floor, where there is also a Baroque Hall. In the basement, reached by a staircase from the entrance hall, is the Gold Room with priceless exhibits from prehistoric times to the medieval period.

Stairs
descending to
the Gold Room

★ **Maria from Viklau**
This Madonna figure without child is the best-preserved example from Sweden's early medieval period. The colourful wooden sculpture is richly gilded.

Main entrance

KEY

🟦	Prehistoric Era
☐	Middle Ages and Baroque
☐	Temporary exhibitions
☐	Non-exhibition space

★ **THE GOLD ROOM**
Since the early 1990s the museum's many priceless gold artifacts have been on show in Guldrummet (the Gold Room), a 700-sq m (7,500-sq ft) underground vault built with 250 tons of reinforced concrete to ensure security. The room is in two circular sections. The inner section houses the main collection, with 50 kg (110 lb) of gold treasures and 250 kg (550 lb) of silver from the Bronze Age to the Middle Ages.

The Elisabeth Reliquary was originally a drinking goblet which was mounted with gold and precious stones in the 11th century. In about 1230 a silver cover was added to enclose the skull of St Elisabeth. In 1631 it was seized as a trophy for Sweden during the Thirty Years War.

The Gold Collars were found between 1827 and 1864; the three-ringed collar in a stone quarry in eastern Sweden, the five-ringed in a ditch on the island of Öland, and the seven-ringed hanging on a spike in a barn.

The underground Gold Room in Historiska Museet

Berwaldhallen, concert hall of the Swedish Radio Symphony Orchestra

Berwaldhallen ❺

Dag Hammarskiölds väg 3.
Map 6 A2. **Tel** 784 18 00.
🚇 Karlaplan. 🚌 56, 69, 76.
◯ noon–6pm Mon–Fri. 🎫 🖥 🍴
www.berwaldhallen.se

On 30 November 1979 the Swedish Radio Symphony Orchestra and the Radio Chorus acquired their own concert hall, Berwaldhallen. Since then the hall has become a national showcase for Swedish music. It is named after Franz Berwald (1796–1868), one of Sweden's greatest composers. The architects Erik Ahnborg and Sune Lindström won an award for their "wonderful and sensitively designed concert hall". Hans Viksten, Hertha Hillfon and other artists undertook the decoration of the foyer. Nature has made its own contribution in the form of untouched areas of rock which were blasted out to accommodate two-thirds of the six-sided building.

The Swedish Radio Symphony Orchestra and Radio Chorus give between 70 and 80 performances every season in the hall, which has established it as an internationally renowned concert stage, attracting audiences of 150,000 a year. Visiting ensembles from all over the world also perform here and the hall is often used for other types of events, as well as corporate functions and conferences.

Diplomatstaden ❻

Map 6 A2. 🚇 Karlaplan. 🚌 56, 69, 76.

The elegant villas which gave the area of Diplomatstaden its name stretch along Nobelgatan and the eastern part of Strandvägen (from No. 74). The first house for a foreign diplomat was built in the 1910s, when the British ambassador moved into Nobelgatan 7. Nearby is Engelska Kyrkan (the English Church), which was built in the city centre in the 1860s but was moved to the diplomatic quarter in 1913. In the 1980s the church was finally completed with the addition of an octagonal parish hall. Villa Bonnier at No. 13 was designed by Ragnar Östberg and was a gift to the State by a prominent publishing family. It is now used by the Government for official functions.

The embassies of Hungary, Turkey, South Korea, Norway, Germany, the UK and USA are all located in or near the area. Nobelparken, the park adjoining the embassies, is named after the scientist Alfred Nobel (1833–96). In the early 20th century plans for a Nobel Palace in the park were drawn up by the architect Ferdinand Boberg, but the project never came to fruition. On the north side of Strandvägen is the Törner Villa, a heritage wooden house built in 1880. The villa is named after a firemaster at Nobel's gunpowder factory.

Sjöhistoriska Museet ❼

Djurgårdsbrunnsvägen 24.
Map 6 C2. **Tel** 519 549 00. 🚌 69.
◯ 10am–5pm Tue–Sun. 🎫 📷
⛄ 🖥 🍴 www.sjohistoriska.se

The National Maritime Museum's architectural design and location on Djurgårdsbrunnsviken are worthy of a country with a long coastline and numerous archipelagos and lakes. Sjöhistoriska Museet focuses on shipping, shipbuilding and naval defence, and there are fascinating exhibits, both permanent and temporary, on these themes.

There are some 100,000 exhibits, including more than 1,500 model ships. The oldest ship was built in the 17th century and the oldest Swedish vessel is a reproduction of the so-called "Cathedral ship" from the early 1600s. The collections include every conceivable type of ship – from small coasters and Viking longboats to oil tankers, coal vessels, dinghies, full-riggers and sub-

Majestic buildings in the diplomatic quarter at Djurgårdsbrunnsviken

The galley *Lodbrok*, one of many maritime models at Sjöhistoriska Museet

marines. A series of models on a scale of 1:200 show the development of ships in Scandinavia from the Iron Age to the present day.

There are also full-scale settings which give a good idea of life on board the ships. Among them are the beautiful original cabin and elegant stern from the royal schooner *Amphion*. The ship was built at the Djurgården shipyard and designed by the leading shipbuilder F H Chapman. It was Gustav III's flagship in the 1788–90 war with Russia. Contrasting with this is the cramped and damp-preserved forecastle from the schooner *Hoppet*, where four crew members ate, slept and spent their time off watch.

The museum has some notable examples of ship decoration from the late 17th century. They include part of the national coat of arms recovered by divers in the 1920s from the stern of the *Riksäpplet*, which sank at Dalarö in 1676. When *Carolus XI*, an 82-cannon ship, was launched from the shipyard in Stockholm in 1678 the stern had a large relief portrayal of Karl XI on horseback. The relief was possibly removed some years later when the ship was renamed *Sverige*, but it was saved and is now in the museum. There are many fine figureheads in the collection, including one depicting Amphion, the son of Zeus, playing his lyre, which once adorned the schooner of the same name.

Linked to the museum is the Swedish Marine Archaeology Archive, which contains a mass of information, including a complete listing of shipwrecks with 10,000 entries from 1720 to the present day. The ship-design archive has documents covering most eras of maritime history and is used extensively by researchers. The photographic collection has 300,000 pictures, while the library covers all aspects of seafaring and war at sea. There is a special children's section with a workshop which is open on Saturdays, Sundays and during school holidays. During the summer a dinghy-sailing school is arranged for children aged 8–14.

Figurehead, about 1850

The attractive museum building was one of the architect Ragnar Östberg's last works and was opened in 1938. On the gable facing Djurgårdsbrunnsviken is *The Sailor*, a monument to the victims of naval war by Nils Sjögren.

Tekniska Museet 8

Museivägen 7. **Map** 6 C2.
Tel *450 56 00.* *69.* *10am–5pm Mon–Tue, Thu–Fri, 11am–8pm Wed, 11am–5pm Sat & Sun.* *by appointment.*
www.tekniskamuseet.se

Anyone planning to visit the Museum of Science and Technology should allow plenty of time. Throughout the 20th century it accumulated a wealth of exhibits connected with Sweden's technical and industrial history. It has 12,000 sq m (129,000 sq ft) of well-stocked exhibition space plus a library with 50,000 volumes and a large collection of technical magazines. It is also the home of Sweden's first Science Centre, Teknorama, with many "hands on" experiments aimed particularly at children and young people.

The machinery hall is the largest exhibition area with many powered machines from different eras. Among them is the country's oldest preserved steam engine, built in 1832 and once used in a coal mine in southern Sweden. The classic T-Ford is there, too, as well as early Swedish cars from Volvo, Scania and Saab.

The museum also has sections on the history of telecommunications and the computer, electric power, book-printing and the Swedish forestry industry. The mining and processing of iron and steel is also highlighted.

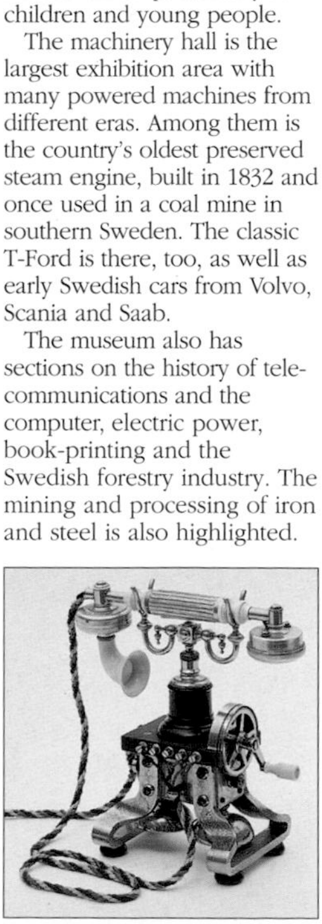
Ericsson telephone made in 1903 for Czar Nicholas II

Gärdet ➒

Rindögatan. Ⓣ *Gärdet.*
www.housingprototypes.org

Gärdet, one of the largest
residential neighbourhoods in
Stockholm, was built as the
result of a design competition
in the late 1920s, at a time
when the Swedish Modern
movement was in full swing.
The competition was won by
the architect Arvid Stille and
this area exhibits the graceful
form of Functionalism for
which Sweden became known
at the time, and which
continues to exert a strong
influence to this day. One
characteristic of Swedish
architecture from that period
was the emphasis it placed on
decoration whilst still adhering
to the basic principles of
Functionalist ideology.

   The individual buildings in
Gärdet were designed and
built between 1935 and 1939
by a variety of architects,
including Sture Fröhlén, Albin
Stark, Ernst Grönwall, Wolter
Gahn, Björn Hedvall and
Swen Wallander, all within
Stille's overall plan.

Etnografiska Museet ➓

Djurgårdsbrunnsvägen 34. **Map** 6 C2.
Tel 519 550 00. 🚌 69. 🕐 *10am–
5pm Mon–Tue & Thu–Fri, 10am–8pm
Wed, 11am–5pm Sat & Sun.* 🎫 ♿
🍴 🖥 📷 www.etnografiska.se

The National Museum of
Ethnography is a showcase
for the collections brought
home to Sweden by travellers
and scientists from the 18th
century to the present day.
The imaginative displays are
intended to offer visitors not
only a better understanding of
the unknown or unfamiliar
from around the world,
but also of the cultural
connections between
such far-off places
and Sweden
through explaining
how and why the
objects came into
the museum's
collection.

   The explorer Sven
Hedin (1865–1952),
who was the last
Swede to be ennobled (in
1902), contributed many
exhibits, including Buddha
figures and Chinese costumes,
as well as Mongolian temple
tents donated by leaders of
the Kalmuck people in western
China to King Gustav V.

   A Japanese tea house, built
by 15 Japanese craftsmen to a
design by Professor Masao
Nakamura, was opened in
1990. It is a work of art in
itself, offering a space for
reflection and meditation
within a traditional setting.
During the summer months
visitors can take part in tea
ceremonies, while at other
times the house can be
viewed from outside.

   Another section of interest
is dedicated to the native
peoples of North America.
Here there are masks, textiles
and ceramics from various
tribes, as well as totem poles
from western Canada.

   Closer to home, the
museum also reflects upon
the multicultural influences

**Religious mask from
British Columbia**

on Sweden brought about by
the large-scale immigration
into the country in the late
20th century.

   Alongside the permanent
displays, the museum puts on
a changing series of
temporary exhibitions
highlighting different
aspects of the
collection. Every
year since 1936 it
has published the
international
magazine *Ethnos*.
There is also a good
reference library.

   Visitors can
sample foods from
around the world in the
museum's bar-restaurant
"Babajan". Here you can try
one of 20 kinds of tea or
choose from an impressive
list of international beers. The
food is mainly African, Asian
and Middle Eastern.

Kaknästornet ⓫

Ladugårdsgärdet. **Map** 7 D1.
Tel 667 21 05. 🚌 69. 🕐
*May–Aug: 9am–10pm daily, Sep–Apr:
10am– 9pm daily.* 🕐 *by
appointment.* 🔊 📷 ♿ 🍴 🖥 📷

Anchored by 72 steel poles,
each one driven 8 m (26 ft)
into the rock, the 34-storey
Kaknästornet soars to a height
of 155 m (508 ft). The tower,
designed by the architects
Bengt Lindroos and Hans
Borgström, was opened in
1967. It was erected as a
centre for the country's
television and radio broadcasting and also contains
technical equipment to
conduct conferences by

The Japanese tea house in the gardens of the Etnografiska Museet

Kaknästornet with the buildings of Sjöhistoriska Museet, Tekniska Museet and Folkens Museum Etnografiska in the foreground

satellite between European cities. Five dishes to the left of the tower – the largest of which has a diameter of 13 m (43 ft) – relay signals to and from satellites. The main hall containing the transmitters and receivers has been blasted out of the rock below the dishes.

The observation points on levels 30 and 31 provide a spectacular view of the city, and the restaurant on the 28th floor has panoramic windows. It is reached by two lifts, travelling at 18 km/h (11 mph). The restaurant also runs a busy tourist information office at the entrance level, selling souvenirs, maps and the Stockholm Card (see p191). Decorative features include a wall relief by Walter Bengtsson, which was inspired by the tower's daunting technology.

Ladugårdsgärde ⓬

Map 6 C1. 🚌 *1, 69, 76.*

As early as the 15th century there was a royal farm on the site where the Nobel Park now stands. After 250 years it had outlived its usefulness and for a few centuries it was used as a training area for the Stockholm garrison. Between Kungliga Borgen (Royal Fortress) and Hakberget are the remains of Karl XI's fort from 1672, which was largely rebuilt in time for the World Equestrian Championships, held here in 1990. During the 20th century what became

known simply as Gärdet lost its military role. In the early 1900s the area was used for May Day processions, and car races were staged here around 1920.

The fortress of Kungliga Borgen is a relic of the military training era, and it was from here that Karl XIV Johan used to watch his troops manoeuvring. He rode from here to Rosendal Palace on Djurgården (see p98) via a pontoon bridge near the present-day National Maritime Museum. The fortress was badly damaged by fire in October 1977, but it has since been rebuilt to its original appearance. A restaurant is open during the summer.

Something is always going on in Gärdet. It is the starting point for major fun runs and the venue for kite-flying festivals, and is used by the city's balloonists. It is also a favourite place to exercise horses and dogs.

Filmhuset ⓭

Borgvägen 1–5. **Map** 6 B1.
Tel *665 11 00.* 🚇 *Karlaplan.* 🚌
56, 72, 76. ⏰ *8am–6pm Mon–Thu, 8am–5pm Fri.* **Film club, library & archives** *ring for details.* ♿ 🍴 📷
www.sfi.se

The production of quality Swedish films is supported by the Swedish Film Institute. The institute also acts as guardian of the country's cinematic heritage and promotes Swedish films both at home and abroad. From 1971, all its activities were brought under one roof in Filmhuset, a Modernist structure by P Celsing.

The institute's archives include more than 18,000 films. Also there is a comprehensive library and a film database, accessible on the Internet. The institute publishes the *Film Annual*, and organizes the Film Gala at which the Gold Beetle prizes are presented. The film club shows Swedish and international films daily in their original languages.

Filmhuset, home of the Film Institute and Dramatic Institute

INGMAR BERGMAN

The playwright and producer Ingmar Bergman was born at Östermalm in 1918. His long series of masterly films have made him world-famous, but he started his career in the theatre. From 1963–6 he was Director of Dramatiska Teatern, where he is still a guest producer. He has created more than 100 theatrical productions. His international breakthrough as a film producer came with *Smiles of the Summer Night* (1955), and *The Seventh Seal* (1957) was a cinematic milestone. Bergman completed this stage of his career with *Fanny and Alexander* (1982).

Ingmar Bergman at a press conference, 1998

Tessinparken, surrounded by Functionalist-style housing dating from the late 1930s

Tessinparken & Nedre Gärdet ⑭

Map 3 F2. 🚇 *Karlaplan, Gärdet.*
🚌 *1, 4, 72.*

Three generations of the Tessin family of architects *(see p37)* have given their name to this park opened at Lower Gärdet in 1931. Tessinparken runs from north to south and is attractively designed with lawns, play areas, paths and ponds. The adjoining houses, built between 1932–7, have their own gardens and blend in such a way that they give the impression of being part of the park itself.

The earliest houses, nearest to Valhalla-vägen, still show signs of 1920s Classicism, although Gärdet's real hallmark is Functionalism *(see p37)*. The lower white houses along Askrikegatan are Functionalist in style and noticeably different from other buildings in Gärdet. They mark the northern boundary of the park. Some 60 different architects were involved in designing the Gärdet development, including Sture Frölén.

A granite statue of a woman with a suitcase, *Housewife's Holiday*, stands in the part of Tessin Park adjoining Valhallavägen. It was made by Olof Thorwald Ohlsson in the 1970s. At the other end of the park is a colourful concrete statue, *The Egg*, by Egon Möller-Nielsen.

Functionalist façade at Tessinparken

Försvars-högskolan ⑮

Valhallavägen 117. **Map** 3 E2.
🚌 *4, 62, 72.* 🚇 *Stadion.*
⬤ *to the public.*

Two decorative cannons, an aircraft propeller and an 18th-century anchor guard the entrance to Försvarshögskolan (the Military Academy). The building has been sympathe-tically renovated and appears to be lower than it really is because the adjoining Valhalla-vägen was built at a higher level.

It was originally the base for the Svea Artillery Regiment and is one of many notable military buildings designed by the architect Ernst Jacobsson. After Nybrogatan was blasted out through the Tyskbagarbergen hill, the regimental building provided a backdrop to the newly extended street.

The regiment moved out in 1949 to make way first for Swedish Radio and later for the Military Academy, in whose present gym Swedish

The restored façade of Försvarshögskolan (Military Academy) on Valhallavägen

TV started. A plaque reads: "From this building the first regular television programme was transmitted on 24 October 1954."

Stadion ⑯

Lidingövägen 1–3. **Map** 3 E2.
Tel 508 260 00. 🚇 *Stadion.* 🚌 *4, 55, 72, 73.* ⬤ *15 Apr–15 Oct.*
📷 *during events.* ♿ 🍴 🖥

A new arena was built for the 1912 Olympic Games in Stockholm. The architect of Stadion, Torben Grut (1871–1945), followed the National Romantic influences of the day. His design was based on his own interpretation of the commission to build a stadium "using modern construction methods adapted from traditional medieval brick-building techniques". It is no coincidence that the arena, which is the world's oldest Olympic stadium still in use, is often known as the "Stadium Fortress".

In addition to the 1912 Olympics, the stadium has also been the venue for ice hockey and bandy (a type of hockey) championships, the European Athletics Championships in 1958, and the World Equestrian Championships in 1990. The stadium is renowned for athletics events, and stages an international athletics gala every summer.

Stadion is listed as a heritage building and its twin towers are a familiar landmark. The complex is richly decorated. The clock tower has two figures by Carl Fagerberg, *Ask and Embla*, the counterparts of Adam and Eve in Nordic mythology. There are also busts of Victor Balck, the man behind the 1912 Olympics; P H Ling, the father of Swedish gymnastics; and Edwin Wide, the "flying teacher",

Bruno Liljefors's statue *Play* outside Stadion

who was a leading opponent of the Finnish master-athlete Paavo Nurmi in long-distance races during the 1920s.

Four notable sculptures were added in the 1930s. The painter and gymnast Bruno Liljefors created *Play* at the main entrance, Carl Eldh made *The Runners*, and Carl Fagerberg provided *Relay Runners* and *The Shot-Putter*.

Tekniska Högskolan ⓱

Valhallavägen 79. **Map** 3 D1.
🅣 *Tekniska högskolan*. 🚌 *4, 72, 73.*

The renowned higher education establishment, Tekniska Högskolan, accounts for one-third of Sweden's technical research and engineering education at university level. It has 15,000 students, 1,000 active research students and a staff of 2,500. It was founded in 1827, and since 1917 its campus has been housed in heritage buildings on Valhallavägen, as well as in

the suburbs of Haninge and Kista, and outside Stockholm in Södertälje, Gävle and Visby.

The main building on Valhallavägen was designed by Erik Lallerstedt and its opening in October 1917 was a milestone in Sweden's technological development.

The architect commissioned several contemporary artists to decorate the austere technical environment, so it has become something of an artistic treasure trove. The sculptors and painters whose works adorn the buildings included Einar Forseth, Olle Hjertzberg, Georg Pauli, Ivar Johnsson, Axel Törneman, Hilding Linnqvist and Carl Milles. Milles was also responsible for the fountain sculpture, *The Industrial Monument*, which rests on a marble base in the courtyard facing Valhallavägen.

Early in the 20th century the main building underwent a painstaking renovation. The surrounding park was also restored to its original state.

Engelbrektskyrkan & Lärkstaden ⓲

Östermalmsgatan 20. **Map** 3 D2.
🅣 *Tekniska högskolan*. 🚌 *1, 42.*
Engelbrektskyrkan *Tel* 406 98 00.
🅞 *11am–3pm Tue–Sun.* 🕇 *11am Sun, 11:30am Thu.* ♿ 🅟

One of Sweden's leading Jugendstil architects, Lars Israel Wahlman, designed the Engelbrekt Church as a result of winning an architectural competition in 1906. The church was opened on 25 January 1914 in the presence of King Gustaf V.

Engelbrektskyrkan gives the appearance of thrusting out from the rocks, and it dominates the surrounding area with its slender brick tower. In the chancel, the monumental paintings are by Olle Hjortzberg (1872–1959). The sculptor Tore Strindberg (1882–1968) was commissioned for the stucco reliefs both in the chancel and above the main entrance. Filip Månsson executed the frescoes in the west portico and elsewhere. The nave is the highest in Scandinavia, and the arches inside the church are supported by eight granite pillars.

Engelbrektskyrkan is located in Lärkstaden, a quarter which was developed around 1910 and is characterized by dark red façades and tiled roofs that blend in well with the church. The area has winding streets and natural differences in level – inspired partly by Austrian patterns.

Engelbrektskyrkan, dominating the surrounding area of Lärkstaden

---

ARENA FOR RECORDS

No other athletics arena can compete with Stockholm's Stadion when it comes to world records. The 1912 Olympics gave the statistics a flying start with 11 world records. The gold medallist Ted Meredith's time of 1 min 51.9 sec in the 800-m event can be compared with Wilson Kipketer's 1997 time of 1 min 41.73 sec over the same distance; the last world record set at Stadion. It has recorded a total of 83 world records. London is second with 68 and Los Angeles is third with 66 records. The top Swedish runner of the 1940s, Gunder Hägg, set seven world records and the Finn, Paavo Nurmi, had six.

Running track at Stadion, 1912

Kungsholmen

Once best known for its handicrafts and small industries, Kungsholmen changed in the late 19th century with the emergence of new apartment blocks and institutional buildings. By the early 1900s the area had a different status, exemplified by Ragnar Östberg's Stadshuset (city hall) – Stockholm's most notable architectural project of the 20th century – and Carl Westman's majestic Rådhuset (law court). These were followed by the elegant waterfront houses along Norr Mälarstrand. The area has a high concentration of government buildings, but it also offers many venues for entertainment and nightlife.

Stately buildings on Norr Mälarstrand line the Riddarfjärden waterfront

SIGHTS AT A GLANCE

Marieberg **6**
Norr Mälarstrand **3**
Rådhuset **2**
Rålambshovsparken **4**
Stadshuset (see pp114–15) **1**
Västerbron **5**

KEY

■ Central Stockholm
═ Motorway
━ Major road
━ Minor road
🔵 Tunnelbana station

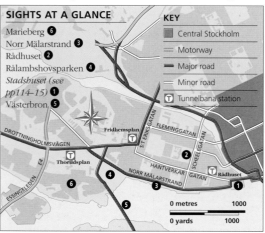

0 metres   1000
0 yards   1000

Stadshuset **1**

See pp114–15.

Rådhuset **2**

Scheelegatan 7. **Map** 2 A5.
🔵 *Rådhuset.* 🚌 *40, 52.*

In the early 20th century, the intention was to build a combined city hall and law court, but the plans changed when two separate architectural competitions were launched. The winning entry for Rådhuset (the law court), was a design by Carl Westman (1866–1936), who became a leading exponent of the National Romantic School along with Ragnar Östberg (1866–1945), architect of Stadshuset. Building began in 1911, and

Rådhuset was opened in December 1915. In his design, Westman drew inspiration from the Vasa Renaissance of the 16th century and was probably influenced by Vadstena Castle in southern Sweden. Rådhuset, with its prominent tower, is one of the best examples of the National Romantic style, but its solid scale also shows Jugendstil influences.

The sculptors Christian Eriksson and the brothers Aron and Gustaf Sandberg were responsible for the decoration, which also includes paintings by Olle Hjortzberg and Filip Månsson. Beside the staircase on the fifth floor is a copy of *Kopparmatte*, the pillory which once stood on Stortorget in Gamla Stan. The original pillory is at Stockholms Stadsmuseum (*see p127*).

Rådhuset, exterior detail

Norr Mälarstrand **3**

Map 1 C3. 🔵 *Rådhuset, Fridhemsplan.* 🚌 *40, 52.*

When industries like textiles and dyeing left Norr Mälarstrand in the early 20th century, work began on exploiting Kungsholmen's attractive location along the bay of Riddarfjärden. Gradually an exclusive residential area emerged. During World War II a sculpture park was developed along the waterfront, where the excursion boats and vintage coasters are moored today. Willow, poplar, alder and birch trees thrive along the shoreline. A pavilion with a summer café stands on pillars above the water. It was designed by Erik Glemme, assistant to the city's master gardener Holger Blom (born 1906).

The architect of Stadshuset, Ragnar Östberg, designed Norr Mälarstrand 76. Cyrillus Johansson, Sven Wallander and J Norberg were the architects of Nos. 26, 28 and 30, where the figures on the gables above the steps were created by the metal craftsman Ragnar Myrsmeden. There is much to see in the small side streets, including the façades of No. 5 Jacob Westins Gata (architect Harald Wadsjö) and No. 9 Skillinggränd. The original service-flat building at No. 6 John Erikssongatan was designed by Sven Markelius, who was influenced by the ministerial couple Gunnar and Alva Myrdal. It is the first residential building in the Functionalist style typical of the 1930s to be listed as a heritage site.

Rålambshovs-parken ❹

Map 1 B3. 🚇 *Fridhemsplan.* 🚌 *1, 4, 40, 56, 57, 62, 74.* 🚃

Rålambshovparken was created in 1935, when the Västerbron bridge was built. It adjoins other green areas, including Smedsudden and Marieberg and Fredhäll parks. These open spaces attract joggers and sun-bathers. In summer it is possible to swim from the beach at Smedsudden or the cliffs at Fredhäll.

When the city celebrated its 700th anniversary in 1953 an amphitheatre was opened in Rålambshovsparken, and a paddling pool and playgrounds were added. The park has been enhanced with Elli Hemberg's sculpture *The Butterfly*, Eric Grate's *Monument to an Axeman*, *Judgement* by Egon Möller-Nielsen and Lars Erik Falk's *Colour Tower*.

Rålambshovsparken on the north side of Västerbron bridge

Västerbron ❺

Map 1 B4. 🚌 *4, 40, 74.*

As Stockholm expanded and car use increased in the 1920s, it became necessary to build an additional bridge between the northern and southern shores of Lake Mälaren. German experts dominated the architectural competition launched in 1930, but their plans were implemented by Swedish architects and engineers and the bridge was completed in 1935.

The attractive design blends well with the landscape. The bridge is built in two spans of 168 m (551 ft) and 204 m (669 ft) with a vertical clearance of 26 m (85 ft). It is used by an average of 12,000 vehicles daily. A walk to the centre of Västerbron is rewarded with a magnificent view of central Stockholm.

Marieberg ❻

Map 1 A3. 🚇 *Thorildsplan.* 🚌 *1, 49, 56, 62.* **Riksarkivet** *Tel* 737 63 50.

The area at the northern end of the Västerbron bridge, Marieberg, was once known for its porcelain factory and military installations. But since the early 1960s it has become the city's main newspaper district and the home of three of the four Stockholm dailies.

The architect Paul Hedqvist's 98.6-m (323-ft) high building for *Dagens Nyheter* and *Expressen* is one of the city's landmarks. The neon sign which tops the building at Görwellsgatan 30 was designed by P O Ultvedt, who also created the relief at the entrance. Works of art include Lennart Rodhe's walls made from glazed stoneware, *Day and Night*, and Arne Jones' sculpture *Nova*. Some older works of art were brought from the papers' original building in the central Klara district, including Stig Blomberg's copper sculpture,

The Orb by Elli Hemberg (1970) in front of Riksarkivet

Freedom our Watchword, made in 1951.

The offices of *Svenska Dagbladet* are not as richly decorated as their neighbours', but they are no less interesting architecturally. The building was inspired by Pirelli's high-rise offices in Milan and designed by Tengbom Architects in 1960–2.

The third interesting building in Marieberg is Riksarkivet, the state archive. It was built in 1968 by architects Åke Ahlström and Kjell Åström. Riksarkivet is one of Sweden's oldest public bodies, dating from the Middle Ages. At the entrance is Elli Hemberg's iron sculpture, *The Orb*. The main hall, which has 56 seats for researchers and 18 individual study rooms, is dominated by Lennart Rodhe's tapestry, *Symbol in the Archive*, which was created by the Friends of Handicrafts. In a smaller adjoining room the public has access to archive documents, microfilm and microfiche.

Among the archives is one of the world's largest books – the accounts for the province of Östergötland dating from 1813. It has 12,390 pages, weighs 42 kg (92 lb) and is 1.13 m (3.7 ft) wide.

Guided tours of Riksarkivet can be arranged.

Västerbron bridge, opened in 1935, linking Kungsholmen with Södermalm across Lake Mälaren

Stadshuset ❸

Probably Sweden's biggest architectural project of the 20th century, the City Hall was completed in 1923 and has become a symbol of Stockholm. It was designed by Ragnar Östberg (1866–1945), the leading architect of the Swedish National Romantic style, and displays influences of both the Nordic Gothic and Northern Italian schools. Several leading Swedish artists contributed to the rich interior design. The building contains the Council Chamber and 250 offices for city administrative staff. The annual Nobel Prize festivities take place in the Blue Hall.

Engel-brekt

★ The Golden Hall
The Byzantine-inspired wall mosaics by Einar Forseth (1892–1988) have 19 million fragments of gold leaf. The theme of the norther wall is Queen of Lake Mälaren.

Norra Trapptornet, crowned by a sun.

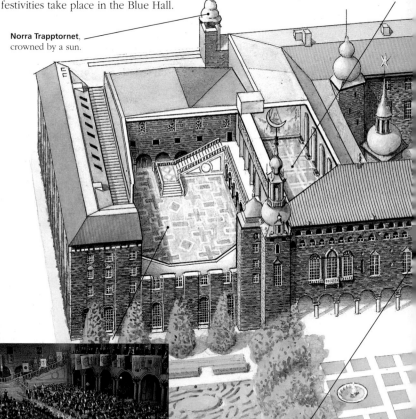

★ The Blue Hall
The banqueting room is made from hand-shaped dark bricks. The name comes from the original plan to use polished blue-painted bricks.

★ The Prince's Gallery
A fresco, The City on the Water, *in the Prince's Gallery, was painted by Prince Eugen (see p99), who donated it to the City Hall.*

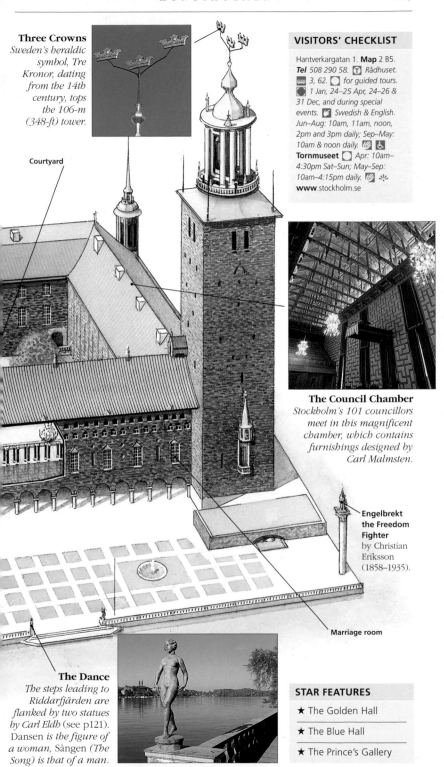

Three Crowns
Sweden's heraldic symbol, Tre Kronor, dating from the 14th century, tops the 106-m (348-ft) tower.

Courtyard

VISITORS' CHECKLIST

Hantverkargatan 1. **Map** 2 B5.
Tel 508 290 58. 🚇 Rådhuset.
🚌 3, 62. ⬜ for guided tours.
⬤ 1 Jan, 24–25 Apr, 24–26 &
31 Dec, and during special
events. 📷 Swedish & English.
Jun–Aug: 10am, 11am, noon,
2pm and 3pm daily; Sep–May:
10am & noon daily. 📷 ♿
Tornmuseet ⬜ Apr: 10am–
4:30pm Sat–Sun; May–Sep:
10am–4:15pm daily. 📷 ❄
www.stockholm.se

The Council Chamber
Stockholm's 101 councillors meet in this magnificent chamber, which contains furnishings designed by Carl Malmsten.

Engelbrekt the Freedom Fighter by Christian Eriksson (1858–1935).

Marriage room

The Dance
The steps leading to Riddarfjärden are flanked by two statues by Carl Eldh (see p121). Dansen is the figure of a woman, Sången (The Song) is that of a man.

STAR FEATURES

★ The Golden Hall

★ The Blue Hall

★ The Prince's Gallery

Vasastan

Building started in Vasastan, the most northerly part of Norrmalm, in the 18th century. Today it is both a residential area, with houses built around 1900 for manual workers and craftsmen, and a lively part of the city with a wide choice of bars and restaurants. The area also includes some of Stockholm's most agreeable green open spaces, including Vasaparken and Vanadislunden. Stadsbiblioteket, the city library *(see p117)*, is one of Stockholm's most distinctive buildings, and there are several architecturally outstanding churches.

The old observatory (1748–53) at the top of the Observatory hill

SIGHTS AT A GLANCE

Gustav Vasa Kyrka **5**
Handelshögskolan **3**
Judiska Museet **6**
Karlbergs Slott **9**
Observatoriemuseet **2**
Röda Bergen **10**
Rörstrandsgatan **8**
Spökslottet **1**
Stadsbiblioteket **4**
Vanadislunden **11**
Vasaparken **7**

KEY

■ Central Stockholm
— Motorway
— Major road
— Minor road
Ⓣ Tunnelbana station

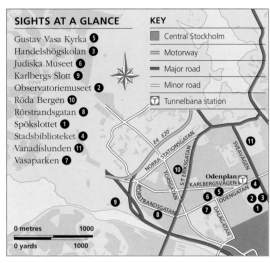

0 metres 1000
0 yards 1000

Spökslottet **1**

Drottninggatan 116. **Map** 2 B3.
Tel 16 47 07. Ⓣ *Rådmansgatan.*
📧 *52.* ◯ *only during prearranged tours.* 🎫 *groups only, by appt.* 📷
♿ *limited access.* 📷

Until about 1900 the most northerly section of Drottninggatan formed the main road into the city from the north. Here is Spökslottet (the "haunted palace"), built in the grand style popular during Sweden's time as a great power, thus dating it to around 1700. It has been suggested that it was designed by Tessin the Elder, but it is more likely that it was by his step-son, Abraham Winantz, who was ennobled in 1693 for his

services as an architect. On show in the palace is Stockholm University's collection of 370 paintings from the 16th to the 19th century, and the Hellner collection of 700 pieces made at the Orrefors glassworks. Pehr Hilleström's painting *With the Fortune Teller* is included in the collection, but the emphasis is on foreign works such as *The Assault*, attributed to Pieter Bruegel the Elder (1567), and *Danae Banquet* and *Cleopatra's Banquet* by Tiepolo. The property was acquired in 1925 by the College of Higher Education, later Stockholm University, which handed it over to the State in 1960. Legend has it that the house has a ghost.

**Orrefors bowl
by Simon Gate, 1925**

Observatoriemuseet **2**

Drottninggatan 120. **Map** 2 B2.
Tel 545 483 90. Ⓣ *Odenplan.* 📧
52. ◯ *during guided tours.* 🎫
guided tours in English by appointment.
♿ 📷 www.observatoriet.kva.se

A number of institutions connected with science and education can be found on and around the hill of Brunkeberg. The oldest is the former observatory designed by Carl Hårleman for the Royal Scientific Academy and opened in 1753. In 1931 its astronomical research was moved to Saltsjöbaden in the Stockholm archipelago. The building has since become Observatoriemuseet (the Observatory Museum), where visitors can see the observation room with its instruments, the two median rooms, the weather room and the instrument workshop. In good weather one can view the stars. There is a splendid view of Stockholm from the museum's dome.

The grove which surrounds the old observatory began to take shape in the 18th century. It is an idyllic enclosed area which was first opened to the public in the 20th century.

On top of Brunkeberg is Sigrid Fridman's statue *The Centaur*. A park stretches down to Sveavägen, where a large pond is fed by water from a stream running down the hillside. The statue *Dancing Youth* is by Ivar Johnsson. At the southern entrance of the park is Nils Möllerberg's sculpture *Youth*.

Handelshögskolan ❸

Sveavägen 65. **Map** 2 C2. Ⓣ *Rådmansgatan.* 🚌 *52.*

When the architect Ivar Tengbom (1878–1968) designed Handelshögskolan, Stockholm's School of Economics, in the early 1920s he was inspired mainly by the Renaissance and Neo-Classical styles. Tengbom himself took charge of the construction and the building was officially opened in 1926 in the presence of King Gustav V. The façade has stone reliefs and a gilded Mercury – the god of commerce – all by Ansgar Almquist, who also contributed a stucco relief with a lion gate based on the one in ancient Mycenae in Greece.

The school was founded in 1909 and was previously based in premises at Brunkebergstorg before moving to the newly built Handelshögskolan.

Entrance of Handelshögskolan, the School of Economics

Vasastaden with Stadsbiblioteket (top left) and Gustav Vasa Kyrka

Stadsbiblioteket ❹

Sveavägen 73. **Map** 2 B2. **Tel** *508 311 00.* Ⓣ *Rådmansgatan.* 🚌 *4, 42, 46, 52, 53, 72.* 🕐 *mid-Jun–mid-Aug: 9am–7pm Mon–Fri, noon–4pm Sat; mid-Aug–mid-Jun: 9am–9pm Mon–Thu, 9am–7pm Fri, noon–4pm Sat & Sun.* ♿ 📱

Gunnar Asplund's master work, Stadsbiblioteket (City Library), is one of the capital's most architecturally important buildings *(see p36)*. Asplund, the champion of the Functionalist style prevalent in the 1930s, designed a library which was dominated by Classic ideals. It was opened in 1928.

Internally, the furnishings and many of the lightfittings were designed by Asplund himself. In the entrance hall are Ivar Johnsson's stucco reliefs with themes from Homer's *Iliad*. The sparkling mural painting in the children's section, *John Blund*, is by Nils Dardel, and the depiction of the stars in the heavens by Ulf Munthe. The door lintels, fine door handles and drinking fountains are by Nils Sjögren. Hilding Linnquist was responsible for the giant-sized tapestry, and also for four mural paintings using ancient fresco techniques.

The library lends more than a million books every year.

Gustav Vasa Kyrka ❺

Odenplan. **Map** 2 B2. **Tel** *508 886 00.* Ⓣ *Odenplan.* 🚌 *4, 40, 42, 46, 53, 69, 72.* 🕐 *11am–6pm Mon–Thu, 11am–3pm Fri–Sun; Jun–Aug: 11am–6pm daily.* 🕐 *noon Mon & Fri, 8:30am Wed, 6pm Thu, 11am Sun, in Swedish.* ♿

Sweden's largest Baroque sculpture forms the altar in Gustav Vasa Kyrka, which was opened in 1906. The piece, by the court sculptor Burchardt Precht (1651–1738), was made for Uppsala Cathedral, from where it was removed in the late 19th century. It was bought by the Gustav Vasa parish congregation, whose church immediately gained a notable attraction.

The architect Agi Lindegren designed the central part of the church in Italian Neo-Baroque style with a 60-m (197-ft) high dome. Lindegren himself designed the marble pulpit and the font was created by Sigrid Blomberg. In the baptismal chapel there is a 15th-century painting by an unknown Dutch artist. The paintings on the dome are by Vicke Andrén, who also portrayed the four evangelists in the transepts. The organ was built with the help of the composer Olle Olsson, the church organist for 50 years.

GUNNAR ASPLUND

Gunnar Asplund (1885–1940) was the dominant figure among Swedish and internationally renowned architects between the two world wars. His first major commission was the chapel at the Skogskyrkogården Cemetery, designed in National Romantic style. His last work was Heliga Korsets Kapell, the cemetery's crematorium (1935–40). Regarded as a masterpiece in the Functionalist style, it has earned a place on the UNESCO World Heritage list *(see p133)*. Asplund also designed Stadsbiblioteket (City Library, 1920–28). He pioneered the Functionalist style as chief architect for the Stockholm Exhibition in 1930.

Stockholm Exhibition, by Gunnar Asplund, 1930

An eight-stemmed *chanuki* (candlestick) in the collection of Judiska Museet

Judiska Museet ❻

Hälsingegatan 2 **Map** 2 A2. **Tel** 31 01 43. Ⓣ Odenplan. 🚌 4, 47, 72. ◯ noon–4pm Mon–Fri & Sun. ◪ in English by appointment. 🏛 ♿ ⬛ ▣ **www**.judiska-museet.a.se

In 1774 Aaron Isaac became the first Jewish immigrant to settle in Stockholm and practise his religion. Half of Sweden's Jewish population of around 18,000 live in the Stockholm area. Judiska Museet depicts the history of the Swedish Jews from Isaac's time up to the present day. It focuses on Judaism as a religion, its integration into Swedish society and, naturally, the Holocaust. A comprehensive collection of pictures and other items provide an insight into Jewish life in Sweden with its important traditions and customs. The beautiful *Torah* (the five books of Moses), the bridal canopy, and the collection of eight-stemmed *chanukis* (candlesticks) are just some of the museum's remarkable spiritual artifacts.

Vasaparken ❼

Map 2 A3. Ⓣ S:t Eriksplan. 🚌 3, 4, 47, 72.

Vasaparken dates from the early 20th century. It was typical of parks of its time with its emphasis on sport exemplified by the inclusion of a spacious grass sports field. During World War I the field was used for growing potatoes. A playground area was added in 1911.

It is a leafy and pleasant park. With few exceptions the trees were planted when the

park was opened, but a lime tree in the shape of a candelabra is believed to be more than 200 years old.

During a major face-lift in the 1940s, the appearance of the section along Torsgatan was changed. Three terraced gardens were added with granite and concrete walls and reliefs. Gottfrid Larsson's bronze statue *The Workman* has stood in this part of the park since 1917. On the opposite side of the park is *Romeo and Juliet*, a small granite sculpture by Olof Th Ohlsson.

Vasaparken, a green lung in the built-up area of Vasastan

Rörstrandsgatan ❽

Map 1 C1. Ⓣ S:t Eriksplan. 🚌 3, 4, 42, 57, 72.

This street takes its name from the no longer existing Rörstrand palace, built in the early 1630s. In the summer of 1726 the manufacture of Delft-style porcelain started in the building. Two hundred years later the now-famous

Rörstrand porcelain factory was moved to the Gothenburg area and then to its current home at Lidköping in south-west Sweden.

Rörstrandsgatan has become a popular street for restaurants and pubs, and it was the site of one of the city's first Chinese restaurants. Today a wide range of restaurants offer cuisine from all over the world. The many outdoor cafés give the street a colourful atmosphere during summer.

Karlbergs Slott ❾

Map 1 B1. **Tel** 514 390 00. 🚌 42, 72 to the station of Karlberg, then 15 min walk. ◪ groups only, by appointment.

Admiral Karl Karlsson Gyllenhielm started to build Karlbergs Slott in the 1630s, during the Thirty Years War. From 1670 the palace was extended and rebuilt by Magnus Gabriel de la Gardie, with Jean de la Vallée as his architect. When Karlberg became royal property in 1688, it was one of Sweden's most majestic palaces. It was where the "hero King" Karl XII (1682–1718) grew up, and it was here that he lay in state after his death at the Battle of Fredrikshald (*see p19*).

In 1792 the architect C C Gjörwell converted the property into the Royal War Academy, which later became the Karlberg Military School, and since 1999 it has been one of the country's military academies.

Cadet balls at Karlberg are unforgettable experiences, not

Rörstrandsgatan, a popular area for restaurants and pubs

Karlbergs Slott, a palace dating from the 1630s – now one of Sweden's military academies

least because of the magnificent setting. The interior decorations include Carl Carove's magnificent stuccowork which can be seen in the grand hall. The palace church has been renovated, but the 17th-century lamps are original. De la Gardie's "rarities room" is now the sacristy but once housed his collection of valuables.

Röda Bergen ⑩

Map 2 A2. Ⓣ *S:t Eriksplan.*
🚌 *3, 42, 47, 57, 69.*

Turning off from Sveavägen into Vanadisvägen one soon reaches Matteus Kyrka which dates from 1902–3. This church was designed by Erik Lallerstedt, who 20 years later undertook its renovation. The figure of St Matthew at the entrance, as well as the reredos figures, are the work of Ivar Johnsson. The mural paintings are by the artist Olle Hjortzberg.

The Röda Bergen ("Red Mountains") district starts at Vanadisplan with a sculpture made from reinforced plastic, *Transformation*, by Chris Gibson (1984). The area is a typical 1920s garden city where, as in Lärkstaden *(see p111)*, the architects abandoned the normal rigid road layout and allowed the

street plan to follow the terrain. After the rose gardens of Rödabergsbrinken, flanked by the parkland oases of Hedemora and Sätertäppan, comes Rödabergsgatan, an avenue of horse chestnut trees typical of the area. A Modernist sculpture in steel has sneaked in here – Björn Selder's *1 1/2 Spheres* (1979). In the background is a playground with Bo Englund's sculpture *Genesis* (1984).

Vanadislunden ⑪

Map 2 B1. 🚌 *2, 40, 52.* **Vanadisbadet Tel** *34 33 00.* ◯ *mid-May–Sep: 10am–6pm daily.* 📷 ♿ 🚻 ⬜

Many places in Vasastan are named Vanadis, which derives from Norse mythology. It was not until the late 19th century that the area around the northern end of Sveavägen started to be developed. In the 1880s a park was laid out on the nearby hillside in which

the cultivated areas were created from a landfill site. A chapel, Stefanskapellet, at the southern end of the park, was opened in 1904. It was designed by Carl Möller, who was the architect responsible for Johannes Kyrka. During renovation in 1925–6 the chapel acquired its painted altar by Einar Forseth depicting the Passion.

It took almost a half-century to complete Vanadislunden The Vanadisbadet outdoor swimming pool was opened in 1938. Above the pool the sculpture *Girl in the Evening Sun* by Anders Jönsson looks out over Vasastaden. This is the highest part of Vanadislunden, and the streets around here have attractive black and white paving stones.

At one time there were numerous suburban mansions in the area. One of them, Cederdals Malmgård, can still be seen towards the northern end of the park.

Houses in Röda Bergen with their typical façades in warm colours

Norrtull & Ekoparken

Large parts of Ekoparken, the world's first National City Park, are spread around the Brunnsviken inlet, only a few kilometres north of the city centre. The English-style park, Hagaparken, with its many 18th-century buildings, extolled by the poet Carl Bellman *(see p98)*, is located in this oasis. To the north lies the majestic Baroque Ulriksdals Slott. In stark contrast, to the south visitors come abruptly to the inner city's built-up area at the old Norrtull gateway. The area has several museums, including Naturhistoriska Museet, Sweden's largest.

The Wenner-Gren Center's main building, Pylonen

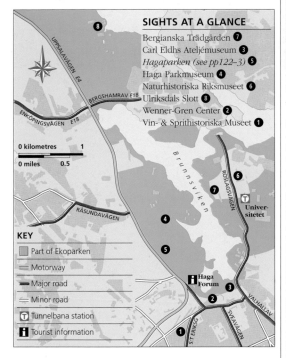

SIGHTS AT A GLANCE

Bergianska Trädgården ❼
Carl Eldhs Ateljémuseum ❸
Hagaparken (see pp122–3) ❺
Haga Parkmuseum ❹
Naturhistoriska Riksmuseet ❻
Ulriksdals Slott ❽
Wenner-Gren Center ❷
Vin- & Sprithistoriska Museet ❶

0 kilometres   1

0 miles   0.5

KEY

▭ Part of Ekoparken

═ Motorway

▬ Major road

⚊ Minor road

Ⓣ Tunnelbana station

🛈 Tourist information

Wenner-Gren Center ❷

Sveavägen 166. **Map** 2 B1. 🚌 2, 40, 52, 69.

The industrialist Axel Wenner-Gren (1881–1961) had an almost religious faith in the potential of science. "Let us use science to solve mankind's problems" is an expression attributed to him. During the 1920s he launched products like vacuum cleaners and refrigerators through his company, Electrolux, which he founded in 1919. His name is preserved in three foundations and in the Wenner-Gren Center, whose 24-storey headquarters, Pylonen, stands like an exclamation mark at the northern end of Sveavägen.

It was opened in 1962, but Wenner-Gren lived only long enough to see the topping-out ceremony in 1961. In the semi-circular Helicon are 155 apartments for the use, at subsidized rents, of foreign scientists undertaking long-term research in Sweden.

The Wenner-Gren Foundation was set up to encourage scientific exchanges between Sweden and other countries. About 250 scientists take part in these every year, and international symposiums are arranged.

Vin- & Sprithistoriska Museet ❶

Dalagatan 100. **Map** 2 A1.
Tel 744 70 70. Ⓣ S:t Eriksplan.
🚌 65. ⏱ 10am–9pm Tue, 10am–4pm Wed–Fri, noon–4pm Sat & Sun.
🎫 🖼 ♿ 🏠 🏠
www.vinosprithistoriska.se

Swedish punsch and schnapps are the themes of Vin- & Sprithistoriska (Wine and Spirits Historical Museum), located in an old wine warehouse. It was designed by Cyrillus Johansson and built in 1923. As the wine trade decreased over the years, the building was used for other purposes until 1967, when the first exhibition was staged. Today's museum dates from 1989 and covers 1,700 sq m (18,300 sq ft). It shows how a wine shop would have looked around 1900. From the same era is a typical southern Swedish distillery in which potatoes were used to make the best schnapps. There is also a collection of spices used for schnapps and liqueurs, and over 50,000 labels are on show.

Visitors can listen to some 200 "schnapps songs" via a computer which also has the texts of 2,000 drinking songs.

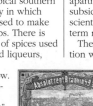

Schnapps label, Vin- & Sprithistoriska Museet

Carl Eldhs Ateljémuseum ❸

Lögbodavägen 10, Bellevueparken.
Tel 612 65 60. 🚌 2, 40, 52, 53.
⬜ Apr: noon–4pm Sun; May: noon–
4pm Sat & Sun; Jun–Aug: noon–4pm
Tue–Sun; Sep: noon–4pm Sat & Sun;
Oct: noon–4pm Sun. 📷 🍴 ♿
🚫 📱 💻

It is not easy to find Löge-
bodavägen, but those who
do are richly rewarded. It has
a viewpoint looking out over
the Brunnsviken inlet and
is close to the monument
*The Young Strindberg in
the Archipelago* by Carl Eldh
(1873–1954). The sculptor's
studio, now Carl Eldh's
Ateljémuseum, is only a few
metres from the viewpoint.

In his time Carl Eldh was
one of Sweden's most prolific
sculptors. Like his colleague
Carl Milles, he lived in Paris
for several years and was influenced by Rodin's Impres-
sionist style. Later his works
were characterized by a more
robust Realism. Eldh's
sculptures can be seen at 16
public sites in Stockholm. The
gypsum forms of these works

Carl Eldh's Ateljémuseum containing gypsum originals of his works

are on show in the studio.
Examples include the
Branting Monument at Norra
Bantorget, the statue of
Strindberg in Tegnérparken,
and *The Runners* at Stadion
(see pp110–11). The original
studio, built in 1918–19, was
designed by the City Hall's
architect, Ragnar Östberg.

Haga Parkmuseum ❹

Mellersta Koppartältet, Hagaparken.
Tel 730 39 81. 🚇 Odenplan then
bus. 🚌 515. ⬜ Jan–14 May:
11am–4pm Thu–Sun; 15 May–30
Sep: 11am–5pm Tue–Sun. 📷

Reopened in 2003, this
museum is housed in the
largest of the three copper-
clad "tents" situated in the
northwest corner of
Hagaparken. It is dedicated
to the history of the park and
includes exhibits on the plans
for its original design, its
unusual collection of buildings,
and the people associated
with them, from the time of
Gustav III to the present.

Originally built in 1787–90
as an open stable yard, the
building housing the museum
was completely destroyed by
fire in 1953. The tent-like
façade was restored to its
former glory in the 1960s,
including the painted copper
cladding, but it was not until
the 1970s that the stables
behind were rebuild as a
covered structure, in keeping
with the original design.

Today, the museum has its
own café, whilst the "tents"
on either side contain a
restaurant and accomodation.
The large rolling lawn in front
of the museum is popular
with locals for sunbathing
and and picnics in summer.

EKOPARKEN – THE NATIONAL CITY PARK

Ekoparken – the world's first National City Park – was
established by the Swedish Parliament in 1995. This has
enabled the capital to safeguard the ecology of its "green
lung", a 27-sq km (10.5-sq miles) area for recreation and
outdoor activities in an urban setting. In fact, the park
covers an area that is as large as Stockholm's inner-city.
Ekoparken includes central districts like Skeppsholmen and
the southern part of Djurgården, and continues north-west
to northern Djurgården, Hagaparken, Brunnsviken and
Ulriksdal. Much of the park was a royal hunting ground as
early as the 16th century, scattered with beautiful palaces
and other sights. The archipelago is represented by the

**Isbladskärret in Ekoparken with its rich
bird-life, including breeding herons**

Fjäderholmarna
islands in the south.
Information on the
park is available at
Haga Forum *(see
map p120)*, which is
a natural entry point.
From here there are
guided boat tours
around Brunnsviken,
with stops at some
of the more impor-
tant sights. For more
information on
Ekoparken and
bookings inquiries,
telephone 587 140 40.

Hagaparken ⑤

In the mid-18th century King Gustav III decided to create a royal park in the popular Haga area. The king's vision was realized by the fashionable architect Fredrik Magnus Piper (1746–1824) with the help of leading architects and decorators, and the result was an English-style park with some unusual buildings. A royal palace inspired by Versailles in France was also planned, but construction halted after the king's death and it remained unfinished. Today Hagaparken is part of Ekoparken *(see p121)*, the world's first national city park – an oasis of nature and culture in the city centre.

Gustav III's Pavilion **painted in 1811 by A F Cederholm**

Fjärils- & Fågelhuset
Hundreds of exotic butterflies and birds fly freely around the greenhouses containing humid tropical rainforest with waterfalls and luxuriant growth at a temperature of 25°C (78°F).

Haga Park-museum

These ruins are all that remain of Gustav III's unfinished royal palace.

★ Koppartälten
These "Roman battle tents" designed by Louis Jean Desprez were completed in 1790. They were originally used as stables and accommodation, but now house a restaurant, café and the Haga Parkmuseum.

Stora Pelousen
The lawns stretching down from Koppartälten to Brunnsviken are popular with Stockholmers for sun-bathing and picnics in the summer, and skiing or sledging in the winter. At the rear is Gustav III's Paviljong.

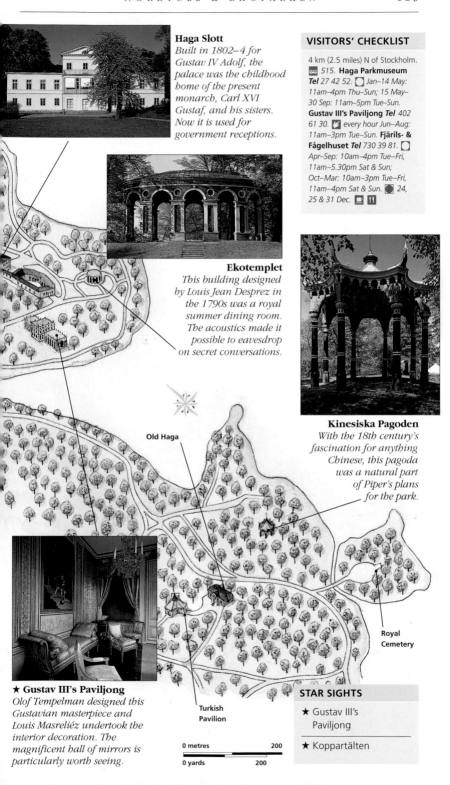

Haga Slott
Built in 1802–4 for Gustav IV Adolf, the palace was the childhood home of the present monarch, Carl XVI Gustaf, and his sisters. Now it is used for government receptions.

Ekotemplet
This building designed by Louis Jean Desprez in the 1790s was a royal summer dining room. The acoustics made it possible to eavesdrop on secret conversations.

Kinesiska Pagoden
With the 18th century's fascination for anything Chinese, this pagoda was a natural part of Piper's plans for the park.

Old Haga

Royal Cemetery

★ **Gustav III's Paviljong**
Olof Tempelman designed this Gustavian masterpiece and Louis Masreliéz undertook the interior decoration. The magnificent hall of mirrors is particularly worth seeing.

Turkish Pavilion

0 metres   200
0 yards   200

STAR SIGHTS

★ Gustav III's Paviljong

★ Koppartälten

Polar bear in a natural setting at Naturhistoriska Riksmuseet

Naturhistoriska Riksmuseet ⑥

5 km (3 miles) N of Stockholm. *Tel* 519 540 00. Ⓣ *Universitetet.* ⬚ *40, 540.* ◯ *10am–7pm Tue–Wed & Fri, 10am–8pm Thu, 11am–7pm Sat & Sun.* ◪ *by appointment.* ♿ ◻ ◻ ◻ www.nrm.se

Completed in 1916, the vast Naturhistoriska Riksmuseet (Natural History Museum) was designed by Axel Anderberg and decorated by Carl Fagerberg. The museum is a venerable institution, founded in 1739 by Carl von Linné (1707–78) as part of Vetenskapsakademien (the Academy of Science). It is one of the 10 largest museums of its kind in the world. Over the centuries, the number of exhibits has risen to about 17 million.

During the 1990s it was modernized with the aim of providing "experience-based knowledge". There are permanent collections, such as "Treasures from the Earth's Interior" and "Marvels of the Human Body", along with temporary exhibitions. In "1.45 Billion Years" visitors can get acquainted with the dinosaurs and the earliest

human beings. "Life and Water" presents both the smallest creatures and the giants of the sea, while penguins, sea lions and polar bears await visitors in "The Polar Regions".

During the 1980s the restaurant and museum courtyard were given an artistic facelift by Nils Stenqvist, Gunnar Larsson and Pål Svensson, and a major extension was added in the early 1990s. This also saw the opening of Cosmonova, which is both a planetarium and an IMAX cinema. The architects were Uhlin & Malm. The dome-shaped cinema screen is 25 times the size of a normal screen. It is largely due to Cosmonova that the museum is now a major visitor attraction.

The *Vega Monument* was erected in front of the museum in 1930 to mark the 50th anniversary of explorer Adolf Erik Nordenskiöld's first voyage through the North-East Passage in his ship *Vega*. Designed by Ivar Johnsson, it is an obelisk in dark granite topped with a copper ship.

Lumpfish, Naturhistoriska Riksmuseet

Bergianska Trädgården ⑦

5 km (3 miles) N of Stockholm. *Tel* 545 917 00. Ⓣ *Universitetet.* ⬚ *40, 540.* **Edvard Andersons Växthus** ◯ *11am–5pm daily.* **Victoriahuset** ◯ *May–Sep: 11am–4pm Mon–Fri; 11am–5pm Sat & Sun.* ◪ ◻ ♿ ◻ ◻ www.bergianska.se

Bergianska Trädgården features more than 9,000 types of plants in beautiful natural settings, and provides an attractive display throughout the year. The most important parts of the gardens are the herb area with its botannical planting scheme, the park with its flower borders, Victoriahuset and the conservatories of Edvard Anderson Växthus, and the fruit and berry beds. There is a kitchen garden in the shade of 100-year-old spruce hedges, and an area for spices and medicinal plants.

There are also trees and shrubs from northern Europe, Asia and America, as well as flowerbeds with both Nordic and Mediterranean plants, and rhododendrons. The spring spectacle of seas of flowering bulbs is the result of 100 years of dedicated care. The Japanese pool was added in 1991 to mark the 200th anniversary of the Bergius foundation which made these gardens possible.

The Victoriahuset conservatory (1900) houses tropical water plants, utility plants and epiphytes. Edvard Andersons Växthus (1995) has large sections for Mediterranean and tropical plants.

An environmental trail offers information on subjects linked with the garden.

Edvard Andersons Växthus in Bergianska Trädgården featuring Mediterranean and tropical plants

Ulriksdals Slott with its magnificent 18th-century Baroque exterior, seen from the palace park

Ulriksdals Slott ⑧

7 km (4.3 miles) N of Stockholm.
Tel 402 61 30. 🚌 503. **Palace** ◯
*Jun– Aug: noon–4pm Tue–Sun.
Guided tours only in this period at
noon, 1, 2 and 3pm.* **Orangery** ◯
*Jun–Aug: noon–4pm Tue–Sun for pre-
booked groups.* **Coronation carriage**
◯ *For pre-booked groups.* 🚫 ♿
♿ 🏠 🍴 💻 www.royalcourt.se

Ulriksdals Slott is situated
between the two main roads
in the northern outskirts of
Stockholm – the E4 and
Norrtäljevägen. The palace
sits on a headland in the bay
of Edsviken. Its attractive
buildings and lush and leafy
surroundings are well worth a
visit. At the entrance to the
grounds is one of Stockholm's
best-known restaurants,
Ulriksdals Wärdshus *(see p170)*.

The original palace was
built in the 1640s and designed by Hans Jakob Kristler in
German/Dutch Renaissance
style. The owner, Marshal of
the Realm Jakob de la Gardie,
named the palace Jakobsdal.
It was bought in 1669 by the
Dowager Queen Hedvig
Eleonora. When she had a
grandson, Ulrik, 15 years later
she donated the palace to
him as a christening gift, and
it was renamed Ulriksdal.

Around this time the architect Tessin the Elder *(see p37)*
suggested some rebuilding
work, but only a few of his
proposals saw the light of
day. However, the stucco
work by Carlo Carove in the
southern wing can still be
seen. In the 18th century the
palace acquired its Baroque

exterior. After being a popular
place for festivities in the time
of Gustav III (1746–92), it
began to lose its glamour and
at one time was used as a
home for war invalids.

Interest in the palace was
revived under Karl XV
(1826–72), and furnishings
and handicrafts many
hundreds of years old are on
show in his rooms. The living
room of Gustav VI Adolf
(1882–1973) in the rebuilt
Knights' Hall, contains furnishings by the great architect
and designer Carl Malmsten.
The suite was a gift from the
Swedish people in 1923 to the
then Crown Prince when he
married Louise Mountbatten.
A new staircase was built at
the same time to designs
which Tessin the Elder had
suggested 250 years earlier.

The park was laid out in the
mid-17th century. It has 300-
year-old lime trees, as well as
one of Europe's most
northerly beechwoods. Carl
Milles's two sculptures of wild
boars stand by the pool in

front of the palace. A stream
is crossed by a footbridge,
which is supported by Per
Lundgren's *Moors Dragging
the Nets*. More art can be seen
in the orangery, designed by
Tessin the Elder in the 1660s
and rebuilt in 1705. It now
houses a sculpture museum.

The palace chapel, a popular
place for weddings, was designed by F W Scholander and
built in 1865 in Dutch Neo-
Renaissance style. It has some
notable medieval stained-
glass windows.

It was from Ulriksdal that
Queen Kristina's Coronation
procession departed in 1650.
Legend has it that by the time
the queen reached the city,
some of her retinue had still
not left Ulriksdal. In one of
the stables there is a replica
of Kristina's carriage. A riding
school, built in 1671, was
converted into a theatre by
Carl Hårleman and C F
Adelcrantz in the 1750s. Performances are staged in the
theatre, named Confidencen,
every summer *(see p176)*.

Sculpture on display in the 17th-century orangery at Ulriksdals Slott

Södermalm & South of Söder

The Södermalm area, generally known as "Söder", rises steeply from the water and is something of a city in itself with its own character, charm and dialect. The slopes are lined with old wooden cottages with an unrivalled view of Stockholm. The dramatic topography has provided some hilly parks, and allotments are scattered among the built-up areas. The area has plenty of shops, bars and restaurants and a lively nightlife, as well as the latest in modern architecture. South of Söder is Globen, a spectacular indoor arena, and Skogskyrkogården Cemetery which is on the UNESCO World Heritage list.

The towers of Mariaberget on a steep hillside close to Slussen

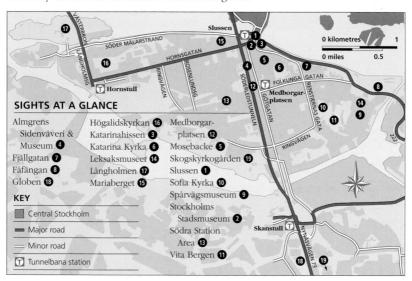

SIGHTS AT A GLANCE

Almgrens Sidenväveri & Museum **4**
Fjällgatan **7**
Fåfängan **8**
Globen **18**
Högalidskyrkan **16**
Katarinahissen **3**
Katarina Kyrka **6**
Leksaksmuseet **14**
Långholmen **17**
Mariaberget **15**
Medborgarplatsen **12**
Mosebacke **5**
Skogskyrkogården **19**
Slussen **1**
Sofia Kyrka **10**
Spårvägsmuseum **9**
Stockholms Stadsmuseum **2**
Södra Station Area **13**
Vita Bergen **11**

KEY

- ◼ Central Stockholm
- ▬ Major road
- — Minor road
- Ⓣ Tunnelbana station

Slussen **1**

Map 4 C4. Ⓣ *Slussen.* 🚌 *2, 3, 43, 53, 55, 59 76.* 🚢 *Djurgårdsfärja.*

Steadily increasing traffic in the early 1900s turned the narrow road between Södermalm and Gamla Stan into a bottleneck. All the boats sailing between Lake Mälaren and the Baltic had to pass through the locks here, and land traffic was confined to a narrow bridge. The congestion was eased in 1928, when some of the boat traffic was transferred to a new canal, but the problem needed a more radical solution. This took the form of a clover-leaf system of roundabouts devised by Tage William-Olsson and Gösta Lundborg. It was opened in 1935 and was so well designed that it was able to cope with the change to right-hand driving in 1967.

At Slussplan, facing Södermalm and the lock that bears his name, is a bronze statue of Karl XIV on horseback by Bengt Fogelberg, unveiled in 1854 by Oscar I on the 40th anniversary of the union between Sweden and Norway (1814–1905). Around the same time, the locks were rebuilt. New machinery devised by the inventor Nils Ericsson was installed. Today the locks are used mostly by pleasure boats, whose erratic manoeuvres provide entertainment for onlookers.

Although the construction of Västerbron bridge and Söderleden road have eased the traffic burden, Slussen is still a busy junction and is in need of a thorough facelift.

The intricate traffic system at Slussen, opened in 1935

Stockholms Stadsmuseum ❷

Ryssgården. **Map** 4 B5.
Tel 508 316 00. Ⓣ Slussen. 🚌 2,
3, 43, 53, 55, 59, 76. ◯ 11am–5pm
Tue–Sun (Sep–May: also 5pm–9pm
Thu; Jun–Aug: also 5pm–7pm Thu).
🎦 ⌀ ♿ 🛈 🖥
www.stadsmuseum.stockholm.se

Hemmed in between the traffic roundabouts of Slussen and the steep hill up to Mosebacke Torg is Stockholms Stadsmuseum (City Museum). It is housed in a late 17th-century building originally designed by Tessin the Elder as Södra Stadshuset (Southern City Hall). After a fire, it was completed by Tessin the Younger in 1685. It has been used for various purposes over the centuries, including law courts and dungeons, schools and city-hall cellars, theatres and churches. It became the city museum in the 1930s.

The museum documents the history of Stockholm. The city's main stages of development are described in a slideshow and a series of four permanent exhibitions. The first starts with the Stockholm Bloodbath of 1520 (see p54) and continues through the 17th century. The eventful 18th century is illustrated with exhibits that include the Lohe treasure – 20 kg (44 lb) of silver discovered in Gamla Stan in 1937. The other sections depict the industrialization in

Stomatol neon-sign Katarinahissen

the 19th century and the tremendous growth in the 20th century with the emergence of a new city centre and new suburbs.

The library has a large archive of pictures and a reference room where visitors can find out virtually anything they want to know about Stockholm. There are also children's activities, concerts and lectures.

Almgrens Sidenväveri (silk mill), now a museum with working 19th-century looms

Katarinahissen ❸

Stadsgården. **Map** 4 C5.
Ⓣ Slussen. 🚌 2, 3, 43, 53, 55, 59,
76. ◯ 7.30am–10pm Mon–Sat,
10am–10pm Sun. ♿ 🍴 ♒

Katarinahissen is the oldest of Stockholm's "high-rise" attractions. The 38-m (125-ft) high lift was opened to the public in March 1883 and is still a prominent silhouette on the Söder skyline. The first Swedish neon sign was erected here in 1909 – a legendary advertisement for Stomatol toothpaste. Since the 1930s, the sign has been placed on a nearby rooftop.

The original lift was driven by steam, but it switched to electricity in 1915. In the 1930s it was replaced by a new lift when the Cooperative Association (KF) built its large new office complex at Slussen. In its first year the lift was used by more than a million passengers, but its

record year was 1945, when it carried 1.8 million people between Slussen and Mosebacke Torg.

The lift is still used every year by about 500,000 passengers who can enjoy a spectacular view of the city from the top.

Almgrens Sidenväveri & Museum ❹

Repslagargatan 15 a. **Map** 9 D2.
Tel 642 56 16. Ⓣ Slussen. 🚌 59.
◯ 10am–4pm Mon–Fri, 11am–3pm
Sat & Sun. 🎦 during and outside
opening hours, call for details. 🎦 🛈
www.kasiden.se

Karl August Almgren was the founder of Almgren's silk-weaving mill, now a museum, in 1833. While on a study tour to Lyon and Tours in France in 1825, Almgren learned about the punch-card system, which was one of the secrets of France's dominance of the silk business. Armed with this information, he returned to Sweden with designs for modern looms and opened his own mill. It soon became a leader in the market, which in the 1700s had seen the establishment of more than 30 silk-weaving mills in Stockholm.

The Almgren family continued the business until 1974, when the mill finally closed. Everything was left intact, and the mill took on a new role in 1991 as a living museum. In the weaving room there is a museum shop selling textiles. The area where the old steam-driven machinery stood is now used as a banqueting room with well-preserved 19th-century decorations.

Katarinahissen with Stockholms Stadsmuseum in the background

Mosebacke ❺

Map 9 D2. Ⓣ *Slussen, then a short walk or take the lift at Katarinahissen.* 🚌 *59, then a short walk.* 〰

By taking the lift at Katarina-hissen *(see p127)* from Slussen, the district of Mosebacke with its distinctive atmosphere can be reached. The area got its name from a miller and landowner, Moses Israelsson, the son-in-law of Johan Hansson Hök who managed two mills on the hilltop plateau in the 17th century.

In the mid-19th century Mosebacke became increasingly attractive to Stockholmers as a centre for entertainment. A theatre was built in 1852. However, it was destroyed by fire soon after and replaced in 1859 by a new building, Södra Teatern, designed by Johan Fredrik Åbom. The gateway leading to Mosebacke Terrass and its spectacular panoramic views of the city was added at the same time.

Södra Teatern is a classic among Stockholm's stages. Around 1900 the new auditorium was enhanced with a ceiling painting by Vicke Andrén. In the 1930s murals were added, some by Isaac Grünewald. Carl Eldh's bronze bust, *The Young Strindberg*, placed on the theatre's terrace in 1975, shows the author looking across to the city from this very terrace, recalling the character of Arvid Falk in the beginning of Strindberg's novel *The Red Room* (1879).

Nils Sjögren's *The Sisters* stands behind railings on Mosebacke Torg. Attractive

Katarina Kyrka (1695) after its extensive restoration due to a devastating fire in 1990

steps lead up to Fiskargatan. At No. 12 is an experimental fireproof-gable design, *Morning Light*, an *al secco* painting on limestone plaster.

Katarina Kyrka ❻

Högbergsgatan 13. **Map** 9 D2. **Tel** 743 68 00. Ⓣ *Medborgarplatsen, then 3 min walk.* 🚌 *2, 3, 53, 76.* ◯ *11am–5pm Mon–Fri, 10am–5pm Sat & Sun.* 🎨 *by appointment.* ✝ *11am Wed, 11am Sat, 11am Sun.* ♿ 🎫

The buildings on Katarina-berget date partly from the 18th century and surround a hilltop where various churches have been sited since the late 14th century. The earlier chapels were replaced in the 17th century by a more impressive and appropriate building, Katarina Kyrka, de-signed by one of the era's greatest architects, Jean de la Vallée (1620–96). King Karl X Gustaf was also deeply involved in the project, and he insisted that the church should have a central nave with the altar and pulpit right in the middle. The church was founded in 1656, although it was not completed until 1695. In 1723 it was badly damaged by fire, along with large parts of the surrounding built-up area, but it was restored over the next couple of decades. Major restoration was also carried out in the 20th century, and a new copper roof was added in 1988. Two years later, on the night of 16 May 1990, there was another fire and, apart from the outer walls, the church and virtually all its fittings were destroyed.

The architectural practice of Ove Hidemark was commissioned to design a new church which, as far as possible, would be a faithful reconstruction of the original. It was not just the outer shell of the building that had to undergo detailed restoration. In order to make the best use of the surviving walls it was necessary to adopt 17th-century building techniques throughout the new building. Experts and craftsmen managed to join heavy timbering on to the central dome in the traditional way, and the collapsed central arch was rebuilt with specially made bricks in 17th-century style.

In 1995, the church was reconsecrated, more beautiful than ever in the view of many people, with the altar sited exactly where it was originally planned.

The reconstruction cost 270 million kronor, of which 145 million kronor was covered by insurance. Such was the popularity of the project that the rest was raised through public donations.

Mosebacke Torg with Södra Teatern in the background

Fjällgatan ❼

Street light, Fjällgatan

Per Anders Fogelström (1917–98), probably Söder's best-known author, wrote: "Fjällgatan must be the city's most beautiful street. It's an old-fashioned narrow street which runs along the hilltop with well-maintained cobble-stones ... and with street lights jutting out from the houses. Then the street opens up and gives a fantastic view of the city and the water..." This area offers an experience of the authentic Söder and its unique atmosphere.

The Heights of Söder
With its 300-year-old houses and terraced gardens, the Söder hilltop stands like a giant stage-set behind Stadsgården harbour.

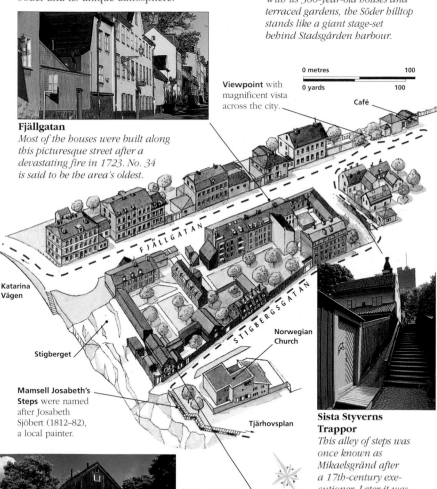

Fjällgatan
Most of the houses were built along this picturesque street after a devastating fire in 1723. No. 34 is said to be the area's oldest.

Viewpoint with magnificent vista across the city.

| 0 metres | 100 |
| 0 yards | 100 |

Café

Katarina Vägen

FJÄLLGATAN

STIGBERGSGATAN

Stigberget

Norwegian Church

Mamsell Josabeth's Steps were named after Josabeth Sjöbert (1812–82), a local painter.

Tjärhovsplan

Sista Styverns Trappor
This alley of steps was once known as Mikaelsgränd after a 17th-century executioner. Later it was named after the inn on the harbour, Sista Styvern ("The Last Penny").

Söder Cottages
Typical well-preserved cottages can be found along Stigbergsgatan. One of them is No. 17, the house of the block-maker Olof Krok during the 1730s.

KEY

– – – Suggested route

Fåfängan

Map 6 A5. 🚌 53. ☐ ☼

Fåfängan, at Södermalm's most easterly point, provides a grandstand view of the boats sailing in and out of Stockholm's harbour. In the 1650s, Field Marshal Erik Dahlberg made full use of its strategic location on a hilltop to build a defensive fortress. Some relics of this period can still be seen.

Sofia Kyrka and Vita Bergen park with its 18th-century cottages

The hill and its park were given the name Fåfängan in the 1770s. The wholesale merchant Fredrik Lundin owned the area at that time, and he built a pavilion which still stands on the hilltop in a square garden filled with flowerbeds. The word "Fåfängan" ("Vanity") originally denoted an area of land which was not worth using. But in Stockholm it has a special meaning: "The pavilion on the hilltop with a marvellous view." It is a delightful place for a coffee break while exploring Söder.

Spårvägsmuseet 🅐

Tegelviksgatan 22. **Map** 9 F3.
Tel 462 55 31. 🚌 2, 55, 66.
☐ 10am–5pm Mon–Fri, 11am–4pm Sat & Sun. 🎟 by appt. 🅰 🅑 🅾
🖥 www.sparvagsmuseet.sl.se

The Tram Museum, Spårvägsmuseet, covers the development of the Stockholm public transport system, SL, from the horse-drawn buses of the 19th century to the high-tech underground trains of today. Visitors can try out old and new trams and buses for

Horse-drawn tram from the 1890s on display in Spårvägsmuseet

comfort and can experience a driver's-eye view of the city traffic on film.

The museum has three permanent exhibitions covering 5,000 sq m (53,800 sq ft). One shows the history of public transport with the help of some 50 vehicles. Another section traces technical developments from different eras. The third section focuses on the artistically decorated underground stations *(see p203)*. There is also a library and archive. On Saturdays and Sundays for most of the year visitors can take two free round trips on a vintage bus.

Sofia Kyrka 🅐

Vitabergsparken. **Map** 9 F3.
Tel 641 83 01. 🚌 3, 46, 76.
☐ 9.30am–4pm Mon–Fri, noon–4pm Sat & Sun. 🕆 noon Wed, 6:30pm Thu, 11am Sun. 🎟 by appt. 🅑 🅾
Concerts 3pm Sat.

High up on Vita Bergen, surrounded by a leafy green park, is Sofia Kyrka, named after Oscar II's consort and built in 1902–06.

The 35-year-old architect Gustaf Hermansson, who had already designed several churches, including Oscars-kyrkan at Östermalm, created a monumental design with both National Romantic and Gothic influences and tall spires, the highest reaching 78 m (256 ft).

Three windows by Olle Hjortzberg are all that remain of the original decorations. The early 1950s saw

the addition of the large altar fresco by Hilding Linnqvist with themes from the Old and New Testaments. The interior acquired its present appearance as part of a major renovation in the early 1980s when the layout of the church was radically altered.

Vita Bergen 🅐

Map 9 F3. 🚌 2, 3, 55, 66, 76.

Vita Bergen (White Mountains) is best known as a park, largely because of Swedish TV broadcasts from its open-air theatre. But it is more than just a park. Houses for workers at Söder's harbours and factories were built on and around the hilltop in the 18th century. They were simple homes, often with a small garden and surrounded by a fence. In 1736 the building of new wooden houses was forbidden because of the fire risk, but the slum districts were exempted. As a result, areas like Bergsprängargränd still have houses which have retained their original character and give a good idea of life in bygone days.

Around 1900, when Sofia Kyrka was built, the area was turned into a leafy hillside park. This was complemented to the east by an area of allotment-garden cottages. Towards Malmgårdsvägen is the 300-year-old Werner Groen Malmgård (suburban mansion). The park has a bronze statue, *Elsa Borg*, by Astri Bergman Taube (1972), wife of the great troubadour Evert Taube *(see p57)*.

Medborgar-platsen ⓬

Map 9 D3. Ⓣ *Medborgarplatsen.*
🚌 *59, 66.*

Södermalm's natural centre is Medborgarplatsen. The square had been called Södra Bantorget for more than 100 years, but in 1939 it was renamed Medborgarplatsen (Citizen's Square) on completion of Medborgarhuset. The building, designed by Martin Westerberg in Functionalist and Neo-Classical styles, contains an auditorium, gym, swimming pool and library.

On the west side of the square is Söderhallarna, a complex of restaurants, delicatessens and a cinema. In 1984 the Göta Ark offices, designed by Claes Mellin and Willy Hermansson, were added on the north-west side.

Alongside the stairway to Södra Station is the Södertorn apartment block designed by the Danish architect Henning Larssen. At the entrance is *Nana's Fountain* by Niki de Saint-Phalle, who also created a large sculpture group at the Moderna Museet *(see pp80–81)*. The western corner of Medborgarhuset features a 17th-century gateway. Closer to Götgatan is Gustaf Nordahl's *The Source of Life* (1983).

Göran Strååt's sculpture *Kasper* can be seen at the 17th-century Lillienhoffska Palatset. Stefan Thorén's sculpture *Dawn* in welded iron is a dominant feature on the square outside.

Södertorn tower and Ricardo Bofill's curved building near Södra Station

Södra Station Area ⓭

Map 8 C3. Ⓣ *Medborgarplatsen or Mariatorget, then a short walk.*
🚌 *43, 55, 66.*

In the mid-19th century Fatburen lake existed to the west of Medborgarplatsen. It was filled in and in the 1860s a train station called Södra Station was opened nearby. In the 1980s the track site was transformed into a new residential area with about 3,000 apartments.

The district became a test-bed for the design concepts of the 1980s shaped by architects' efforts towards Stockholm's urban renewal. The most interesting developments were the work of the Spanish architect Ricardo Bofill. He designed the tower blocks near to the station building as well as the curved residential building – the area's most impressive Neo-Classical feature – which adjoins the new Fatbur Park.

The park has an open section close to Bofill's curved building with a wooded area further away. It is crossed by a path which links Medborgarplatsen with Södermalmsallén and the rail-shuttle station. A 200-m (660-ft) long avenue with 16 sculptures cuts diagonally across the park with a fountain and pool in the middle. In the northern part of the park a flower garden has been named after the Swedish composer Johan Helmich Roman (1694–1758). The arches of Bofill's curved building shelter some interesting works of art.

Leksaksmuseet ⓮

Tegelviksgatan 22. **Map** 8 F3.
Tel 641 61 00. Ⓣ *Slussen.* 🚌 *3, 55, 66.* 🕐 *10am–5pm Mon–Fri. 11am–4pm Sat & Sun.* 📷 *by appt.*
🎫 ♿ 🏠 🖥

Toys which have delighted children and adults alike over the past century are on show at Leksaksmuseet (the Toy Museum). The museum was opened in 1980, and the main exhibition changes continuously as new toys are added to the collection.

One floor features musical instruments, including musical boxes, barrel organs and accordions. Another floor is devoted to mechanical toys, models and dioramas. A third section has dolls, dolls' houses, wooden toys, steam engines, and several working model railways. Private collections are also on show. There is a playroom and children's theatre.

Medborgarplatsen, central Södermalm, with Lillienhoffska Palatset, once a poorhouse

Bastugatan, one of Mariaberget's well-preserved 18th-century streets

Mariaberget **⑮**

Map 8 C2. Ⓣ *Mariatorget.*
🚌 *43, 55.*

A fire in 1759 destroyed the
old buildings of Mariaberget.
The area was rebuilt
according to a 1736 law for-
bidding the construction of
wooden houses in this part
of Söder. The result of this
purposeful 18th-century town
planning remains intact.
Mariaberget's stone buildings
on the slopes down towards
Riddarfjärden are among
Stockholm's most distinctive,
and the character of the steep
winding streets and alleys
has been well preserved.

Towards the end of the 20th
century a conservation programme was implemented to
safeguard the area's cultural
heritage, including the view
over Riddarfjärden. Near
Bastugatan an attractive
promenade, Monteliusvägen,
has been built along the
rock's edge. A new flight of
steps leads down to the Söder
Mälarstrand quayside.

The author Ivar Lo-Johansson
(1901–90) lived in this area
for more than half a century.
A small park with a bust of
the artist bears his name.
The 18th-century poet C M
Bellman *(see p98)* was born at
Mariaberget, although he is
more usually associated with
Haga and Djurgården.

Mariaberget presents a pleasant contrast to the busy traffic
artery of Hornsgatan. When
the street was widened and
levelled in 1901 a number of
18th-century buildings came
into view. The area now
features galleries and antique
shops. On the opposite side
of Hornsgatan is Maria

Magdalena Kyrka on a site
where there have been religious buildings since the 14th
century. The predecessor of
the present building was constructed in 1634. It burnt
down in 1759 and was rebuilt
four years later.

Högalidskyrkan **⑯**

Högalids Kyrkväg. **Map** 1 C5.
Tel *616 88 00.* Ⓣ *Hornstull.*
🚌 *4, 66, 74.* ◯ *11am–6pm
Mon–Fri, 10am–4pm Sat & Sun.* 🚻
noon Wed, 11am Sun. ♿ 🅿

The octagonal twin towers of
Högalidskyrkan make the
church easy to identify from
many parts of the city. The
impressive brick building in
National Romantic style was
completed in 1923. It was
designed by Ivar Tengbom.
He also put his mark on the
interior decoration, which
involved a number of leading
artists and craftsmen.

Tengbom was enlisted to
design the columbarium
which was added in 1939.
The most prolific artist was
Gunnar Torhamn, who
provided the Crucifix – the

**The distinctive twin towers of
Högalidskyrkan, built in 1923**

largest in Scandinavia – as
well as the frescoes in the
baptismal chapel and the
decoration of the pulpit and
organ loft. Erik Jerke created
the reredos in Byzantine style.
In the cemetery chapel below
the chancel, Einar Forseth
designed an apse mosaic
using the same techniques
that he employed for Gyllene
Salen (the Golden Room) in
Stadshuset *(see p114).*

By no means everything in
the church is new. The font is
from the 16th century, and
the seven-stemmed candle-
stick on the altar dates from
the 18th century.

**Exercise yard in the former royal
prison on Långholmen**

Långholmen **⑰**

Map 1 B5. Ⓣ *Hornstull, then 3 min
walk.* 🚌 *66.* ⛴

Below the majestic Västerbron bridge *(see p113)* is the
island of Långholmen, which
is linked to Södermalm by
two bridges. Långholmen is
best known for the various
prisons which have been located here since 1724. During
the 20th century the prison
here was the largest in
Sweden, housing 620 inmates.
When it closed in 1975, the
island became a popular
recreational area.

The prison buildings were
demolished in 1982, but the
old royal jail dating from 1835
remains. The one-time cells
now form part of a hotel, as
well as a prison museum.
There is also a youth hostel
and an excellent restaurant, as
well as a small museum to
the poet C M Bellman with a
café in the gardens which run
down towards Riddarfjärden.

Långholmen's park has an
open-air theatre, and offers
excellent swimming both from
the beaches and the rocks.

Globen ⑱

3 km (1.9 miles) S of Stockholm.
🚇 Globen. **Tel** 50 83 53 00.
🅾 during events. 📷 by appt. ♿
📧 🖥 www.globen.se

In 1989 Stockholm acquired a new symbol in the shape of the indoor arena Globen. It is the world's largest spherical building and has given the southern part of the city a completely new silhouette.

Globen offers a wide programme, including 125 annual events. The ice hockey world championship in 1989 was the first major competition to be staged here. It has been followed by other world championships, including handball, boules, wrestling and indoor bandy (a type of hockey). Globen has also hosted European championships in gymnastics, athletics and volleyball and key equestrian events.

Concerts at Globen have featured international stars like Pavarotti, Sinatra and the Rolling Stones, as well as Bruce Springsteen, who attracted a record audience of 16,357. World figures who have appeared here have included Pope John Paul II and Nelson Mandela.

Chapel of the Holy Cross by Gunnar Asplund at Skogskyrkogården

Globen, designed by Berg Architects, has a circumference of 690 m (2,260 ft) and a height of 85 m (279 ft). The viewing screens each cover 13 sq m (140 sq ft). Globen City has sprung up around the arena with more than 150 shops, hotels and other services.

The silhouette of Globen arena dominating the surrounding area

Skogskyrko-gården ⑲

6 km (3.7 miles) S of Stockholm. **Tel** 508 301 93. 🚇 Skogskyrkogården. 📷 May–Sep: 5pm Mon. ♿ 📧

Nature and the splendid buildings have combined to provide a harmonious setting which has placed Skogskyrkogården Cemetery on the UNESCO World Heritage list. It is sited amid pine-woods which provide a justly sombre frame-work for the chapels and crematorium.

The winners of a competition to de-sign the cemetery in 1914 were Gunnar Asplund *(see p117)* and Sigurd Lewerentz, whose proposals were considered the most likely to safeguard the area's special character. Asplund's first significant work, Skogs-kapellet (Woodland Chapel), with its steep shingled roof,

Epitaph to Gunnar Asplund

was opened at the same time as the cemetery in 1920. This was followed five years later by Uppståndelsekapellet (Resurrection Chapel), designed by Lewerentz.

In 1940 Asplund's last great work, Skogskrematoriet (Woodland Crematorium), was opened, along with its three chapels representing Faith, Hope and the Holy Cross. They are sited along Korsets Väg. John Lundqvist's *The Resurrection* stands in the pillared hall of Heliga Korsets Kapell – the largest of the three. Adjoining the chapel is Asplund's black granite cross.

A memorial park was added in 1961 on the wooded slopes to the north-west of the chapel. The Hill of Meditation lies to the west. The chapel has been decorated by artists like Carl Milles, Sven Erixson and Gunnar Torhamn.

Skogskyrkogården is the last resting place of both the unknown and the celebrated, among whom is Greta Garbo.

GRETA GARBO

The legendary Greta Garbo, one of the 20th century's out-standing film stars, was born in 1905 in a humble part of Södermalm. At the age of 17 she joined the theatre academy of Dramaten and made her film debut in *Peter the Tramp*. Her breakthrough came in 1924 in Mauritz Stiller's film of Selma Lagerlöf's book *The Atonement of Gösta Berling*. The following year she moved to Hollywood, where she soon became the reigning star. Garbo appeared in 24 films, including *Anna Karenina* (1935) and *Camille* (1936). She never married and lived a solitary life until her death in 1990. Her ashes were interred at the Skogskyrkogården Cemetery in 1999.

Garbo in *As You Desire Me* (1932)

THREE GUIDED WALKS

Stockholm is a perfect city for walking. Not only is it flat, but it is also one of Europe's less crowded capital cities, making it ideal for stress-free strolling through the streets and thoroughfares. Many of Stockholm's pedestrian areas also have cycle paths running alongside them, so take care to observe the painted signs on the ground, indicating which side of the line you should walk. These guided walks have been devised to cover

The top of Kaknästornet TV tower

some of the city's most appealing districts: discover residential Södermalm (also known as "Söder") south of the centre, with great views of the city centre; take in some of Stockholm's best parkland on Djurgården – the perfect destination for a picnic; and finally, explore the commercial heart of the Swedish capital, following a route which takes you past leading department stores and boutiques, as well as more sedate churches and monuments.

A view of Stockholm from Södermalm *(see p135)*

Stadsbiblioteket (the city library) in central Stockholm *(see p139)*

KEY

••• Walk route

0 kilometres 1

0 miles 1

A 90-minute walk around the city centre *(pp138-9)*

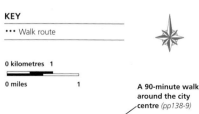

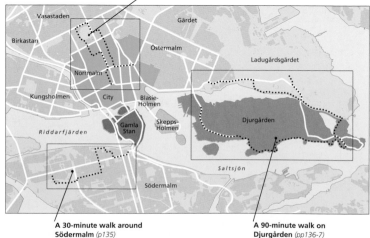

A 30-minute walk around Södermalm *(p135)*

A 90-minute walk on Djurgården *(pp136-7)*

A 30-Minute Walk around Södermalm

Winding through a charming mix of narrow residential streets and neighbourhood allotments with their red and white summer cottages, this walk also offers the best views of Stockholm from anywhere in the city. There is also the chance to browse in some of the more quirky stores or stop at a streetside café whilst exploring this largely undiscovered side of Stockholm.

Begin at Södermalms torg ①, the heart of one of Stockholm's main traffic interchanges, Slussen. Before leaving the square, glance up at the roofs of the surrounding buildings and you'll see

Boats serving as floating hotels lining Söder Mälarstrand ⑦

head north towards Söder's northern shore, then take a left into pretty, cobbled Bastugatan ④, full of 18th-century houses. Turn right into Blecktornsgränd ⑤ to see some of the finest views in the city, with open vistas out over Riddarholmen, Gamla Stan and the city centre. Follow the narrow path of Monteliusvägen ⑥ west, enjoying the sweeping views on your right; several of the

View of Riddarholmen from Blecktornsgränd ⑤

| 0 metres | 500 |
| 0 yards | 500 |

[Map of Södermalm walk route]

Riddarfjärden

KEY

••• Walk route

☼ Good viewing point

🚇 Tunnelbana station

Sweden's first ever neon sign for the now defunct Stomatol toothpaste. From Södermalms torg, head west along Hornsgatan ②. Söder has a plethora of good restaurants and unusual shops, and on the initial stretch of this long road you will also find many small, interesting art galleries. On the left as you make your way along Hornsgatan you'll soon pass the 17th century Maria Magdalena Kyrka ③ designed by the same architects as the Royal Palace.

Now leave the main road to walk along some of Söder's residential streets which are among Stockholm's most sought after addresses. Turn right into Bellmansgatan and

house-boats below on Söder Mälarstrand ⑦ now serve as floating hotels. At Timmermansgatan head south until you reach Wollmar Yxkullsgatan ⑧, considered by some to be the heart of Södermalm.

Now head right along Wollmar Yxkullsgatan until you reach Ringvägen. Cross this road and take the delightful Zinkens Väg ⑨ through an area of allotments and small summer cottages in the Zinkensdamm area ⑩. Owners often spend several days at a time here pottering in their gardens. After passing the Zinkensdamm youth hostel, head north up the steps of Pipmakartrappan back to Hornsgatan and the end of the walk ⑪.

TIPS FOR WALKERS

Starting point: *The easiest way to get to the start of the walk is to take the T-bana to Slussen; Södermalms torg is just outside the main exit.*
Length: *2.5 km (1.6 miles)*
Duration: *Half an hour*
Stopping-off points: *There are plenty of cafés and shops along Hornsgatan for a break or rest.*
Ending the walk: *At the end of the walk you can take the Zinkensdamm T-bana located on Hornsgatan (two stops west of Slussen).*

A 90-Minute Walk on Djurgården

This delightful walk offers a chance to explore the
former royal hunting grounds of Djurgården, an island
which forms the northern side of Stockholm harbour.
Heavily wooded and dotted with grand old houses, the
island offers peace, tranquility and some of the city's
most striking museums. There are also stunning views
across Stockholm from the top of the Kaknäs TV tower.

The greenery of Djurgården as seen
from the air

Nordiska museet to Ryssviken

The walk starts at the palatial
Nordiska museet ①, one
of the city's best museums,
which provides a good
grounding in the history
of everyday Swedish life.
From the museum, follow
Djurgårdsvägen south,
looking out for the boat-
shaped building behind the
Nordiska museet. Here resides
the former warship, Vasa,
who sank in Stockholm
harbour on her maiden
voyage in 1628 (see pp92–5).

Continuing on, you will
soon come to the eclectic
Liljevalchs Konsthall art
gallery ② (see p95) which
hosts frequently-changing
exhibitions of art and
sculpture. Once at Almänna
Gränd, you are entering the
pleasure zone: there are often
crowds of children here
heading for the amusement
park, Gröna Lund ③ (see
p95), which features several

hair-raising rides including the
"Free Fall", a vertical drop of
around 100 m (330 ft). From
here Djurgårdsvägen swings
east on its way around
Djurgården. Follow the road
to the small inlet, Ryssviken
④, where you could end the
walk if you wish and take
the 47 bus back to the city.

Ryssviken to Blockhusudden

From Ryssviken, take the
path south to the promontory
known as Waldemarsudde ⑤
(see p99) with its good views
across the harbour and
excellent art gallery

The Vasa Museet, home to the
former warship, the Vasa

specialising
in late 19th-century
Nordic art. From here, it is
a pleasant walk along the
waterfront to another small
promontory, Biskopsudden ⑥.

Heading east a short
distance along Biskopsvägen,
pick up another path along
the shore which begins just
south of the junction with
Djurgårdsvägen ⑦. This path
leads to the eastern end of
Djurgården, Blockhusudden ⑧,
which gives views of the hi-
tech business centre, Nacka

TIPS FOR WALKERS

Starting point: Tram number 7
or buses 44 and 47 will bring you
closest to the Nordiska museet.
Length: 8.5 km (5.3 miles)
Duration: One and a half to
two hours
Stopping-off points: A great
spot for lunch or a cup of coffee
is the Blå Porten, Djurgårdsvägen
64, near the Liljevachs Konsthall
art gallery. The café at the top of
the Kaknästornet TV tower has
the best views of Stockholm.
End point: You could end this
walk early at Blockhusudden,
which is conveniently the
terminus for the 69 bus which
runs all the way back into the
centre of the city via Strandvägen
and Sergels torg. From the end
of the walk at Strandvägen
buses 69 and 79 run back to
the centre.

Strand, on the southern side of the harbour and the residential area, Jarlaberg, high on the cliffs above. The arcing sculpture of a boy atop a crescent of steel that you can see across the water, is *Gud på himmelsbågen*, by Stockholm sculptor Carl Milles *(see p150)*.

Blockhusudden is also home to Thielska Galleriet ⑨ *(see p99)*, a superb art gallery with a fine collection of 19th-century Scandinavian art. If you wish to end the walk at this point, there is a bus from here back to the city.

Carl Milles' sculpture, *Gud på himmelsbågen*

Blockhusudden to Berwaldhallen concert hall

On foot, continue northeast to Lilla Sjötullsbron bridge ⑩. The stretch of path before the bridge runs past a marshy pond, especially preserved for its birdlife. Once over the bridge, head west along the tranquil canal to meet up with Djurgårds-brunnsvägen which leads towards the Kaknästornet TV tower ⑪ *(see p108)*. This is a long diversion from the main route, but worth it if you are feeling energetic. At 155 m (508 ft) high, the tower is one of the tallest buildings in Scandinavia and even boasts a café at around 120 m (390 ft) elevation.

From the tower, backtrack to the main walk and head west along the canal path past a clutch of museums on your right, including the Sjöhistoriska museet ⑫ *(see pp106–7)*, which reveals Sweden's maritime history. Further along the path, the imposing villas on the right are part of Diplomatstaden ("Diplomat's Town", *see p106*), home to several Embassies, including that of the United States of America ⑬. The spire rising from behind the waterfront houses belongs to Engelska Kyrkan ⑭, the English Church. To finish the walk, take the path around Nobel Parken and end at Strandvägen, with its elegant façades lining the waterfront ⑮.

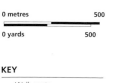

DJURGÅRDEN

0 metres 500
0 yards 500

KEY

••• Walk route

🔆 Good viewing point

🚌 Bus stop

🚊 Tram stop

🅣 Tunnelbana

Palatial waterfront houses along Strandvägen ⑮

A 90-Minute Walk around the City Centre

This walk will take you right through the heart of Stockholm, giving you a chance to browse in the city's best shops or to enjoy a coffee and pastry in one of the many cafés you'll pass. It also provides a chance to see some of the imposing buildings that Stockholm has to offer, such as the magnificent Konserthuset or the architecturally interesting Stadsbiblioteket. The route also includes a park or two where you can take a break and escape the bustling streets.

Mille's Orpheus

Plaque in memory of Olof Palme ⑤

Sergels torg to Adolf Fredriks Kyrka

This walk begins at Sergels torg *(see p67)* ①, a split-level square widely regarded as the very centre of the modern city. It is

Strindberg's study at Strindbergsmuseet Blå Tornet (The Blue Tower) on Drottninggatan ⑦

marked by a tall glass obelisk which is illuminated at night. From this point, take pedestrianised Sergelgatan north to reach the city's main market square, Hötorget *(see p68)* ②, full of vegetables and flowers for sale. It was in the PUB department store here in

the square that film legend Greta Garbo sold hats in the millinery department; there is a small exhibition devoted to her by the ground floor entrance.

On the opposite side of Hötorget is the grand Konserthuset *(see p68)* ③,

home to the Swedish Royal Philarmonic. In front of Konserthuset stands Carl Mille's sculpture, *Orpheus*. Across Kungsgatan you will see the Kungshallen shopping mall ④ which also contains several cafés and restaurants. From Kungsgatan turn left into Sveavägen. At the junction with Olof Palmes Gata you will find a plaque in the pavement that marks the spot where the former

The colourful Hötorget market, outside Konserthuset ③

Swedish Prime Minister, Olof Palme, was gunned down in 1986 as he left a nearby cinema with his wife ⑤.

A short distance to the north, still on Sveavägen, Palme's grave can be visited in the churchyard at Adolf Fredriks Kyrka *(see p70)* ⑥.

Blå Tornet to Odenplan

Just after the church, turn left into Kammakargatan to reach the former home of writer August Strindberg, now a museum, Blå Tornet *(see p69)* ⑦, at the corner of Drottninggatan. Head uphill on Drottninggatan, past small quirky shops and various popular cafés ⑧.

Once past Kungstensgatan, Drottninggatan becomes Norrtullsgatan and continues north along the side of Observatorielunden ⑨, a leafy park which hides Stockholm's former observatory dating

The imposing Kungstornen (King's Towers) on Kungsgatan ⑮

from 1753. At the end of the road you'll reach another of Stockholm's main squares, Odenplan ⑩, a large open area of superb 19th-century architecture dominated by the Neo-Baroque Gustav Vasa Kyrka *(see p117)* ⑪. There is a T-bana station here if you want to cut the walk short.

Odenplan to Stureplan

From Odenplan, head east along Odengatan past some university buildings to reach the city library, Stadsbiblioteket *(see p117)* ⑫, designed by Gunnar Asplund and widely regarded as one of Stockholm's finest Functionalist buildings. Next take a right into Sveavägen and head south towards the prestigious Stockholm School of Economics ⑬, Handelshögskolan, where competition for places is extremely fierce.

From here turn left into Rehnsgatan and walk a short distance east before turning right into Döbelnsgatan which, leading south, eventually becomes Malmskillnadsgatan. Johannes Kyrka ⑭, a 19th-century Neo-Gothic church set in a small park, can be seen on your

left. The wooden steeple which stands next to it was constructed much earlier in 1692.

Look out for a set of stone steps on the left which lead down onto Kungsgatan beside the Neo-Classical Kungstornen twin towers *(see pp68–9)* ⑮, which dominate this part of the city. Once on Kungsgatan, you will find a good selection of cafés and stylish shops, as well as several cinemas near the Kungstornen bridge.

The walk ends with a short stroll downhill to Stureplan, *(see pp70-71)* ⑯ an open square that is centre of Stockholm's vibrant nightlife and a popular meeting place.

The impressive doorway of the Neo-Baroque Gustav Vasa Kyrka ⑪

TIPS FOR WALKERS

Starting point: *Sergels torg is easily accessible from Stockholm's main T-bana station, T-Centralen. When leaving the platform simply follow the signs for Sergels torg.*
Length: *3.5 km (2.2 miles)*
Duration: *One and a half hours*
Stopping-off points: *For cafés, try the Kungshallen shopping mall at Hötorget or Kungsgatan and Stureplan. The Saluhallen indoor market in Hötorget is the best place in Stockholm for ethnic treats and delicious Middle Eastern snacks.*

HUMLEGÅRDEN

ENGELBREKTS-PLAN

AVID BAGARES GATA

HUMLEGÅRDSGATAN

BRUNNSGATAN

GREV TUREGATAN

KUNGSGATAN ⑯ STURE-PLAN

LÄSTMAKARGATAN

Östermalms-torg

JAKOBSBERGSGATAN

NORRLANDSGATAN

BIBLIOTEKSGATAN

RIDDARGATAN

MÄSTER SAMUELSGATAN

SMÅLANDSGATAN

NYBROGATAN

REGERINGSGATAN

NYBRO-PLAN

BERZELI PARK

AMNGATAN

0 metres 300

0 yards 300

KEY

••• Walk route

🔆 Good viewing point

Ⓣ Tunnelbana station

EXCURSIONS FROM STOCKHOLM

*S*tockholm's strategic location between the Baltic Sea and Lake Mälaren provides the backdrop for a range of excursions which offer an insight into Swedish life and history. To the east lies the beautiful archipelago with its 24,000 islands and skerries. To the west are the more sheltered beaches and islands of Mälaren with a cultural heritage stretching back to the time of the Vikings and before.

The wide stretches of water to the east and west of the capital are markedly different, in terms of both their natural environment and history. The Vikings and their ancestors headed west towards the present-day Lake Mälaren for defensive reasons before the gradual rising of the land transformed what was once a Baltic inlet into a freshwater lake.

A lighthouse in the archipelago

Sweden's first town, Birka, was founded on the island of Björkö in the 8th century, but archaeological finds indicate that the area was used for trading with other countries as long as 1,500 years ago. Evidence of these early residents can be found on Björkö to this day. Along with the royal palace of Drottningholm, on nearby Lovön, Birka is included on the UNESCO World Heritage list.

Around Lake Mälaren's sheltered shores are many other majestic palaces, elegant manor houses and several small towns like Mariefred, which has retained its old-time character.

To the east of the city, the rising of the land since the Ice Age has provided a fantastic and largely untouched archipelago with over 24,000 islands, rocks and skerries. The archipelago has often been the scene of enemy attacks from the sea, so it lacks the wealth of cultural treasures that characterize Mälaren. Instead, visitors are attracted by the natural scenery. The boat trip to the leafy Fjäderholmarna islands takes less than half an hour, but a full day should be allowed for an excursion to the outer archipelago with its smooth rocks and wide bays.

Archipelago boats ready for departure from Strömkajen, outside Stockholm's Nationalmuseum

◁ Gripsholms Slott, King Gustav Vasa's Renaissance fortress at Mariefred, founded around 1540

Excursions from Stockholm

Stockholm is surrounded by a remarkable natural landscape which provides an attractive setting for excursions. Idyllic towns, majestic castles and prehistoric settlements dot the shores of Mälaren to the west. On the eastern side are the islands of the archipelago with their traditional wooden houses, and cosy hotels and youth hostels. Annual sailing regattas attract yachting enthusiasts from all over the world. Everything is easily accessible by scheduled boat services, making the journey itself a memorable experience.

KEY

=== Motorway

— Major road

···· Minor road

⌁ Railway

— Minor railway

Drottningholms Slott on Lovön in Lake Mälaren

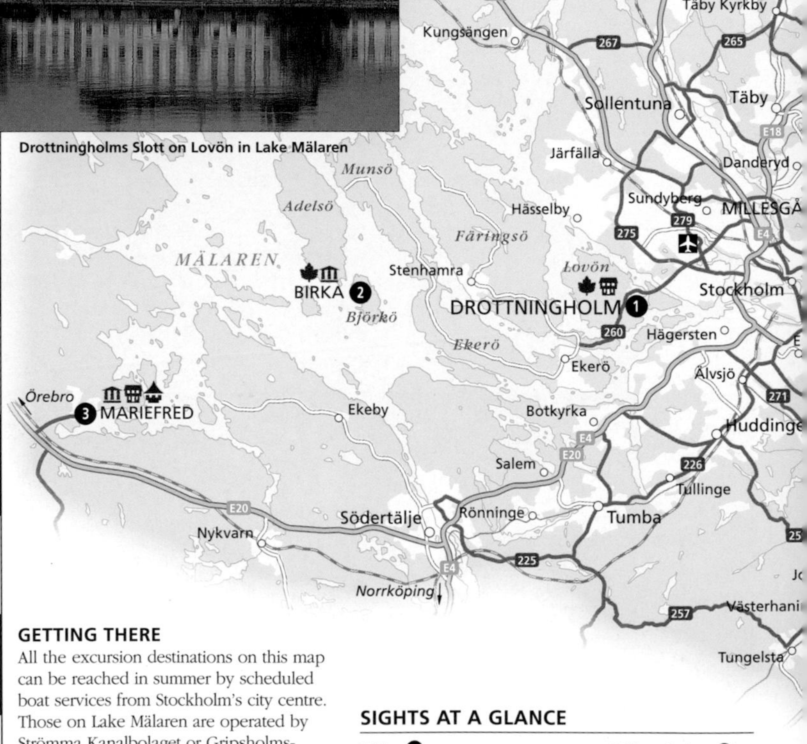

GETTING THERE

All the excursion destinations on this map can be reached in summer by scheduled boat services from Stockholm's city centre. Those on Lake Mälaren are operated by Strömma Kanalbolaget or Gripsholms-Mariefreds Ångf. AB. Most of those in the archipelago are operated by Wax-holmsbolaget *(see p205)*. Other destinations on the mainland can be reached by car or bus, and by train to Mariefred. See also the checklist for individual sights.

SIGHTS AT A GLANCE

Birka **2**

Drottningholm pp146–49 **1**

Finnhamn **9**

Fjäderholmarna **6**

Grinda **8**

Mariefred **3**

Millesgården **5**

Sandhamn **10**

Steninge Slott **4**

Utö **11**

Vaxholm **7**

EXCURSIONS BY STEAMBOAT

Traditional steamboats are a picturesque feature on the waters around Stockholm. Both in the archipelago and on Lake Mälaren visitors can still enjoy the quiet, calm atmosphere of a steamboat voyage. One of the real veterans, *SS Blidösund* (1911), is operated by voluntary organizations and serves mostly the northern archipelago. Some routes, for example Stockholm–Mariefred, are operated partly or completely by steamers. Most of the other passenger boats from the early 20th century have been fitted with oil-fired engines but still provide a nostalgic journey back in time.

SS Blidösund, one of the oldest in Stockholm's fleet of renovated steamboats still in regular service

Huvudskär in Stockholm's outer archipelago

Drottningholm ❶

See pp146–49.

Birka ❷

30 km (19 miles) W of Stockholm.
🚢 *May–Sep from Stadshusbron.*
Birkamuseet *Tel 560 514 45.*
⬜ *May–Sep: 11am–4pm Mon–Fri,
11am–5pm Sat & Sun (Jul–mid-Aug:
11am–6:30pm daily).* 🎫 *of
exhibitions and excavations.* 📷 🖥
🍴 www.raa.se/birka

The 16th-century Gripsholms Slott just outside Mariefred

The first town in Scandinavia was called Birka, on the island of Björkö in Lake Mälaren. It was founded in the 8th century by the king of Svea who then reigned over the central parts of present-day Sweden. His royal residence was on the nearby island of Adelsö. About 100 years later a contemporary writer gave the town this description: "In Birka there are many rich merchants and an abundance of all types of goods, money and valuable items." It was not a large town. There were only about 700 inhabitants, but they included craftsmen, whose work attracted merchants from distant countries.

The town was planned on simple lines. People lived in modest houses which stood in rows overlooking the jetties where ships were moored. These vessels were used by the king's warriors, the Vikings, for their marauding expeditions. In 830 a monk named Ansgar came to Birka, bringing the Christian faith to Sweden. In the 10th century Birka was abandoned in favour of Sigtuna, 15 km (9 miles) to the north, which is now Sweden's oldest town.

Today Björkö is a flourishing island with gardens and juniper-covered slopes. But, most importantly, it is a popular excursion destination with a fascinating museum and continuing archaeological digs. During the early 1990s these excavations provided a lot of new information about Birka and the Vikings. More recently, work has continued around the old fortifications, revealing much about the town's defences and the life of its inhabitants. The museum shows how Birka looked in its heyday, along with some of the archaeological finds. Visitors can also see freshly dug artifacts while excavations are in progress.

Birka crucifix

Mariefred ❸

65 km (40 miles) W of Stockholm.
📱 *0159–297 90.* 🚢 *summer from
Stadshusbron.* 🚌 *from Central-
stationen to Läggesta, then bus.*
Gripsholms Slott ⬜ *15 May–15
Sep: 10am–4pm daily; 16 Sep–14
May: noon–3pm Sat & Sun.*
Grafikens Hus ⬜ *11am–5pm
Wed–Sun.* www.grafikenshus.se

Mariefred should ideally be approached from the water to get the best view of the magnificent Gripsholms Slott in all its splendour. The first fortress on this site was built in the 1380s by the Lord High Chancellor, Bo Jonsson Grip, who gave the castle its name. Work on the present building, initiated by King Gustav Vasa, started in 1537 but parts have been rebuilt or added – most notably during the time of Gustav III in the late 18th century. It was during this period that the National Portrait Gallery was established. It now contains more than 4,000 portraits and covers some 500 years of artistic endeavour, from the time of Gustav Vasa to the present day. It also has a collection of notable foreign portraits which are shown in a separate section.

Gripsholms Slott's well-preserved interiors feature a wide collection of furniture, art and handicrafts. There are about 60 rooms. Highlights include Gustav III's late 18th-century theatre and the White Salon which is also from the same era.

The town of Mariefred, in the shadow of the castle, derives its name from a late

Iron Age burial ground at Birka on the island of Björkö in Lake Mälaren

15th-century monastery, Monasterium Pacis Mariae. It received its charter as a town in 1605, and an inn has stood on the site of the monastery since the early 17th century. The elegantly restored and rebuilt restaurant is an attraction in itself.

Visitors to Mariefred can stroll through the town and admire

Duke Karl's bedchamber, Gripsholms Slott

the 17th-century church and the 18th-century Rådhus (law courts' building) which also houses the local Tourist Information Office. There are a number of specialist shops, galleries and an excellent antiques shop.

The vintage railway attracts visitors of all ages. Those interested in art should head for Grafikens Hus (House of Graphics) on a hill leading up to the former royal farm, where stables and haylofts have been converted into an exhibition area.

The excursion can be made into a varied round trip. From Stockholm to Mariefred one can travel on Sweden's oldest steamboat service, dating from 1832. The steamboat *Mariefred*, which has operated on the route since 1903, travels at 6–7 knots and the journey takes about three and a half hours. Beautiful scenery and a lunch of classic "steamboat

beef" is on offer along the way. For the return journey, a vintage steam railway runs from Mariefred to Läggesta (a 40-minute journey) from where it is possible to catch an express train back to Stockholm (30 minutes).

Steninge Slott ❹

40 km (25 miles) N of Stockholm.
Tel 592 595 00. 🚢 *summer from Stadshusbron to Rosersberg and connecting bus.* **Cultural Centre** ◻ *10am–5pm Mon–Sat, 11am–5pm Sun.* **Palace** ◻ *11am–2pm Sat, 11am–3pm Sun; Jun–Aug: 11am–4pm daily.* 🎫 🏠 ♿
www.steningeslott.com

South-east of Sigtuna, Sweden's oldest town, and only 10 minutes from Arlanda Airport is Steninge Slott, one of the gems of Lake Mälaren. The palace ranks among the finest works of Tessin the

Younger *(see p37)* and was designed a decade before he started on Stockholm's Royal Palace. The roof is that of a traditional Swedish manor house of the time, but otherwise the design is influenced by Tessin's studies, mainly in Italy and France. The result is an Italianate palace in a rural Swedish setting which Carl Gyllenstierna gave to his wife Anna Soop as a wedding gift in 1706. Since then Steninge has had several owners, the best known of whom was Count Axel von Fersen, reputed to have been the lover of the French Queen Marie Antoinette (1755–93). The park, planned by the landscape architect Johan Hårleman, has a monument of Count von Fersen.

In 1999 the estate was transformed into a cultural centre. The biggest attraction is the elegant Baroque palace. The staircase has similarities to its counterpart at the Royal Palace *(see p50)*, and elsewhere there are details which can also be seen in Tessinska Palatset *(see p48)*. The oval hall is a masterpiece of Swedish Baroque, decorated by the Italian stucco artist Giuseppe Marchi. It regained its original splendour as part of restoration work in the early 20th century, planned by the architect G Clason. At the same time Julius Kronberg contributed paintings on the door lintels and ceilings.

A 19th-century stone barn houses a gallery, glassworks, pottery, candle-making workshop, shop and restaurant.

Steninge Palace, one of the most perfect examples of late 17th-century manor house design

Drottningholm ❶

With its palace, theatre, park and Chinese Pavilion, the whole of Drottningholm has been included in UNESCO's World Heritage list. The royal palace on the island of Lovön emerged in its present form towards the end of the 17th century, and was one of the most lavish buildings of its era. Contemporary Italian and French architecture inspired Tessin the Elder (1615–81) in his design, which was also intended to glorify royal power. The project was completed by Tessin the Younger, while 18th-century architects like Carl Hårleman and Jean Eric Rehn put the finishing touches to the interiors. The Royal Family uses part of the palace as its private residence.

Baroque Garden
The bronze statue of Hercules (1680s) by the Dutch Renaissance sculptor Adrian de Vries adorns the parterre in the palace's Baroque Gardens.

The Upper South Bodyguard Room
This ante-room to the State Room, used for ceremonial occasions, was decorated with stucco works by Giovanni and Carlo Carove, and ceiling paintings by Johan Sylvius.

Apartments of the Royal Family

STAR FEATURES

★ The Staircase

★ Queen Lovisa Ulrika's Library

★ Queen Hedvig Eleonora's State Bedroom

Writing Table by Georg Haupt
Standing in the Queen's Room is this masterpiece (1770) commissioned by King Adolf Fredrik as a gift to Queen Lovisa Ulrika. Textiles for the walls and furnishings date from the 1970s.

★ Queen Lovisa Ulrika's Library

The Queen commissioned Jean Eric Rehn (1717–93) to decorate this splendid library which emphasizes her influence on art and science in Sweden in the 18th-century.

VISITORS' CHECKLIST

10 km (6 miles) W of Stockholm. 🚇 Brommaplan, then bus 178, 301, 323. 🚢 May–Sep fr Stadshusbron. **Palace** *Tel* 402 62 80. ◻ May–Aug: 10am–4:30pm daily; Sep: noon–3:30pm daily; Oct–Apr: noon–3:30pm Sat & Sun. ● public hols. 📷 📵 📶 **Chinese Pavilion** ◻ May–Sep. 📷 📵 📶 **Theatre Museum** *Tel* 759 04 06. ◻ May–Sep. 📷 📶 **www.royalcourt.se**

The Palace Church
in the northern cupola was completed by Hårleman in the 1720s.

Entrance

★ Queen Hedvig Eleonora's State Bedroom

Morning receptions ("levées") were held in this lavish Baroque room designed by Tessin the Elder. It took about 15 years for Sweden's foremost artists and craftsmen to decorate the room, which was completed in 1683.

★ The Staircase

Trompe l'oeil paintings by Johan Sylvius adorn the walls, giving the impression that the already spacious interior stretches further into the palace.

Exploring Drottningholm

The Palace of Drottningholm is complemented by the Court Theatre (Slottsteatern), the world's oldest theatre still in active use, the Theatre Museum (Teatermuseum) and the elegant Chinese Pavilion (Kina Slott). The complex is situated on the shores of Lake Mälaren, surrounded by Baroque and Rococo gardens, and lush English-style parkland. In summer there are jousting tournaments; the theatre stages opera and ballet; and the church is used for High Mass and concerts.

Karl XI's gallery at Drottningholm, featuring the victory at Lund, 1667

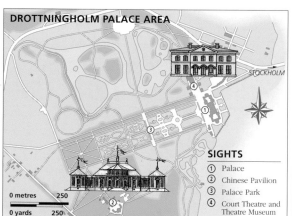

DROTTNINGHOLM PALACE AREA

STOCKHOLM

0 metres 250
0 yards 250

SIGHTS

1. Palace
2. Chinese Pavilion
3. Palace Park
4. Court Theatre and Theatre Museum

THE PALACE APARTMENTS

The first thing that meets the eye on entering the apartments is a Baroque corridor with a view that frames part of the gardens in all their splendour. The central part of the palace is dominated by the staircase, crowned by a lantern with ceiling paintings by Ehrenstrahl. There are examples of Baroque stucco work by Giovanni and Carlo Carove. Marble statues of the nine muses and their protector, Apollo, are placed at the corners of the balustrades.

Medallion showing life and death

The Green Salon is reached from the lower vestibule via the Lower Northern Bodyguard Room. This is the beginning of the main ceremonial suite, which continues with Karl X's Gallery where paintings illustrate his major military exploit, the crossing of the ice in the Store Bælt (Great Belt) by the Swedish army in 1658.

Queen Hedvig Eleonora (1636–1715) held audiences in the Ehrenstrahl Salon, named after the artist whose paintings dominate the walls. More prominent guests were received in the State Bedroom which later in Queen Lovisa Ulrika's time was in fact used for sleeping. Her Meissen porcelain can be seen in the Blue Cabinet; the Library has her collection of more than 2,000 books. Behind the Upper Northern Bodyguard Room with a ceiling by Johan Sylvius is a Gustavian drawing room, with a bureau by Johan Niklas Eckstein. In 1777, following Gustav III's assumption of power, the Blue Salon was decorated in the Neo-Classical style.

The Chinese Salon was used as a private bedroom by King Adolf Fredrik. It is directly above the Queen's State Bedroom and there is a hidden staircase linking the two floors. The "bureau"

opposite the tiled stove is also a sofa bed. The Oscar Room was refurbished by Oscar I (1799–1859) and is adorned by a tapestry dating from the 1630s. After the General's Room, Karl XI's Gallery commemorating the victory at Lund (1667), and the Golden Salon comes the Queen's Salon. Just as the adjoining State Room had portraits of all the European monarchs, the portraits in the Queen's Salon were of European queens. This floor finishes with the Upper South Bodyguard Room, an ante-room to the State Room and lavishly decorated by the Carove stucco artists and the ceiling painter Johan Sylvius.

THE CHINESE PAVILION

On her 33rd birthday in 1753 Queen Lovisa Ulrika was given a Chinese pavilion by her husband, King Adolf Fredrik. It had been manufactured in Stockholm and the previous night it was shipped to Drottningholm and assembled a few hundred metres from the palace. It had to be taken down after 10 years because rot had set in, and was

The Chinese Pavilion, an extravaganza in blue and gold

replaced by the Chinese Pavilion (Kina Slott) which is still one of the major attractions at Drottningholm. The polished-tile building was designed by D F Adelcrantz (1716–96).

At this time there was great European interest in all things Chinese. In 1733 the newly formed East India Company made its first journey to China. After Lovisa Ulrika's death in 1782 this interest waned, but it was rekindled in the 1840s. The Chinese Pavilion is a mixture of what was considered 250 years ago to be typical Chinese style along with artifacts from China and Japan. Efforts have been made to restore the interior to its original state with the help of a 1777 inventory.

Four smaller pavilions belong to the building. In the north-eastern pavilion the king had his lathe and a carpenter's bench. Alongside is the Confidencen pavilion, where meals were taken if he wished to be left undisturbed. The food was prepared in the basement, the floor opened and the dining table hauled up. The adjoining Turkish-style "watch tent" was built as a barracks for Gustav III's dragoons. It now houses a museum about the estate.

THE PALACE PARK

The palace's three gardens are each of a completely different character but still combine to provide a unified whole. The symmetrical formal garden started to take shape in 1640. The garden was designed to stimulate all senses with sights, sounds and smells. It starts by the palace terrace with its "embroidery" parterre and continues as far as the Hercules statue. The water parterre is situated on slightly higher ground and is broken up with waterfalls and topiaries. The sculptures, mainly carved by the Flemish

sculptor Adrian de Vries (1560–1626) were war trophies from Prague in 1648 and from Fredriksborg Castle in Denmark in 1659.

The avenues of chestnut trees were laid out when the Chinese Pavilion was completed, as well as the Rococo-inspired garden area – a cross between the formal main garden and the freer composition of the English park. The English park has natural paths and a stream with small islands, along with trees and bushes at "natural" irregular intervals. Gustav III is reputed to have been responsible for its design and also planned several buildings. Not all his plans were realized, but he added four statues which he had bought during his travels in Italy.

Tiled stove in a cabinet in the Chinese Pavilion

The first 300 of a total of 846 lime trees were planted in the avenues flanking the Baroque garden as early as 1684.

THE COURT THEATRE AND THEATRE MUSEUM

The designer of the Chinese Pavilion, Carl Fredrik Adelcrantz, was also responsible for the Drottningholm Court Theatre (Slottsteatern), which dates from 1766. The theatre was commissioned by Queen

Court Theatre stage machinery: the world's oldest still in use

The magnificent 18th-century stage in the Drottningholm Court Theatre

Lovisa Ulrika, but Adelcrantz did not have the same resources as the architects of the palace itself. This simple wooden building with a plaster façade is now the world's oldest theatre still preserved in its original condition. The interior and fittings are masterpieces of simple functionality. The pilasters, for example, are made from gypsum and the supports from papier maché. The scenery, with its wooden hand-driven machinery, is still in working order.

After Gustav III's death in 1792 the theatre fell into disuse until the 1920s, when the machinery ropes were replaced, electric lighting was installed, and the original wings were refurbished.

The scenery is adapted to 18th-century plays. It can be changed in just a few seconds with the help of up to 30 scene-shifters. The sound effects are simple but authentic: a wooden box filled with stones creates realistic thunder, a wooden cylinder covered in tent cloth produces a howling wind. Every summer there are about 30 performances, mainly opera and ballet from the 18th century. The theatre is open daily for visitors to the palace.

A Theatre Museum and shop are housed in Duke Carl's pavilion, built in the 1780s. The museum focuses on 18th-century theatre, with decoration sketches, paintings, scenery models and costumes. A *Commedia dell'arte* room contains paintings by Pehr Hilleström and sketches for Gustav III's dramatic productions by Louis Jean Desprez.

Millesgården, home of the sculptor Carl Milles in the early 20th century

Millesgården ❺

Herserudsvägen 30, Lidingö.
Ⓣ *Ropsten, then bus 207 or train to Torsvik. **Tel** 446 75 90.* ◯ *May–Sep: 11am–5pm daily (–8pm Thu); Oct–Apr: noon–4pm Tue–Sun (–8pm Thu).* ▨ *by appointment.* Ⓖ Ⓘ ▣ ▯
www.millesgarden.se

Carl Milles (1875–1955) was one of the 20th century's greatest Swedish sculptors and the best known internationally. From 1931 he lived for 20 years in the USA, where he became a prolific monumental sculptor with works like the *Meeting of the Waters* fountain in St Louis and the *Resurrection* fountain in the National Memorial Park outside Washington DC. In Stockholm visitors can see 15 of his public works, including the *Orpheus* fountain in front of Konserthuset *(see p68)*.

In 1906 Milles bought land on the island of Lidingö on which he built a house, completed in 1908. He lived here with his wife until 1931, and also after his return from the USA. In 1936 he and his wife donated the property to the Swedish people.

Millesgården covers 18,000 sq m (194,000 sq ft) in a series of terraces and includes Milles' studios with originals and replicas of his work. It has a magnificent garden – a work of art in itself – and a fine view over the water.

Fjäderholmarna ❻

6 km (4 miles) E of Stockholm. ▦ *53.* ▧ *May–Sep from Nybrokajen and Slussen.* **Baltic Aquarium Tel** *718 40 55.* ◯ *May–mid-Sep.* ▨ *ring to book: 715 80 65.* ▯ ▮

With the inclusion of the Fjäderholmarna islands in The National City Park *(see p121)* the city's "green lung" has acquired a small part of the archipelago. The main island, Stora Fjäderholmen, is only a 25-minute boat journey from Nybrokajen or Slussen.

The island already boasted an inn in the 17th century, conveniently sited for the archipelago islanders on their way to and from the city to sell their wares. The inn was closed during World War II when the area was taken over by the military and landing was forbidden.

Access to the public was restored in the mid-1980s and the main island now has an attractive harbour, three restaurants and an ice-cream parlour. There are also three museums, two of which are devoted to traditional and recreational boating. The third covers angling in conjunction

The Fjäderholmarna islands, a popular summer excursion just 25 minutes by boat from the city

with the Baltic Aquarium, which has some interesting displays showing where different types of fish can be found in the archipelago.

Various handicrafts are practised on the island, including metalwork, weaving, textile printing, wood-carving, pottery and glassmaking. There is also an art gallery. During the summer there are popular theatre weeks for children.

The other three islands have a rich bird-life and one of them, Libertas, has Sweden's last remaining gas-powered lighthouse.

Vaxholm Fortress, strategically sited on the approach to Vaxholm

Vaxholm ❼

25 km (16 miles) NE of Stockholm.
▥ *541 314 80.* ▦ *670.* ▧ *from Strömkajen and Nybrokajen.* **Vaxholm Fortress** *and* **Vaxholm Fortress Museum Tel** *541 721 56/57* ◯ *mid-Jun–Sep: 11:30am–5:30pm daily.*

The archipelago's main community, Vaxholm, has been a strategic point for shipping since the 19th century. It is easily reached by boat from Stockholm on a delightful one-hour journey through the inner archipelago. Vaxholm has been inhabited since the 16th century. In 1548 Gustav Vasa ordered that the nearby island of Vaxholmen should be fortified. Some 300 years later a new fortress was built here, but it soon lost its military importance and was used as a civil prison. Today the imposing citadel houses an interesting military museum.

Two of Stockholm's best-known architects have left their mark on Vaxholm town. The 100-year-old law-courts' building was given its present appearance in 1925 by Cyrillus Johansson. On the headland nearest to the harbour is a rather stately hotel designed in 1899 by Erik Lallerstedt, and traces of its Jugendstil ornamentation can still be seen.

The wooden buildings around the square and along Hamngatan with their souvenir shops provide a pleasant stroll, and the harbour is always busy.

Grinda ❽

30 km (19 miles) E of Stockholm.
☎ 542 490 72. 🚌 670 from Östra station to Vaxholm, then boat.
🚢 from Strömkajen and Nybrokajen.
🍴 (summer only).

Grinda is a leafy island, typical of the inner archipelago. It has some excellent beaches and rocks for swimming, as well as good fishing. Boats and bicycles can be hired, making it an ideal place to visit while exploring the archipelago. It takes about one and a half hours by boat from the city.

The architect Ernst Stenhammar, who designed the Grand Hôtel *(see p79)*, built a large Jugendstil villa here, which is now a restaurant and pub and has guest rooms. There are chalets for rental, a campsite and a youth hostel in a former military barracks.

Finnhamn ❾

40 km (25 miles) NE of Stockholm.
☎ 542 462 12. 🚢 from Strömkajen and Nybrokajen. 🅿 🍴

Finnish ships used to moor at Finnhamn on their way to and from Stockholm. This attractive group of islands lies two and a half hours by boat from the city at the point where the softer scenery of the inner archipelago gives way to the harsher landscape of the outer islands. As on Grinda, the main island has a wooden villa designed by Ernst Stenhammar (1912). Today it is the largest youth hostel in the archipelago. There is a restaurant, chalets for rental and a campsite. Smaller islands nearby are accessible by rowing boat.

Sandhamn, the yachting centre in Stockholm's outer archipelago

Sandhamn ❿

50 km (31 miles) E of Stockholm.
☎ 57 03 45 67. 🚌 433, 434 from Slussen to Stavsnäs, then boat. 🚢 from Strömkajen and Nybrokajen. 🅿 🍴

Over the past 200 years Sandhamn, on Sandön, has been a meeting point for sailors, particularly yachting enthusiasts. The Royal Swedish Yacht Club has been based at Seglarrestaurangen (Sailors' Restaurant) for more than 100 years. Every year the world's yachting elite flock to Sandhamn to take part in the Round Gotland Race.

Once a pilot station, Sandhamn is a charming village with narrow alleys and houses adorned with decorative carvings. There are now about 100 permanent residents. The Customs House, built in 1752, is a listed heritage building. A

Smooth rock formations at Utö in the southern archipelago

customs inspector who worked here, Elias Sehlstedt (1808–74), made his name as a poet and artist.

Sandhamn has shops, handicraft centres, and a swimming pool. Guided tours can be arranged. Camping is not permitted, but hotel, bed-and-breakfast and chalet accommodation is available.

Utö ⓫

50 km (31 miles) SE of Stockholm.
☎ 501 574 10. 🚢 in summer, from Strömkajen. 🅿 🍴
www.utoturistbyra.se

No other island in the archipelago has as rich a history as Utö, which was inhabited before the Viking era. In the 12th century the islanders started to mine iron ore, and this activity continued until 1879. Their story is told in the Mining Museum adjoining the hotel. Today's holiday homes along Lurgatan were built as miners' cottages in the 18th century. A windmill, built in 1791, provides an unrivalled view of the island.

Utö is one of the best seaside resorts in the Stockholm area, and is ideal for a weekend or full-day excursion. Its facilities include a variety of restaurants. The hotel's restaurant is sited in the old mine offices.

Hotel, youth hostel, camping, chalet and bed-and-breakfast accommodation are all available. Bicycles, rowing boats and canoes can be hired, and there are also regular fishing trips and archipelago safaris.

TRAVELLERS' NEEDS

WHERE TO STAY

Doorman

Stockholm's hotel scene could be said to revolve around Blasieholmen, where the Grand Hôtel offers accommodation which is just as princely as the Royal Palace on the opposite side of Norrström. Only a short distance away is *af Chapman*, a ship which is probably one of the world's most beautiful youth hostels. Stockholm's hotels are not usually built in the same grandiose style as their counterparts in southern Europe, but they offer a high level of comfort and service and often have magnificent views or locations.

The listings on pages 156–59 cover about 40 hotels in Stockholm and the immediate area, from budget accommodation and youth hostels to luxury hotels, with the large medium-price chain hotels in between.

Exterior of the elegant Hotel Diplomat (see p158)

CHOOSING A HOTEL

When you stay at a beautifully located classic hotel, you pay for the quality. But although most of Stockholm's hotels fall into the rather expensive category, it also has perfectly acceptable budget accommodation, maybe with a shower and toilet along the corridor.

The cheapest accommodation is offered by the dozen or so youth hostels, most of which have high standards. Other value-for-money options include the many Bed & Breakfast establishments.

Stockholm has become one of the world's most important cities for conferences, so occupancy at the city's hotels is high – around 80 per cent between May and November but much lower in July. Visitors are strongly advised to book hotel accommodation well in advance.

You should also try to avoid the peak seasons for trade fairs, or events like the Stockholm Marathon in June. The **Stockholm Information Service** (SIS) events calendar posted on the Internet (www.stockholmtown.com) is useful for finding out when the busiest periods are.

HOW TO BOOK

If you do not book a hotel through your travel agent, you can easily make your own reservation through SVB's **Hotellcentralen** agency, either over the counter or on the SVB/Hotellcentralen website. This user-friendly site includes a simple booking form (in English) which you complete and send back to Hotellcentralen by e-mail. The agency makes bookings for hotels in the whole of Greater Stockholm, including the archipelago and the Mälardalen area. Advance booking on the Internet and by telephone or fax is free of charge, but a small fee is charged for bookings over the counter.

Of course, reservations can also be made directly with the hotel by telephone or fax, and in most cases also on the Internet. Web addresses for the larger hotel chains' reservation centres are listed opposite.

HOTEL CHAINS

Several international and national hotel chains are represented in Stockholm. **Scandic Hotels**, with more than 100 hotels, is the leading Scandinavian chain and it puts emphasis on its environmentally friendly policies. It has eight hotels in the city and six outside, including two on the way to Arlanda Airport.

Radisson SAS, a chain partly owned by Scandinavian Airlines, has three large hotels in Stockholm and two at Arlanda Airport.

Choice Hotels Scandinavia has two hotels in Stockholm under the "Comfort" banner, indicating a high-standard room-and-breakfast hotel. It also has a hotel near Arlanda and three conference hotels in the "Quality" category.

The environmentally conscious Scandinavian chain **First Hotels** has three categories – First Hotel, First Express and First Resort. There are three First Hotels in the city centre and three First Express properties outside the city.

Rica City Hotels, a partner chain of Braathens and Supranational Hotels, has three centrally located hotels in Stockholm, two near Hötorget and one in Gamla Stan.

Tre Hotell i Gamla Stan is a group of three small and exclusive hotels located in the Old Town – Victory, Lord Nelson and Lady Hamilton – which all have artistic and maritime features.

The lobby at the Victory Hotel in Gamla Stan (see p156)

◁ **Östermalmshallen houses an abundance of delicacies in a well-preserved 1880s setting**

Grand Hôtel's Bernadotte Suite *(see p157)*

PRICES AND PAYMENT

Prices in the hotel listing are for the cheapest double room, including breakfast, service and VAT. All hotels offer rooms at much reduced rates at weekends year-round and daily in the summer. For the cheaper hotels this involves a price reduction of 100–300 kr per night; for the medium-priced hotels about 500 kr; and for de luxe hotels up to 1,000 kr.

Nearly all hotels accept the main credit cards. The larger hotels will also change foreign currency, but the best and cheapest way of changing money is to use one of the bureaux de change *(see p194)*.

YOUTH HOSTELS

There are 13 youth hostels in Stockholm, the four largest of which are affiliated to the **Swedish Touring Club** (STF/IYHF). Apart from the city's flagship, *af Chapman*, three more floating hostels are moored right in the city centre: *Gustav af Klint* at the Stadsgården quay, and *MS Rygerfjord* and *Den röda båten Mälaren* at Söder Mälarstrand. The ships each

Cabin at the floating youth hostel *af Chapman (see p157)*

have about 100 beds, as well as fully licensed restaurants and superb views.

The standard of Stockholm's youth hostels is generally high, especially the four affiliated to STF. Some hostels are open only in the summer.

Prices are around 200 kr per night in a double room, with a discount of about 40 kr for STF members, but come down to about 100 kr in a larger room or dormitory. Prices usually exclude breakfast and bed linen hire.

The **Hotellcentralen** agency can book youth hostel accommodation, but only over the counter and for a stay the same night. Beds can be booked directly with the hostel. A complete list of hostels is available from Hotellcentralen or on the Internet.

BED & BREAKFAST

Bed & breakfast accommodation is widely available in central Stockholm and the suburbs, as well as the archipelago. There is usually a choice between a single room, double room or a whole apartment. Breakfast is normally included in the price – apart from apartments, where self-catering is the rule – and bed linen and hand towels always are. B&B prices range from 300–500 kr per person per night. A double room costs 500–700 kr while an apartment, which often has to be rented for four or five days, costs from 600 kr per night.

B&B can be booked in advance through **Bed & Breakfast Service Stockholm** directly or via the Internet. A small booking fee is charged.

DIRECTORY

CENTRAL BOOKING

Hotellcentralen
(Central booking agency for hotels and youth hostels)
Centralstationen, Vasagatan.
111 20 Stockholm. **Map** 2 C5.
Tel 08-508 285 08.
Fax 08-791 86 66.
www.stockholmtown.com
@ hotels@svb.stockholm.se

HOTEL CHAINS

Choice Hotels Scandinavia
Tel 223 342 00.
www.choicehotels.se

First Hotels
Tel 020-411 111.
Fax 08-669 40 46.
www.firsthotels.com

Radisson SAS
Tel 020-238 238.
Fax see individual hotel.
www.radissonsas.com

Rica City Hotels
Tel 08-723 72 10.
Fax see individual hotel.
www.rica.se

Scandic Hotels
Tel 08-517 517 00.
Fax 08-517 517 11.
www.scandic-hotels.com

Tre Hotell i Gamla Stan
Tel 08-506 400 50.
Fax 08-506 401 71.
www.victory-hotel.se

YOUTH HOSTELS

Swedish Touring Club (STF)
Tel 08-463 21 00.
Fax 08-463 21 06.
www.meravsverige.nu
@ info@stfturist.se

BED & BREAKFAST

Bed & Breakfast Service Stockholm
Sidenvägen 17,
178 37 Ekerö.
Tel 08-660 55 65.
Fax 08-663 38 22.
www.bedbreakfast.a.se
@ info@bedbreakfast.a.se

Choosing a Hotel

The hotels listed here have been selected on the basis of their price category, value for money, comfort and location. The listing starts with the central areas and continues with hotels outside the city centre. For map references, see the street finder maps on *pp206–15*. For restaurant listings, *see pp164–71*.

GAMLA STAN

First Hotel Reisen
ⓀⓀ
Skeppsbron 12, 111 30 **Tel** *22 32 60* **Fax** *20 15 59* **Rooms** *144*   **Map** *4 C3*

Housed in three 18th-century buildings and a historic steamship (for the conference facilities) anchored nearby in the harbour, the Reisen is a lively location. It contains the Primo Ciao Ciao restaurant, which serves excellent pizzas, and the hotel's piano bar is a popular meeting place. **www.firsthotels.com/reisen**

Lord Nelson Hotel
ⒽⓀ
Västerlånggatan 22, 111 29 **Tel** *50 64 01 20* **Fax** *50 64 01 30* **Rooms** *29*   **Map** *4 B3*

Built in 1350 and filled with nautical antiques, this is the narrowest hotel in Stockholm as well as being a fascinating museum. The main floor and lobby resemble the inside of a ship, with the rooms decorated along the same lines. Guests can relax on the roof terrace, which is a unique experience in Gamla Stan. **www.lordnelsonhotel.se**

Lady Hamilton Hotel
ⓀⓀⓀ
Storkyrkobrinken 5, 111 28 **Tel** *50 64 01 00* **Fax** *50 64 01 10* **Rooms** *34*   **Map** *4 B3*

Named after Lord Nelson's mistress, exquisite folk art and maritime antiques adorn the rooms and corridors of this delightful 15th-century building. The Lady Hamilton is a superior family hotel located in the heart of Gamla Stan amongst shops, museums, and the hustle-bustle of historic Stockholm. **www.ladyhamiltonhotel.se**

Rica City Hotel Gamla Stan
ⓀⓀⓀ
Lilla Nygatan 25, 111 28 **Tel** *723 72 50* **Fax** *723 72 59* **Rooms** *51*   **Map** *4 B4*

Charming winding streets lead to the doorstep of this cosy establishment. Located close to the Royal Palace, portraits of Swedish royalty dating from the 1650s adorn the walls of the newly renovated rooms. Here you will find all the modern amenities you could wish for, including conference facilities in the historic wine cellars. **www.rica.se**

Victory Hotel
ⓀⓀⓀ
Lilla Nygatan 5, 111 28 **Tel** *50 64 00 00* **Fax** *50 64 00 10* **Rooms** *45*   **Map** *4 B3*

The flagship of the Tre Hotell i Gamla Stan chain and housed in a beautifully maintained townhouse, this exclusive boutique hotel has business facilities in every room. One of Stockholm's finest hotels, the service is exceptional and the maritime design timeless. Includes the landmark Leijontornet Restaurant *(see p164)*. **www.victoryhotel.se**

CITY

Comfort Hotel Stockholm
Ⓚ
Kungsbron 1, 111 22 **Tel** *56 62 22 00* **Fax** *56 62 24 44* **Rooms** *163*   **Map** *2 B4*

Modern business hotel located in the World Trade Center and close to the central train station. The rooms are small, clean and simply furnished. The Comfort does not have a restaurant, but does serve a buffet breakfast. Well-equipped for business travellers with a 24-hour front desk. **www.choicehotels.se/hotels/se030**

Hotel Riddargatan
ⓀⓀ
Riddargatan 14, 114 35 **Tel** *55 57 30 00* **Fax** *55 57 30 11* **Rooms** *48*   **Map** *3 E4*

Refurbished in 2002 but having retained the 1930s Art Deco styling, this hotel has a good location in Stockholm's "golden triangle", just behind the Royal Dramatic Theatre. Close to restaurants, bars and nightlife, sometimes visiting world-famous jazz musicians stay and perform here.

Radisson SAS Royal Viking Hotel
ⓀⓀ
Vasagatan 1, 101 24 **Tel** *50 65 40 00* **Fax** *50 65 40 01* **Rooms** *459*   **Map** *2 C5*

One of Stockholm's best known hotels, the Royal Viking offers two bars, one in the ground floor atrium and the exciting Sky Bar on the top floor, as well as the excellent Stockholm Fisk Restaurant. This hotel maintains high standards suited to both business and leisure travellers. **www.radissonsas.com**

Key to Symbols *see back cover flap*

Rica City Hotel Kungsgatan 🔲P目 ⓚⓚ

Kungsgatan 47, 111 56 **Tel** *723 72 20* **Fax** *723 72 99* **Rooms** *270* **Map** *2 C4*

Located on the upper stories of the PUB department store, the Kungsgatan is one of the largest hotels in Scandinavia and has views of Hötorget *(see p68)*, Stockholm's oldest marketplace. There is no restaurant but breakfast is served in the rooms, which are medium-sized and modern. An ideal location for travellers wishing to shop. **www.rica.se**

Scandic Hotel Sergel Plaza 🔲P❚❚★目 ⓚⓚ

Brunkebergstorg 9, 103 27 **Tel** *51 72 63 00* **Fax** *51 72 63 11* **Rooms** *403* **Map** *4 A1*

Awarded "Hotel of the Year" four times since its opening in 1984, this establishment offers the full range of services for both tourists and business travellers. Guests can relax in the large rooms or comfortable lobby and enjoy the excellent Scandinavian breakfast buffet. Car rental is available within the hotel. **www.scandic-hotels.se**

Sheraton Stockholm Hotel & Towers 🔲P❚❚★▼目 ⓚⓚ

Tegelbacken 6, 101 23 **Tel** *412 34 00* **Fax** *412 34 09* **Rooms** *462* **Map** *4 A1*

A large international luxury hotel, the Stockholm is centrally located overlooking Gamla Stan and the train station. The lively lobby has a piano bar and three restaurants, including a German *Bierstube* serving Bavarian food and German beer. Rooms are of the typically high standard expected from this chain. **www.sheratonstockholm.com**

Berns' Hotel 🔲P❚❚▼目 ⓚⓚⓚ

Näckströmsgatan 8, 111 47 **Tel** *56 63 22 00* **Fax** *56 63 22 01* **Rooms** *65* **Map** *3 D4*

Located in the heart of bustling central Stockholm, this lively boutique hotel first opened in 1863. Fine dining is available in its restaurant or on the terrace, as well as world-class nightlife with five bars and a popular night club in the basement. A favourite venue for international singers and musicians. **www.berns.se**

Hotel Crystal Plaza 🔲P❚❚★▼目 ⓚⓚⓚ

Birger Jarlsgatan 35, 11 45 **Tel** *406 88 00* **Fax** *24 15 11* **Rooms** *111* **Map** *3 D3*

Built in 1895 and situated close to Stureplan *(see p70)*, all the rooms at the Crystal Plaza have been newly renovated in a variety of styles, including speciality rooms in the bell tower (one of which even includes a Finnish spa). The hotel offers the Plaza Studios for travellers looking for long-term stay options. **www.crystalplazahotel.se**

Lydmar Hotel 🔲❚❚★ ⓚⓚⓚ

Sturegatan 10, 114 36 **Tel** *56 61 13 00* **Fax** *56 61 13 01* **Rooms** *62* **Map** *3 D3*

A modern hotel with an emphasis on music and art. The lobby of the Lydmar often acts as a gallery, as do some of the individually-designed rooms, all of which boast a flat screen TV and spa products. Excellent location and unfailing attention to design have made it a top choice for visiting celebrities. **www.lydmar.se**

BLASIEHOLMEN & SKEPPSHOLMEN

af Chapman & Skeppsholmen (STF/IYHF) P❚❚★ ⓚ

Flaggmansvägen 8, 111 49 **Tel** *463 22 66* **Fax** *611 71 55* **Rooms** *293 beds* **Map** *5 D3*

One of the most beautiful youth hostels anywhere in the world offering beds on board a classic ship *(see p79)* permanently moored across from the Royal Palace or in Hantverkshuset. The gangway to the ship is raised at 2am and a healthy breakfast is served in the morning. Book early – it fills up quickly. **www.stfchapman.com**

Grand Hôtel Stockholm 🔲P❚❚★▼目 ⓚⓚⓚⓚ

Södra Blasiehomshamnen 8, 103 27 **Tel** *679 35 00* **Fax** *611 86 66* **Rooms** *300* **Map** *4 C1*

Magnificently located just a stone's throw from the National Museum *(see pp82-3)* and Kungsträdgården *(see pp 62-3)*, the Grand is one of the world's great hotels. In addition, the Cadier Bar and Franska Matsalen Restaurant *(see p166)* are unrivalled in Stockholm. **www.grandhotel.se**

Radisson SAS Strand Hotel 🔲P❚❚★▼目 ⓚⓚⓚⓚ

Nybrokajen 9, 103 27 **Tel** *50 66 40 00* **Fax** *50 66 40 01* **Rooms** *152* **Map** *5 D1*

Exceptional waterfront location, with views over Nybroviken from the piazza restaurant and piano bar, the Strand offers wireless internet throughout and many other amenities for the business traveller. Discount entry for guests to the nearby Sturebadet spa is a bonus. Excellent buffet breakfast. **www.strand.stockholm.radissonsas.com**

DJURGÅRDEN

Scandic Hotel Hasselbacken 🔲P❚❚★目 ⓚⓚ

Hazeliusbacken 20, 100 55 **Tel** *51 73 43 00* **Fax** *51 73 43 11* **Rooms** *112* **Map** *5 D3*

A beautifully restored traditional hotel dating from 1765 and adjoining Skansen *(see pp96-7)*, the Hasselbacken is close to the city centre, but surrounded by woodland in a peaceful location. Medium-sized rooms are a mixture of Swedish design with wooden features. Excellent restaurant, terrace grill and summerhouse bar. **www.scandic-hotels.se**

ÖSTERMALM & GÄRDET

Clarion Collection Hotel Tapto
⊗⊗

Jungfrugatan 57, 115 31 **Tel** *664 50 00* **Fax** *664 07 00* **Rooms** *117* **Map** *3 F2*

This is a comfortable, homely hotel, located just a short walk away from the city centre. It offers a 24-hour front desk service and has a relaxation area with both men's and women's saunas. Rooms are elegantly decorated and all mod-cons are provided. An evening meal is included in the price.

Villa Källhagen
⊗⊗

Djurgårdsbrunnsvägen 10, 115 27 **Tel** *665 03 00* **Fax** *665 03 99* **Rooms** *20* **Map** *6 B2*

Elegant establishment with outstanding location on Djurgårdsbrunnsviken Bay. All rooms have a view of the Djurgårdsbrun canal. There are beautiful conference facilities in this historic hotel, which also has a top-class restaurant, summertime garden café, and its own bakery. A peaceful retreat. **www.kallhagen.se**

Esplanade, Hotel
⊗⊗⊗

Strandvägen 7A, 114 56 **Tel** *663 07 40* **Fax** *662 59 92* **Rooms** *34* **Map** *3 E4*

Frequented by representatives of nearby embassies and others who enjoy its traditional charm, the Esplanade is a cosy tourist hotel set in a majestic patrician house. It is located on fashionable Strandvägen, close to Stockholm's best boutique shopping, and has individually decorated rooms in Jugendstil style. **www.hotelesplanade.se**

Hotel Diplomat
⊗⊗⊗

Strandvägen 7C, 104 40 **Tel** *459 68 00* **Fax** *459 68 20* **Rooms** *128* **Map** *3 E4*

With a prestigious address on Strandvägen, this hotel offers every amenity and a renowned standard of service to its guests. In a well-preserved Jugendstil building that dates from 1911, the rooms have typical Swedish décor and elegant bathrooms. Weekend highlights include a "tea house" and the T/Bar's popular brunch. **www.diplomathotel.com**

Mornington Hotel
⊗⊗⊗

Nybrogatan 53, 102 44 **Tel** *50 73 30 00* **Fax** *50 73 30 39* **Rooms** *215* **Map** *3 E3*

British-themed, newly renovated hotel with tartan-clad staff and interior design inspired by the theatre world. The Mornington is located across from Stockholm's largest auction house and many antique shops. Guests can enjoy the British-style restaurant or the Library Bar where more than 4,000 books line the walls. **www.mornington.se**

KUNGSHOLMEN & VASASTAN

Vanadis Hotel
⊗

Sveavägen 142, 113 46 **Tel** *30 12 11* **Fax** *31 23 91* **Rooms** *67* **Map** *2 B2*

Efficient budget hotel located on the outskirts of Stockholm with easy access to motorways. Family friendly, it is connected to Stockholm's largest water park, a popular destination in summer – hotel guests can use the facilities for free. Note that not all rooms are *en suite*. **www.vanadishotell.com**

August Strindberg Hotel
⊗⊗

Tegnergatan 38, 113 59 **Tel** *32 50 06* **Fax** *20 90 85* **Rooms** *27* **Map** *2 C3*

Newly renovated, small boutique hotel with its own courtyard, the August Strindberg lies in a quiet location on top of a ridge in Tegnerlunden Park, one of the highest points in Stockholm. For the cheaper rooms, shower and toilet facilities are along the corridor. Kitchenettes and family apartments are also available. **www.hotellstrindberg.se**

Elite Palace Hotel, Best Western
⊗⊗

St Eriksgatan 115, 100 31 **Tel** *56 62 17 00* **Fax** *56 62 17 01* **Rooms** *216* **Map** *2 A1*

Large and comfortable hotel with triple and 4-bed rooms, particularly good for families. This establishment is close to Hagaparken *(see pp122–3)* and has easy access to motorways. The hotel's own pub, the Bishop's Arms, found at street level, serves beer and whisky. Great gym and sauna facilities also available. **www.elite.se**

Hotel Tegnerlunden
⊗⊗

Tegnerlunden 8, 113 59 **Tel** *54 54 55 50* **Fax** *54 54 55 51* **Rooms** *102* **Map** *2 B3*

Near to the August Strindberg museum on Drottninggatan *(see p69)*, the Tegnerlunden offers a family atmosphere and a quiet location. Breakfast buffet is served on the roof with spectacular views over the city centre. This hotel is superbly situated for exploring all parts of the city. **www.hoteltegnerlunden.se**

Nordic Hotel
⊗⊗⊗

Vasaplan 7, 101 37 **Tel** *50 56 30 00* **Fax** *50 56 30 40* **Rooms** *542* **Map** *2 B4*

Two hotels in one – Nordic Light and Nordic Sea – both with award-winning rooms. Nordic Sea rooms are individually decorated in Scandinavian style; Nordic Light rooms are decorated in black and white with unique lighting designs. The famous Ice Bar, completely constructed of ice, is a must-see. **www.nordichotels.se**

Key to Price Guide *see p156* **Key to Symbols** *see back cover flap*

SÖDERMALM

Långholmen Hotel
Kronohäketet, Långholmen, 102 72 **Tel** *720 85 00* **Fax** *720 85 75* **Rooms** *102* **Map** *1 B5*

A converted former prison, the Långholmen offers accommodation in modernised "cells" on a leafy island in the city centre. The restaurant is in the warden's residence, dating from the 1670s, and there is also a pub, a wine cellar, a prison museum, and even a private bathing beach. Youth hostel available from 19 June to 9 August. **www.langholmen.com**

The Red Boat Mälaren
Söder Mälarstrand 6, 117 20 **Tel** *644 43 85* **Fax** *641 37 33* **Rooms** *97 beds* **Map** *1 C5*

Two converted boats moored where Lake Mälaren meets the Baltic Sea make up this youth hostel. The rooms and lobby are decorated to resemble a ship and have been well maintained. The Red Boat is within walking distance of all parts of downtown Stockholm. Breakfast is not included. **www.theredboat.com**

Tre Små Rum Hotel
Högbergsgatan 81, 118 54 **Tel** *641 23 71* **Fax** *642 88 08* **Rooms** *7* **Map** *8 C3*

This inexpensive but cosy modern hotel was started by a traveller hoping to offer an economical and friendly option with a central location. All the rooms are non-smoking, and none *en suite*. Healthy breakfasts are created to your individual order. Early booking is essential. Bicycles are available for hire. **www.tresmarum.se**

Columbus Hotel
Tjärhovsgatan 11, 116 21 **Tel** *50 31 12 00* **Fax** *50 31 12 01* **Rooms** *40* **Map** *9 E3*

This building from 1780 had been used as a brewery, a barracks and a hospital before becoming a hotel in 1976. Voted one of the city's best hotels in 2005, the Columbus is in the popular Södermalm area near restaurants, shopping and nightlife. Enjoy breakfast in the courtyard in the summer at this hidden treasure. **www.columbus.se**

Ersta Konferens & Hotel
Erstagatan 1K, 116 91 **Tel** *714 63 41* **Fax** *714 63 51* **Rooms** *22* **Map** *9 F2*

Good value for money, this small hotel is located in a large, busy complex in a historic setting. It offers comfortable Scandinavian-style rooms, conference facilities, café, restaurant, bookshop, museum and a church. Professional and accommodating staff make this an excellent choice for conferences. **www.erstadiakoni.se**

Hilton Hotel Slussen
Guldgränd 8, 104 65 **Tel** *51 73 53 00* **Fax** *51 73 53 11* **Rooms** *289* **Map** *9 D2*

Well-equipped modern international hotel with two restaurants, two bars and a wine cellar. High on a hill overlooking Gamla Stan and Riddarfjärden, the Slussen has magnificent views from the summertime terrace bar. Pets welcomed by prior arrangement. Excellent gym facilities. **www.hilton.com**

FURTHER AFIELD

Ibis Hotel Stockholm Hägersten
Västertorpsvägen 131, 129 44, Hägersten **Tel** *55 63 23 30* **Fax** *97 64 27* **Rooms** *190*

Located on the southern approach to Stockholm, near the world's largest IKEA. This hotel was completely renovated in 2001 and offers high standards at reasonable prices. Friendly, multi-lingual staff help make this hotel a popular choice for business and leisure travellers alike. Approximately 15 km (9 miles) from the city centre.

Ariston Hotel Lidingö
Stockholmsvägen 70, 181 42, Lidingö **Tel** *54 48 13 00* **Fax** *54 48 13 33* **Rooms** *27*

Three sisters run this pleasant hotel in a quiet part of the residential island of Lidingö, about 15 minutes from the city centre. Close to several golf courses, it has its own tennis court as well as a full indoor gym. The rooms are spacious and individually decorated. Pets allowed by arrangement. **www.aristonhotel.com**

First Hotel Royal Star
Mässvägen 1, 125 30, Älvsjö **Tel** *99 02 20* **Fax** *99 39 09* **Rooms** *103*

Personable business and conference hotel, close to Stockholm International Fairs exhibition centre. This establishment is 10 minutes from the city centre by shuttle train. The large clean rooms have basic amenities. Connecting rooms are available for families and large groups. The restaurant serves traditional Scandinavian cuisine.

Quality Hotel Globe
Arenaslingan 7, 121 26 **Tel** *686 63 00* **Fax** *686 63 01* **Rooms** *287*

Well-equipped large hotel near the Globe Arena and a large shopping mall, with women-only rooms and facilities for conferences and special events. Breakfast is served in the Arena Restaurant, one of the hotel's two restaurants. There is also a lounge/bar area. A convenient eight minutes by subway to the city centre. **www.globehotel.se**

RESTAURANTS, CAFES AND PUBS

Stockholm has become one of Europe's liveliest and most varied cities for eating out. Swedish cuisine has won many international awards in recent years, and seven of the country's restaurants have been awarded Michelin stars. Many of the best restaurants are relatively small and informal as a number of top chefs have opened their own establishments. Various ethnic styles of cooking are often combined to

Swedish hot dog

create innovative and delicious dishes in what is called "cross-over" cuisine. Traditional Swedish dishes are frequently served at lunchtime and are excellent value for money. If you want to eat inexpensively in the evening there are plenty of fast-food outlets, pubs, Chinese restaurants, pizzerias and kebab houses. Hot-dog kiosks, providing filling snacks, can be found dotted all over the city.

WHERE TO EAT

There is a wide choice of restaurants all over the capital, not just in the city centre or the busiest shopping streets. Restaurants and cafés can also be found in the larger department stores and shopping malls, as well as at most museums. Hot meals can be had on many of the archipelago ferries, and several of the boats offering sightseeing tours also include dinner *(see p205)*.

The market halls at Östermalmstorg, Hötorget and Medborgarplatsen have some excellent restaurants and cafés but they are not open in the evening for dinner.

Sandwiches with a variety of fillings can be bought at cafés and cake shops, which often serve inexpensive hot dishes at lunchtime as well.

Outdoor cafés spring up in the summer on many streets and squares, and also in green areas like Djurgården and Hagaparken *(see p122)*.

TYPES OF RESTAURANT

Fashionable restaurants usually attract a young clientele, and the most trendy places sometimes have a rather stark decor and extremely high noise levels. If you are looking for somewhere quieter which also has good service, it is often best to choose an established restaurant. There are many specialist restaurants serving cuisine from abroad, or "cross-over" cooking, which is a combination of styles.

Inn sign, Gamla Stan

Most restaurants charge roughly the same prices, regardless of quality. If you are looking for somewhere cheaper to eat, there are plenty of pizzerias, pubs, kebab houses, hamburger joints or cafés to choose from.

Those with a sweet tooth will be well-catered for in

Stockholm's many modern cafés or traditional cake shops, which offer delicious Danish pastries, cinnamon buns, cakes and gateaux.

Stockholm has few bars *(see pp178–79)* as such and the best can be found at the most popular restaurants *(see pp164–71)*.

Dress is usually informal, even at the more elegant restaurants, although shorts are not acceptable. Men are not normally required to wear a tie.

Smoking was banned in all public bars and restaurants in June 2005.

OPENING TIMES

Most restaurants open for lunch at 11.30am and close at around 10pm. Dinner is served from 6pm or even earlier. A number of restaurants are closed on Sundays or Mondays. Smaller restaurants may close for their annual holiday during July.

Prices for lunch are often extremely reasonable, even at the more elegant establishments, so lunchtime can be spent enjoying an inexpensive meal at a pleasant restaurant. *Dagens lunch* (Lunch of the Day) is generally not served after 2pm, even if the restaurant is open in the afternoon.

For those who like to eat late, a number of restaurants and pubs serve food right up to midnight or even later, particularly those which have

Magnificent interior of Café Opera, next to Operakällaren *(see p165)*

Outdoor café in Riddarhustorget in Gamla Stan

entertainment, music or a disco. Anyone still hungry during the night can find 24-hour hot-dog kiosks.

VEGETARIAN FOOD

Interest in vegetarian food is increasing in Sweden, and this is reflected by the fact that excellent vegetarian cuisine now is served at most Stockholm restaurants. There are also several completely vegetarian restaurants.

BOOKING A TABLE

Reservations should be made for evening meals, but many restaurants do not accept bookings for lunch. If you want to be sure of a table at midday, it is best to arrive at the restaurant before 11.30am or after 1pm, by which time most of the lunchtime clientele will have left.

CHILDREN

All children are welcome in restaurants without exception. They will usually be offered a special children's menu, or half portions from the normal menu. Highchairs are generally available.

PRICES

Prices of meals at Stockholm restaurants are very similar. At most places hot dishes cost from about 100 kr, or 200 kr at the more expensive restaurants. Lunch prices are around 70 kr, and that often includes bread, salad, a soft drink and coffee. However, the price of beer, wine and

other alcoholic drinks can vary considerably. It generally follows that the more expensive the restaurant, the higher the price of the wine. The house wine is usually the cheapest, with a bottle normally costing from 150 kr. Beer is cheaper in pubs than in restaurants. Tap water is free of charge, and Stockholm's drinking water is of excellent quality.

Tips are always included in the price, but if you want to reward good service you can round up the bill. If the restaurant has a manned cloakroom, the normal price is 10 kr per person. A number of restaurants do not allow guests to take their outdoor clothing into the dining room. Credit cards are accepted in virtually every restaurant.

READING THE MENU

Dinner at a Stockholm restaurant usually includes a starter, hot main course and dessert. Most offer one or more fixed-price meals with a choice of two or three dishes at a lower price than the à la carte menu. It is perfectly acceptable to have just a starter or main course. At lunchtime most people order only one course. The meal is nearly always served on the plate, but the more elegant restaurants often have dessert or cheese trolleys. Many restaurants

have menus in English. But if they don't, the serving staff are usually familiar with English and will be pleased to explain the menu. A number of menus have a section labelled *Husmanskost*, which features traditional dishes of Swedish "home-cooking".

Some restaurants serve a typical Swedish *smörgåsbord*, usually on Sundays. During December a *Julbord* is usually available. This is similar to the normal *smörgåsbord*, but with a lavish buffet selection of traditional seasonal dishes. You can eat as much as you like at a fixed price, but drinks are not included.

WHAT TO DRINK

Wine and beer are the normal accompaniments to a meal, as well as mineral water. The wine list often features wine from countries outside Europe, along with a house wine. Vintage wines are usually not available at medium-price restaurants.

Beer is graded into three classes, with class I the weakest. Many pubs and restaurants offer a wide selection, often with one or more on draught. A few smaller Swedish breweries make an excellent non-filtered beer.

Herring or "home-cooking" is usually washed down with beer, sometimes accompanied by one of the many varieties of schnapps as well.

Spirits and wines are more expensive in Swedish restaurants than in most other countries because of the high duty on alcohol and the State retail alcohol monopoly.

Café Tranan in Vasastan, one of Stockholm's many popular small restaurants *(see p169)*

The Flavours of Stockholm

Thanks to strict regulations, Sweden is one of most unpolluted countries in Europe and produces some of the purest food. Salmon can be caught in the heart of Stockholm, zander and herring are fished from the nearby coastal waters and the lakes and rivers are full of crayfish and other delicacies. Fish is a staple, but other gastronomic treats are also on offer. Wild game, such as grouse, reindeer and elk, is abundant in autumn and winter. The forests are full of berries and mushrooms, and the rich pastures produce superlative dairy produce, including several fine cheeses.

Fresh dill

Fresh anchovies on offer at Östermalmshallen food market

THE SMÖRGÅSBORD

The *smörgåsbord* made its first appearance on Swedish tables sometime in the 18th century, when it consisted of a spread of hot and cold hors d'oeuvres that would be served as a prelude to a grand lunch or dinner. All this was washed down with ice-cold "schnapps" (vodka). Gradually, however, it has grown into a full-scale meal. A traditional *smörgåsbord* will start with a selection of different herring appetizers, followed by a variety of cold dishes such as hard-boiled eggs, meat pies and salads. Then a number of hot dishes are served, including such offerings as meatballs, fried potatoes and Jansson's Temptation (a gratin of potatoes, onions, anchovies and cream). Finally an array of desserts will be placed on the table. Diners help themselves, changing their plates between courses.

Some Swedes will prepare a *smörgåsbord* as a good way of using left-overs. Inventive cooks often improvise a very simple version when unexpected guests arrive, using larder staples, such as eggs, slices of cheese and cooked meats, and tinned or pickled fish.

Beetroot & orange salad **Rye crispbread** **Pickled herring** **Egg with lumpfish roe** **Cucumber salad** **Cheese** **Lingonberry tartlets** **Pork liver pâté** **Smoked ham**

Selection of items typically found on a cold *smörgåsbord*

LOCAL DISHES AND SPECIALITIES

A typical Swedish breakfast often includes yoghurt or *filmjölk* (a type of soured milk yoghurt) with cereal. Many Swedes, however, prefer a more savoury start to the day and cheese, ham and even liver paté may be on offer. Bread spread with *kaviar* (a cod's roe paste) is also eaten at breakfast. For lunch, most people reach for something quick and simple to prepare. Salad, perhaps served with a seafood, ham **Lingonberries** or vegetable quiche, is common and pasta is popular too. As well as the main meals, a break for coffee and pastries, known as *fika*, is taken at any time of the day. This strong Swedish tradition is a sociable event as much as an occasion to eat. In the evening, families usually get together for the main meal of the day, dinner, a more elaborate, but still homely, affair.

Gravad Lax, *a salmon fillet, marinated for two days in sugar, salt and dill, is served with a creamy mustard sauce.*

A colourful vegetable stall at Hötorget market

The turn of the 21st century has witnessed a renaissance of gourmet cooking in Sweden, with people now visiting Stockholm for its food as well as its culture. Traditional dishes, made with the finest – usually organic – ingredients are being given an original, modern twist. Instead of simple meatballs with lingonberries, chefs are increasingly offering delights such as *foie gras* with a spiced mixed berry and apple chutney and turning cheap staples, such as pig's offal, into magnificent, melt-in-the-mouth mousses.

During the Christmas season, many Stockholm restaurants serve a special *smörgåsbord*, known as a *Julbord*, which will include dishes using nearly every part of the pig, such as various ham, trotters and a special brawn called *sylta*, made from the head.

RUSTIC FARE

The Swedes are very good at using cheap cuts to prepare delicious dishes and seasoning is usually kept simple with salt, pepper and fresh dill. Such homely fare, known as *husmanskost*, is central to the Swedish diet and regularly features on the menus of many Stockholm restaurants. One favourite is yellow pea soup, traditionally served on Thursdays, accompanied by sausages or lightly salted meat and mustard. This is generally followed by pancakes with jam, washed down with hot *punsch*. Other popular dishes include *pytt i panna* (a hash of meat, onions and potatoes) and meatballs, served with lingonberry jam.

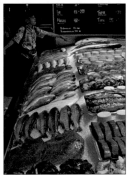
A selection of fine fish from Sweden's pristine coastal waters

WHAT TO DRINK

Beer Along with vodka, beer is the most popular drink to accompany a *smörgåsbord*. Until recently, little was on offer other than insipid lagers, but a recent beer-making revival has made styles from dark porters to pale ales available, including some interesting fruit beers.

Vodka About 60 types of "schnapps", each flavoured with different herbs and spices, are made in Sweden.

Punsch This sweet arak spirit is often taken with coffee or served hot with pea soup.

Wine A huge variety of fine wines are imported, but are usually very expensive.

Jansson's Temptation *is a dish of layered potato, anchovy and onion with cream, baked until golden.*

Meatballs *made from beef or pork are drenched in a rich meaty sauce and served with lingonberries.*

Apple cake *is a delicious buttery dessert traditionally served piping hot with cold vanilla sauce.*

Choosing a Restaurant

This listing covers over 80 restaurants in all the price categories, which have been selected for good value, excellent food and/or their setting. The restaurants are listed area by area, starting with the inner city. For map references, see the maps on *pp206–15*. Note that alcohol, particularly wine, is expensive in Sweden.

PRICE CATEGORIES
The following price ranges are the average prices for a three-course meal for one, half a bottle of house wine and unavoidable charges such as service and cover.
ⓚ under 400 kr
ⓚⓚ 400–550 kr
ⓚⓚⓚ 550–700 kr
ⓚⓚⓚⓚ over 700 kr

GAMLA STAN

Grill Ruby
ⓚ
Österlånggatan 14, 111 31 Stockholm **Tel** *20 60 15*   **Map** *4 C3*

Wonderful grilled steaks at very reasonable prices as well as good classical Swedish dishes, such as *biff rydberg* (thin sliced tenderloin of beef) and *slottstek* (beef stew) with pressed cucumber, are on the menu here. Grill Ruby also offers a special brunch menu on Saturdays. Open daily from 5pm and from 1pm on Saturdays.

Brännvin
ⓚⓚ
Skeppsbrokajen, Tullhus 2, 111 30 Stockholm **Tel** *22 57 55*   **Map** *9 D1*

Featuring an open kitchen with a modern interior, this restaurant serves traditional Swedish dishes with a twist. About 40 dishes are served in small iron pots on a plank, of which *laxpudding* (salmon pudding) is one. There is also a long list of aquavits – a distilled alcoholic drink made from potato or grain – available to try. Closed Sundays.

Brasserie Pontus by the Sea
ⓚⓚ
Tullhus 2, Skeppsbron, 111 30 Stockholm **Tel** *20 20 95*   **Map** *9 D1*

Owned by one of Stockholm's star chefs, Pontus Frithiof, this restaurant offers a reasonably priced, accessible menu including a large seafood platter and the cold meat platter, both of which are worth trying. The food is excellent, as you would expect from this chef. In summer you can sit outside and watch the ships come into port. Closed Sundays.

Pontus in the Greenhouse
ⓚⓚⓚ
Österlånggatan 17, 111 31 Stockholm **Tel** *54 52 73 00*   **Map** *4 C3*

Virtuoso young chef Pontus Frithiof creates culinary masterpieces here, such as Toast Sven Philip Sørensen (beluga caviar and marrowbone on a small slice of toast), with prices to match. The cosy atmosphere upstairs attracts an affluent crowd, while at street level there is a more reasonably priced bistro. Closed at weekends.

Den Gyldene Freden
ⓚⓚⓚⓚ
Österlånggatan 51, 103 17 Stockholm **Tel** *24 97 60*   **Map** *4 C4*

An artists' restaurant with a long tradition, serving excellent Swedish/French cuisine alongside Swedish "home cooking". The fish is well prepared with good sauces. The scallops with mushroom jelly are worth a try. It is quite a tourist trap, but the interior makes it worth a visit. Open evenings Monday to Friday and lunchtime on Saturdays.

Leijontornet
ⓚⓚⓚⓚ
Lilla Nygatan 5, 111 28 Stockholm **Tel** *50 74 00 80*   **Map** *4 B3*

Stylish but slightly eccentric décor in this historic medieval cellar is coupled with a smoky plexiglass ceiling reminiscent of the 1980s. The distinguished eclectic menu uses local ingredients, such as the very traditional lung mousse with cranberries, and is complemented by an interesting wine list. The desserts are masterpieces.

Mistral
ⓚⓚⓚⓚ
Lilla Nygatan 21, 111 28 Stockholm **Tel** *10 12 24*   **Map** *4 B4*

This must be the smallest and one of the best restaurants in town. The menu intrigues with dishes like calves' brisket served with squid and bone marrow, not to mention the *rillettes* made with smoked eel and pig's cheek. Frederik Andersson and Bjorn Vasseur, both chefs and owners, have ensured that without a booking there is rarely a table free.

CITY

Ett litet Hak
ⓚ
Grevx Turegatan 15, 114 46 Stockholm **Tel** *660 13 09*   **Map** *3 E4*

Lively, pleasant local restaurant with trendy Continental cuisine and friendly staff. Ett litet Hak means "a tiny bit", which describes the approach precisely. You can enjoy chorizo or a slice of goat's cheese pie washed down with an ice-cold beer. This open-air restaurant offers great value. Open daily for lunch and dinner.

Key to Symbols *see back cover flap*

Bakfikan

Kungliga Operan, Karl XIIs Torg, 111 86 Stockholm **Tel** *676 58 09*

Map 3 B4

A real little gem for its many regular customers, including artists from the nearby opera house, Bakfikan is ideal if you are looking for a quick bite to eat. The bar menu consists of Swedish "home-cooked" specials, along with a selection of delicious open sandwiches. More complex meals are also available. Closed Sundays.

Bistro Jarl

Birger Jarlsgatan 7, 111 45 Stockholm **Tel** *611 76 30*

Map 3 D4

This small luxurious restaurant serves Mediterranean, Swedish and Asian dishes and is a favourite spot for the hip crowd. The bistro's bar offers vintage champagne in a room filled with crystal chandeliers. One of the best dishes is a beautifully presented beef tartar. The deep-fried taleggio is also delicious. Closed Sundays.

Lydmar

Sturegatan 10, 114 36 Stockholm **Tel** *56 61 13 00*

Map 3 D3

Part of the hotel of the same name *(see p.157)*, this is a lively watering hole for the young and trendy. The food, which is served in three different-sized portions, is excellent, modern and offers value-for-money. You can eat in the bar (known as "the lobby") to the sounds of live jazz or, for a quieter meal, there is the chic dining room.

Nalen

Regeringsgatan 74, 111 39 Stockholm **Tel** *50 52 92 01*

Map 3 D3

Formerly the Grand National, this eatery now has the same name as the jazz club around the corner. The food is traditional Swedish using the best local ingredients such as reindeer, bleak roe and cloudberries. Since Mathias Nordin became the new head chef, it can be difficult to get a table, so book ahead. Closed Sundays.

Prinsen

Mäster Samuelsgatan 4, 111 44 Stockholm **Tel** *611 13 31*

Map 3 D4

Fun but traditional restaurant with wood-panelled walls and attractive paintings, not to mention good food which is mostly Swedish. A classic dish here is *Toast Pelle Jansson* (brioche with bleak roe). Prinsen is a popular meeting place for Stockholm's rich bohemians, artists and writers. Closed on Sundays.

Restaurangen

Oxtorgsgatan 14, 111 57 Stockholm **Tel** *22 09 52*

Map 3 D4

Owner and chef, Melker Andersson, serves small taster-style dishes in his stylish restaurant. You can choose 3, 5, or 7 dishes and the best of these are the desserts. The menu is dominated by strong flavours, from *wasabi* to Swedish anchovies. Choosing from the menu is a tick-box affair, where you mark a cross next to the dishes of your choice.

Sturehof

Stureplan 2, 114 46 Stockholm **Tel** *440 57 30*

Map 3 D4

A classic 19th-century seafood restaurant which was recently rebuilt. There is an oyster bar, elegant restaurant and an outdoor café. Fish and shellfish, delicious snacks and the very best Swedish home cooking are on offer. Located in the very centre of town, Sturehof has a good reputation and is a great place for people-watching.

F12 restaurant

Fredsgatan 12, 111 52 Stockholm **Tel** *24 80 52*

Map 2 C5

Star chefs Melker Andersson and Danyel Couet run this exclusive restaurant with world-class cooking combining the cuisines of many different countries. They have a wonderful *menu dégustation* including sweetbreads. The artichoke hearts and oyster *granité* are also well worth a try. Closed Sundays.

Operakällaren

Operahuset, Karl XII:s Torg, 111 86 Stockholm **Tel** *676 58 01*

Map 4 B1

The capital's temple of gastronomy sports a coveted Michelin star. The chefs are young and creative and the dining room, with its lavish 19th-century ceiling paintings and Jugendstil bar, are attractions in themselves. Café Opera has lower prices and an afternoon cake buffet, and when it is warm you can sit outside. Closed Sundays and Mondays.

Vassa Eggen

Birger Jarlsgatan 29, 111 45 Stockholm **Tel** *21 61 69*

Map 3 D3

The ceiling of this Michelin-starred restaurant has a beautiful, coloured, domed glass cupola. Carefully chosen local ingredients are prepared with sophistication, and there are wonderful reduced sauces. The bouillabaisse and the oxtail tortellini with mascarpone in consommé are musts, and there is also a very good wine list.

BLASIEHOLMEN & SKEPPSHOLMEN

Atrium in the National Museum

Södra Blasieholmshamnen 4, Box 16017, 10321 Stockholm **Tel** *611 34 30*

Map 3 E5

Situated in a unique space in the middle of the National Museum, chef Orjan Klein serves a selection of lovely salads and cold meats. However, it is always the dish of the day that is particularly tempting, such as *laxpudding*, sautéed baltic herring, or poached fish with a great lobster sauce. Closed Mondays.

Pauli in Dramaten Theatre

Nybroplan 2, 102 41 Stockholm **Tel** *665 61 43*   **Map** *3 E4*

A lovely, grand and old-fashioned restaurant on the third floor of this impressive theatre. Traditional *husmanskost* (wholesome home cooking) is served here, such as the delicious Swedish meatballs. George Pauli was a well known Swedish artist and the restaurant is decorated with portraits of famous actors painted by equally famous artists.

Franska Matsalen in Grand Hôtel

Södra Blasieholmshamnen 8, 103 27 Stockholm **Tel** *679 35 84*   **Map** *4 C1*

Roland Persson is the genius behind this Michelin-starred restaurant where the food is both sublime and inventive. The Grand Hôtel has a stunning view of the Royal Palace, so you really get the feel that you are in the heart of Stockholm. On Sundays, when the restaurant is closed, you can always go for a drink on the veranda.

Wedholms Fisk

Nybrokajen 17, 111 48 Stockholm **Tel** *611 78 74*   **Map** *4 C1*

People travel a long way to eat the turbot here, served with a mustard hollandaise that has a nutty, buttery taste. Wedholms Fisk's secret is simplicity, and through this it has become the best fish restaurant in town, not to mention gaining a Michelin star in the process. It is also very prettily located by the old boats on the strand. Closed Sundays.

DJURGÅRDEN

Rosendal's Trädgårds Café

Rosendalsterrassen 12, 115 21 Stockholm **Tel** *54 58 12 76*   **Map** *6 3C*

This is an oasis of delicious homemade cooking located in the trendiest botanical garden in Sweden. The cakes and buns are renowned. You can buy a loaf of their wonderful bread from the "farm shop", which also stocks superb vegetables, wild flowers and their very own recipe book. A "must-visit" in Stockholm.

Hasselbacken Restaurang

Hazeliusbacken 20, 100 55 Stockholm **Tel** *51 73 43 48*   **Map** *6 A3*

Well-prepared traditional Swedish food served in a finely restored 1850s setting. In summer there is an outdoor café, prettily situated next to the Skansen Museum on Djurgården. It has a tendency to be a little touristy, but you will really get a sense of old-time Sweden in this grand building. Open daily 4pm–10pm.

Wärdshuset Ulla Winblad

Rosendalsvägen 8, 115 21 Stockholm **Tel** *663 05 71*   **Map** *6 A3*

Beautifully located restaurant next to the Skansen Museum with an old-fashioned atmosphere and decorated as if out of a Carl Larsson painting. Serves well-prepared classic Swedish cuisine, as well as modern dishes, such as perchpike served with chanterelle sauce. The outdoor café is very popular in the summer. Closed Sundays.

ÖSTERMALM & GÄRDET

Dell'Attore

Skeppargatan 60, 114 59 Stockholm **Tel** *442 61 18*   **Map** *3 F2*

"Dell'Attore" means actors' restaurant – an apt name for this small, buzzing place decorated from floor to ceiling with photographs of famous actors. It boasts the most delicious pizzas in town for which people join lengthy queues to order. It is advisable to book in advance.

Lime 16

Kommendörsgatan 16, 114 48 Stockholm **Tel** *54 56 76 58*   **Map** *3 E3*

Brand new little lunch spot in an elegant part of Stockholm serving delightful salads which will tickle your tastebuds. The décor is understated, with wooden chairs and light coloured walls, and the food is equally simple, though absolutely delicious. Closed weekends.

Teatergrillen

Nybrogatan 3, 114 34 Stockholm **Tel** *54 50 65*   **Map** *3 E3*

One of Stockholm's oldest restaurants, Teatergrillen is beautifully old fashioned; for example you order your desserts from a silver trolley brought to the table, making a refreshing change from the many modern restaurants now in the city. A favourite among celebrities and media workers. Closed Sundays.

Annakahn

Riddargatan 12, 114 35 Stockholm **Tel** *440 30 00*   **Map** *3 E4*

Stockholm's first gourmet Indian restaurant. Its mellow décor of lime-green and walnut has decorations by Jens Fänge. There are recognizable dishes, such as Mulligatawny soup and rogan josh, alongside the less familiar, such as chilli-fried halibut. Stylish and adventurous, Annakahn also serves an interesting tapas menu. Closed Sundays.

Key to Price Guide *see p164* **Key to Symbols** *see back cover flap*

Gerdas Fiskrestaurang

Östermalms Saluhall, 114 39 Stockholm **Tel** *55 34 04 40*

Map *3 E4*

A fun place to visit when looking for good seafood. Located in a lively area close to the Östermalm market (a place where all visiting foodies should go without fail), Gerdas is hugely popular and always busy. Their creamy fish soup is an absolute must. To avoid disappointment, book a table in advance. Closed Sundays.

Brasserie Godot

Grev Turegatan 36, 114 36 Stockholm **Tel** *660 06 14*

Map *3 E3*

This is the new "in" place. The menu has a strong French flavour with such dishes as *moules marinière* and steak and chips. It attracts lots of young people with its great cocktails and substantial food. However, there are Swedish favourites too, including potato blini with bleak roe and sour cream. Closed Sundays.

Cuckoo

Artillerigatan 56, 114 45 Stockholm **Tel** *662 35 62*

Map *3 F3*

Run by the charming Nina von Krusenstierna, this wonderfully quirky and surprising restaurant is full of character. The interior is styled like a French bistro, with checked tablecloths. Walls are decorated with photographs of famous people, and there is even a shelf of climbing boots, which are for sale. The food is delicious. Closed Sundays.

Divino

Karlavägen 28, 114 31 Stockholm **Tel** *611 02 69*

Map *3 D3*

Arguably the best Italian in town, Divino's has a lovely interior and the food is quite superb The *antipasti* is original, and the small slices of lobster and monkfish with fennel and vanilla sauce are worth trying. All this is at a very reasonable price, and there is an extensive wine list. Closed on Sundays (and Mondays in July).

Eriks Bakficka

Fredrikshovsgatan 4, 115 23 Stockholm **Tel** *660 15 99*

Map *3 F4*

Named after Erik Lallerstedt, who also owns the renowned Gondolen *(see p.171)*, Bakficka specialises in Swedish cuisine. The meatballs are the star attraction, with pleasingly reasonable prices as part of the package. Look out for the great desserts and (affordable) champagne by the glass. Open daily.

Halv Grek Plus Turk

Jungfrugatan 33, 114 44 Stockholm **Tel** *665 94 22*

Map *3 E3*

The incongruous Greek-Turkish mix on offer here actually works really well. The menu is tapas-style with a wide selection of *meze* dishes. The décor follows suit, though with an unexpected lean towards the Scandinavian. The bar is worth a visit just for the beautiful design alone. Closed on Sundays.

Undici

Sturegatan 22, 114 36 Stockholm **Tel** *661 66 17*

Map *3 D3*

Owned by footballer Thomas Brolin, who played professionally in Italy, the Undici shows a strong Italian influence, mixed with traditional Swedish food from Norrland. Try the truffle and cauliflower cream with bleak roe and potato *cris*. Undici doubles as a nightclub later in the evening. Closed on Sundays and Mondays.

Beluga Restaurant

Nybrogatan 44, 114 40 Stockholm **Tel** *661 44 74*

Map *3 E3*

Here you will find luxury at its best. The caviar ranges from Swedish Arctic to Iranian beluga, and among the many outstanding dishes on the menu there is smoked lamb with ginger, soya and sesame vinaigrette accompanied by a chanterelle roll. The wine list is unusual with all the wines available by the glass. Closed Sundays.

Paul & Norbert

Strandvägen 9, 114 56 Stockholm **Tel** *08 663 81 83*

Map *3 E4*

A little gastronomic jewel, though on the expensive side, with elegant, discreet and modern décor. Offering superb service and excellent seasonal food, Paul & Norbert is a joy for foodies with an exclusive view of all the old Waxholm boats – just divine when you are feasting on foie gras. The famous Diplomat Hotel is next door. Closed Sundays.

Spring

Karlavägen 110, 104 51 Stockholm **Tel** *783 15 00*

Map *3 E2*

With such a complex mix of influences, including Asian, North African and South American, each item comes with a detailed description on the menu. There are some unusual combinations to be found, such as tapioca with truffles, and cured Japanese freshwater eel with cured duck liver pate, all of which are delicious. Closed Sundays.

KUNGSHOLMEN

Göken & en natt

Pontonjärgatan 28, 112 37 Stockholm **Tel** *654 49 28*

Map *1 C3*

Excellent value for money, this restaurant offers everything from Swedish "home cooking" to French "bistro style" with an oriental touch, not to forget the delicious homemade bread. Owned by the inventive Lena Nygården, this restaurant combines a cosy atmosphere and friendly service with splendid views from the outdoor terrace.

Mälarstrandskrogen

Norr Mälarstrand 30, 112 20 Stockholm **Tel** *653 47 77* **Map** *2 A5*

Though insignificant looking on the outside, this highly popular local restaurant offers classic French and Swedish cuisine at surprisingly low prices. It is great to just pop in if you happen to be in the area, but if you want to be sure of a table it is advisable to book ahead. Good honest cooking. Open daily.

Rosmarin

Hantverkargatan 14, 112 21 Stockholm **Tel** *653 87 63* **Map** *2 A5*

A popular restaurant, best known for its charcoal-grilled meat, which is always top quality, followed by its pork chops. Maria, who runs the place, believes rosemary is particularly good for the brain, so she uses it frequently. Her most famous, and indeed delicious, dish is warm potato salad, which is flavoured with her favourite ingredient.

Salzer

John Ericssonsgatan 6, 112 22 Stockholm **Tel** *650 30 28* **Map** *1 C3*

A lovely restaurant which serves Swedish food mixed with Italian, French and Spanish. Manchego cheese is a popular feature on the menu. A good place to go for brunch on Sunday, and the Salzer, which is named after John Ericsson's invention, the propeller, has a great bar. On Fridays, when there is live music, it is particularly animated. Open daily.

Spisa Hos Helena

Scheelegatan 18, 112 28 Stockholm **Tel** *654 49 26* **Map** *2 A5*

Lit by hundreds of candles, the atmosphere here is cosy and welcoming and the food highly recommended. Do try the tuna steak and Helena's Bookmaker (fillet steak, horseradish, dijon mustard and tomatoes with chips), which has been on the menu since 1996 and is a real favourite. All the main courses are cheaper on Sundays. Open daily.

La Famiglia

Alströmergatan 45, 112 47 Stockholm **Tel** *650 63 10* **Map** *1 B2*

Particularly popular with children, La Famiglia serves classic Italian cuisine at budget prices in a friendly atmosphere. One dish to try is the excellent shellfish pasta. A good place to take the whole family, as the name suggests. Frank Sinatra even made a special visit here just to try the signature dish, sauteed calves' liver. Open daily.

Tabbouli

Norra Agnegatan 39, 112 29 Stockholm **Tel** *650 25 00* **Map** *2 A4*

One of the many Lebanese restaurants that have sprung up in Stockholm in recent years, Tabbouli specialises in grilled meats and *meze*, and makes for a refreshing change if you are enjoying an extended stay in Stockholm. The food is good quality and the atmosphere lively Middle-Eastern.

Terrenos Vinotek

Scheelegatan 12, 112 28 Stockholm **Tel** *653 19 88* **Map** *2 A5*

An original concept lies behind this new venture: a Swede buys an Italian vineyard and sells the wine by the glass along with delicious tapas-style food. You buy a charge card which you put into a slot, and then you order by pressing once for a 4cl taster glass and three times for a full glass. A lovely idea which works exceptionally well.

Mäster Anders

Pipersgatan 1, 112 24 Stockholm **Tel** *654 20 01* **Map** *2 A5*

Specializing in grilled meats and fish, including a delicious chilli bearnaise that leaves a wonderful tingle in the mouth, Mäster Anders also does good traditional Swedish food. The 1913 interior consists of Bentwood chairs, parquet flooring and yellow tiled walls. Closed Mondays.

Stadshuskällaren

City Hall, Hantverkargatan 1, 112 21 Stockholm **Tel** *506 322 00* **Map** *2 B5*

Located in a cellar next to the City Hall where the Nobel Prize ceremony takes place, this restaurant originally opened in 1923 and the décor is typical of that era. The omelettes are delicious if you just want a light snack. For private parties you can choose from any of the past Nobel dinner menus served on the Nobel dinner service.

Lux

Primusgatan 116, 112 62 Stockholm **Tel** *619 0190*

Originally the old canteen for Electrolux, but don't let these humble beginnings put you off. Today Lux sports a Michelin star and is among the top restuarants in Stockholm. The chefs experiment brilliantly with traditional ingredients combining, for example, salt beef with pumpkin, truffle, garlic and pistachio. Closed Mondays.

VASASTAN

Indian Bar

Frejgatan 3, 114 20 Stockholm **Tel** *15 200 30* **Map** *2 C1*

A real find for anyone who enjoys well-prepared Indian food at reasonable prices. It may seem odd to go to Sweden and eat Indian food, but when you come across something as good as this you should not say no. Try the succulent small dishes which are cooked to perfection. Small but perfectly formed restaurant. Closed on Sundays.

Key to Price Guide *see p164* **Key to Symbols** *see back cover flap*

Stockholms Matvarufabrik

Idungatan 12, 113 45 Stockholm **Tel** *32 07 04*

Map *2 B1*

As its name (Stockholm's Food Factory) indicates, this restaurant serves a wide range of classic dishes from a well-planned menu. Very friendly, it is considered one of Vasastan's favourite neighbourhood restaurants. They are well known for making the best omelettes in Stockholm, and the atmosphere is buzzing. Closed Sundays.

Storstad

Odengatan 41, 113 52 Stockholm **Tel** *673 38 00*

Map *2 C2*

This is where people go if they want to be seen, and the bar is usually packed. Here you will find minimalist décor, comfortable seating and courteous staff serving excellent, if a little fanciful, food. Meat and fish are the famed specialities and the dress code is smart and elegant. Closed Mondays; bar menu Sundays.

Döden I Grytan

Norrtullsgatan 61, 113 45 Stockholm **Tel** *32 50 95*

Map *2 B2*

Döden I Grytan literally translates as "death in the pot." However, don't let this strange name put you off – the Italian food here is outstanding, the portions generous and the dishes earthy, such as the polenta and spare ribs, or their succulent carpaccio. You can even take time out to relax on their comfortable sofas after a good meal.

Tranan

Karlbergsvägen 14, 113 27 Stockholm **Tel** *527 281 00*

Map *2 B2*

A bit off the beaten track, this popular and reliable French bistro-style restaurant serves international cuisine and top-class Swedish "home cooking". The menu is in Swedish only, but the waiters are happy to translate. A speciality is fillet of beef with sauteed potatoes and horseradish. There is a lively bar on the floor below.

Claes på Hörnet

Surbrunnsgatan 20, 113 48 Stockholm **Tel** *16 51 36*

Map *2 C2*

This rather decadent-looking building houses a lovely, old fashioned restaurant with extremely good Swedish food. Duck sausage is a speciality, as are the sauteed sweatbreads with leeks and cured ox tongue and the rosehip soup with vanilla ice cream. Head chef Ulf Kappen is a master and no-one can cook fish like he does. Closed Sundays.

Grill

Drottninggatan 89, 113 60 Stockholm **Tel** *31 45 30*

Map *2 C3*

This is another of Melker Andersson and Danyel Couet's success stories – it is an enormous establishment with 200 covers. Most of the food is grilled, but they do serve samosas and Vietnamese delicacies too. There are lots of young people sipping lattes on the sofas and colourful cocktails at the bar, sometimes to live jazz music. Closed Sundays.

Paus Bar & Kök

Rörstrandsgatan 18, 113 40 Stockholm **Tel** *34 44 05*

Map *1 C1*

Local restaurant with sober décor and elegant, modern and advanced cuisine. This street is famous for its restaurants with every other door opening onto a different gastronomic world. The menu at Paus Bar & Kök is quite adventurous, with dishes such as duck liver on toast with figs and apple sauce. Open daily.

Restaurang Hälsingborg

Birger Jarlsgatan 112, 114 20 Stockholm **Tel** *673 34 20*

Map *2 C2*

Wonderful new restaurant which is so popular that it is almost impossible to get a table, but do try as it's well worth the effort. The theme is sea, land and forest. The menu changes daily and you can sample classic Swedish cuisine, such as braised elk tongue. Closed Sundays & Mondays.

Rolf's kök

Tegnérgatan 41, 111 61 Stockholm **Tel** *10 16 96*

Map *2 C3*

Rolf doesn't run this restaurant any more, but those who have taken over do a very good job. The food is imaginative – the elk meatballs are served with parsley root mash and blackcurrant jelly – and the atmosphere and décor fun, with chairs hanging on the walls. If you choose the communal table you never know who you might meet.

Wasahof

Dalagatan 46, 113 24 Stockholm **Tel** *32 34 40*

Map *2 B3*

Friendly brasserie-style restaurant, popular among theatre and opera goers. The speciality here is seafood, and they always have an excellent catch of the day. Swedish and French dishes also feature on the menu. The waiters are good at recommending wines from the well-stocked cellar. Adjoins a pleasant oyster bar. Closed Sundays.

NORRTULL & NORTH OF STOCKHOLM

Stallmästaregården

Norrtull, 113 47 Stockholm **Tel** *610 13 00*

Map *2 A1*

A 17th-century inn set in an idyllic location on Brunnsviken Bay. It serves the epitome of Swedish cuisine, with dishes from the charcoal grill and rotisserie. Specialities include the unusual cocoa-bean soup and their take on beef tartar – smoked elk fillet served with confit of chanterelles. There is also a pleasant outdoor café.

Ulriksdals Wårdshus
Ulriksdals Slottspark, 170 79 Solna **Tel** *85 08 15*

Magnificent location in a beautiful and historic inn. Wårdshus offers elegant top-class cuisine and the largest collection of wines is the world (according to the Guiness Book of Records). Famous for its outstanding *smörgåsbord*, especially at Christmas, for which people book their parties a year in advance.

SÖDERMALM

Crêperie Fyra Knop
Svartensgatan 4, 116 20 Stockholm **Tel** *640 77 27*   **Map** *9 D2*

For a change from local food, try this slice of Normandy in the middle of Stockholm. It is the only crêperie in the city, and has a lovely warm atmosphere, especially in winter. They also serve delicious *galettes*. It is a small popular restaurant so it is worth booking ahead to ensure a place. Good value. Open daily.

Roxy
Nytorget 6, 116 40 Stockholm **Tel** *640 96 55*   **Map** *9 E3*

Nytorget is a very trendy part of Södermalm and great fun in the summer, when it is bustling with young people. At Roxy the food is mainly Mediterranean and the interior cosy and welcoming. The four girls who own it met up in Barcelona and wanted to recreate the tapas and cava in Stockholm. Closed Mondays.

Zucchero
Borgmästargatan 7, 116 29 Stockholm **Tel** *644 22 87*   **Map** *9 E3*

Named after a famous café in Rome, Zucchero is fun and popular with young people, partly because the Italian cuisine served here is very good value. But the main appeal is the retro feel and dishes that are prepared with love. The décor is reminiscent of 1950s Italy and the film *La Dolce Vita*.

Folkoperan Bar & Kök
Hornsgatan 72, 118 21 Stockholm **Tel** *84 50 92*   **Map** *8 B2*

A favourite haunt of those going to the alternative opera house, the food here is good and the bar bustling with activity – worth a visit for the cosy atmosphere alone. There are three menus: the bar offers small starter-size dishes; the other two usually feature either meat or fish. Closed Sundays.

Hosteria Tre Santi
Blekingegatan 32, 118 56 Stockholm **Tel** *644 18 16*   **Map** *9 D4*

Run by Italians who will burst into song if you ask them nicely, Tre Santi is the closest you will get to Italy outside Italy. The interior is rustic, as is the style of food, such as *tortellacci* with artichokes and ricotta. They also do a mouthwatering bruschetta. You'll need to book a table to avoid disappointment. Closed Sundays.

Koh Phangan & Same Same But Different
Skånegatan 57, 116 37 Stockholm **Tel** *642 50 40*   **Map** *9 E3*

Even when it is snowing outside, inside the Oriental décor, bamboo and lanterns makes you feel that you are actually in Thailand – there are even realistic sound effects. The food is delicious with a wide selection of fantastic spicy dishes. Very good value. Book ahead as it is very popular. Closed Saturdays and Sundays.

Lo Scudetto
Åsögatan 163, 116 32 Stockholm **Tel** *640 42 15*   **Map** *9 E3*

The football pictures on the walls make Lo Scudetto popular among sports fans. Top-class Italian dishes, both traditional and innovative, are served with a smile. A couple of good starters are the smoked swordfish and deep-fried pecorino, followed by gnocci with lamb and perhaps a pistachio pie with cherries to finish – just delicious.

Matkultur
Erstagatan 21, 116 36 Stockholm **Tel** *642 03 53*   **Map** *9 F3*

Run by much-travelled enthusiasts who serve food from all over the world. The excellent cuisine in this charming restaurant is exotic in style. The interior is Asian-inspired, as is the menu – some of their Indian specialities are just incredible. Matkultur means "food culture" and that is a true reflection of the ethos to be found here.

Pelikan
Blekingegatan 40, 116 62 Stockholm **Tel** *556 090 90*   **Map** *9 D4*

More than 100 years old, this is a Swedish restaurant through and through, with all the staples such as meatballs and *pytt i panna* (Swedish hash). The interior is very Swedish too, with painted ceilings and wood-panelled walls. Choose beer and schnapps, rather than wine, as they make for perfect accompaniments to the delicious herrings on the menu.

Ringboms
Hornsgatan 90, 118 21 Stockholm **Tel** *429 92 10*   **Map** *8 B2*

Gotland is the culinary home of Ringboms, where the "home cooking" is nearly always a pleasant surprise. With generous portions at low prices and a friendly reception, it serves herrings with almond potatoes, Baltic herrings with honey and mustard sauce and smoked reindeer with cloudberry and juniper berry sauce. Closed on Sundays.

Rival
Mariatorget 3, 118 91 Stockholm **Tel** *545 789 15*   **Map** *8 C2*

Owned by Benny Andersson of the pop group ABBA, this restaurant is great fun and well worth a visit. The cooking is a mix of French and Swedish with dishes such as fried Baltic herrings and a balotine of cornfed chicken. To add to the celebrity appeal, the salad even comes with a Sean Connery dressing. Closed Sundays.

Folkhemmet
Renstiernas Gata 30, 116 31 Stockholm **Tel** *640 55 95*   **Map** *9 E3*

Bohemian in nature, this claims to be Stockholm's favourite Södermalm restaurant. Its gourmet menu combines many different cuisines from around the world. Beetroot with goats cheese and honey is a firm favourite on the menu. This popular restaurant also houses an award-winning bar. Booking essential.

Sjögräs
Timmermansgatan 24, 118 55 Stockholm **Tel** *84 12 00*   **Map** *8 C2*

As well as 167 different types of rum to taste, this Carribean restaurant offers original dishes with grilled meats and fish. Try fish served with a bean ragu flavoured with coconut, tamarind and a pumpkin chutney, and accompanied by deep-fried sweet potato. For dessert you should not miss the chocolate with...rum! Closed Sundays.

Stiernan Restaurang & Bar
Renstiernas gatan 22, 116 31 Stockholm **Tel** *643 97 33*   **Map** *9 E3*

The style here is called "eurofusion", but don't let that put you off – the food is delicious. Try the ravioli with ceps and a pumpkin mash with pancetta. The service is good and the interior is delightful. At the weekends the bar is full and the music can be loud. Stiernan means "star" and this restaurant lives up to its name. Closed Sundays.

Erik's Gondolen
Stadsgården 6, top of Katarinahissen, 104 65 Stockholm **Tel** *644 170 90*   **Map** *9 D2*

Probably one of the best views of the city is to be had from this restaurant. To sample the excellent French food you first need to take a lift, called Katarinahissen *(see p127)*, to get to this elevated establishment. Next door is the Köket restaurant, which also serves superb food in a rustic setting but at significantly lower prices. Closed Sundays.

FURTHER AFIELD

Sjöpaviljongen
Tranebergsstrand 4, 167 40 Bromma **Tel** *704 04 24*

With its own jetty, Sjöpaviljongen is particularly popular with businessmen at lunchtime who want to impress their clients. The view is tremendous, offering a panorama of all the islands around Stockholm. The food is, by comparison, slightly uninteresting, but the service is reliable and the view unbeatable. Open daily.

Båthuset
Hamnen, 193 21 Sigtuna **Tel** *59 25 67 80*

A floating restaurant in Sigtuna's harbour. In the summer you can watch the boats go by whilst you sit at the bar, whilst in the winter there is an open fire and cosy kitchen inside. Their forte is seafood – cod with crayfish sauce is a speciality – but whatever you have will be delicious. Definitely worth a trip out of Stockholm for this. Closed Mondays.

Fjäderholmarnas Krog
Stora Fjäderholmen, 100 05 Stockholm **Tel** *718 33 55*

Situated on an island in Stockholm's archipelago, this restaurant serves delightful Swedish titbits during the summer months. It is a great place for those who haven't been to the archipelago before to get a taste of Sweden's biggest asset. The food is equally fantastic. Boats from central Stockholm take about 25 minutes.

Restaurant J
Värdshusvägen 14–16, 181 63 Lidingö **Tel** *601 34 00*

New England-style food, including clams, oysters and lobster, are the speciality of this American restaurant. The head chef is a master with fish such as turbot and arctic char. In summer, try the fresh salads; in the winter nothing is more warming than a bowl of his delicious soup. Great atmosphere for families.

Edsbacka Krog
Sollentunavägen 220, 191 35 Solentuna **Tel** *96 33 00*

International-class cuisine at an inn dating from 1626, with a setting and service to match. The food is cooked with only the best Swedish ingredients, expertly prepared and beautifully presented by Christer Lingström, who has won a Michelin Star for his efforts. It is definitely worth the 20-minute trip out of Stockholm. Closed Sundays and Mondays.

Oaxen Skärgårdskrog
Oaxen Skärgårdskrog, 153 93 Hölö **Tel** *55 15 31 05*

Awarded two Michelin stars (the only restaurant in Sweden to achieve this) the food at Oaxen – experimental Swedish cuisine – is extraordinary and painstakingly prepared. The chef is Magnus Ek, and his partner, Agneta Green, works at front-of-house. If you want the best meal of your life, this is probably where you will find it in Sweden.

Cafés and Pubs

Swedes love their coffee. At work people take a coffee break at around 3pm, and if they are out and about, they are likely to pop into a café. The cake shops (indicated by the sign "Konditori") have a long tradition. They serve typical Swedish pastries, with everything from sweet small buns to tempting gateaux. The best cake shops have their own bakeries and sell a variety of pastries and sandwiches. Cafés were once cheaper and more popular than the elegant cake shops, but the differences have been evened out and there are now many Continental-style cafés serving espresso, cappuccino and caffe latte. Many cafés open for breakfast early in the morning, and they usually serve lunch as well. The old Swedish "beer cafés" have been replaced by the city's many pubs, which also serve simple dishes at reasonable prices.

CAFES AND CAKE SHOPS

Café culture is flourishing in Stockholm, and the style ranges from American or Italian to traditional Swedish and classic cake shops. The café is a good choice if you feel peckish between meals, need to rest your legs or simply want a meeting place. Apart from coffee, sandwiches and cakes, nearly all serve simple lunches – quiches and salad, for example – soft drinks and ice cream. Typical cafés serve Swedish-style strong coffee, along with sandwiches, buns and cakes. Don't miss the delicious *prinsesstårta* cream cake, by far the most popular one. Cafés usually close at around 6pm.

Many cafés have tables outside in the summer. If you feel like sitting under a fruit tree where you can enjoy the birdsong, **Rosendals Träd-gårdscafé** on Djurgården is the place. The salad buffet is a feast for the eye and the palate, consisting of organically grown vegetables and home-baked bread. It is open only during the summer and in December. **Lasse i Parken** is another rustic idyll in the city with home-baked bread and delicious cheesecakes.

Sturekatten is a classic cake shop decorated in the style of an early 20th-century upper-class home with many small rooms and unrivalled pastries. **Vete-Katten** is one of Stockholm's most authentic cake shops. Its pastries are outstanding and chocaholics won't be able to resist the home-made pralines. After a hectic day's shopping, head for the trendy **Hotel Diplomat T/Bar**, which serves English-style afternoon tea. Another oasis in the shopping district is **Gateau**, one floor up in Sturegallerian. The pastries are delicious and the gentle piano music relaxing.

Rather more unusual is **Legym**, which serves Middle Eastern vegetarian delicacies with biodynamic bread. Another one is **Hemma hos Julia**, where the excellent fresh cheeses are home-made. It also serves excellent hot chocolate and provides a choice of eight different cheesecakes, all of them mouth-watering.

Nilsson's is a genuine traditional Swedish café serving good soup for lunch, and buns or sandwiches with salami sausages. A pleasant place for breakfast is **Cinnamon**, which has its own bakery and serves fresh sandwiches and cakes.

Wayne's Coffee is Söder-malm's most popular meeting place with giant sandwiches and cakes, comfortable arm-chairs and an elegant clientele. **Coffee Cup** serves bagels with various fillings and many different types of coffee. At **Tabac** you can mingle with the locals as you enjoy a café au lait and home-baked brownies. Absolutely the finest espresso is served at **Tinta-rella di Luna**, an authentic Italian café which also has the city's best *panini*.

Coffee connoisseurs should not miss **Robert's Coffee**, where they roast their own beans. They also stock a range of exclusive beans which you can buy to take home.

PUBS

The old Swedish beer cafés have either closed down, transformed into a local restaurant (Tranan at Odenplan is a typical example – *see p169*) or are now pubs with an international flavour. Irish, Scottish or English pubs are all popular, but there are also influences from Belgium, the Czech Republic, Germany, Australia and the USA.

Stockholmers have a great interest in beer, so the pubs usually have a wide selection of brews and the staff are knowledgeable. Try some of the beers from three new small, acclaimed, quality breweries: Tärnö, Stockholm's own brewery; Slottskällan in Uppsala; and Pilgrimstad from northern Sweden.

One of the busiest and most traditional pubs is the **Tudor Arms**, opened in the 1960s, where English is the normal language and many of the regular customers are British. Scots and Americans head for the **Bagpiper's Inn**, where bagpipes are provided on the upper floor and Scottish beers are available. One floor down is the **Bald Eagle** where drinkers can enjoy rock music, and there is usually a queue for the billiards table. The adjoining pub, **Boomerang**, features music from Down Under, everyone is "mate", and the staff are Australian. The steakhouse serves kangaroo or ostrich steaks.

Anyone feeling homesick for Ireland only needs to go through the door of **Limerick** to enjoy some Guinness or Kilkenny. Irish music is performed there at weekends. **O'Leary's** has many expat regulars and also serves excellent food. **The Dubliner** is yet another Irish pub, with a large selection of malt whiskeys. Live music contributes to the atmosphere. On Södermalm, **Soldaten Svejk** specializes in

Czech draught beer and offers rustic country cooking.

Beer connoisseurs or whisky drinkers should head for **Akkurat**, which has about 400 different types of whisky and beer from all over the world, but particularly from Belgium. Mussels are always on the menu, but there is also a good choice of other hot dishes and delicious snacks. Beer and whisky tastings take place frequently, the staff are knowledgeable and service is quick. **Oliver Twist** is reckoned to be one of the city's best pubs for draught beer, imported from all over the world. The staff here are also dedicated and knowledgeable. Business people head for **Man in the Moon** after work, and the atmosphere is rather more refined than at most other pubs. A pleasant rural feel pervades

the **Anchor Pub**, which specializes in unusual beers and has live music 3–4 nights a week.

Lundgrens is one of Sweden's best lagers and can be enjoyed on Kungsholmen, where it is brewed by the Tärnö brewery. It is served on draught at both **Mackinlay's** and **Kings Head**, two pleasant local pubs. **Tennstopet** was once a meeting place for journalists and some have remained loyal customers. It is pleasant but noisy, and there is a darts board. Swedish "home cooking" is available. The clientele is typically in the upper middle-age bracket.

Like their predecessors, the beer cafés, the pubs serve not just drinks but also snacks and value-for-money hot food from lunchtime till late in the evening. Many Stockholmers now regard going out to the

pub as a pleasant and often less expensive alternative to their local restaurant.

Most pubs are open daily. Many open for lunch and usually close at 11pm, while a few remain open to midnight or 1am *(see also pp178–79)*.

FAST FOOD

If you are looking for a quick snack, there are plenty of street kiosks selling hot dogs, hamburgers or kebabs. Several of them are open 24 hours. The Kungshallen complex at Hötorget has a lot of restaurants and fast-food outlets – particularly useful for groups who are undecided on the type of food they want to eat. There are also plenty of pizzerias of varying standards, as well as Chinese restaurants where you can eat well and inexpensively.

DIRECTORY

ENTERTAINMENT IN STOCKHOLM

Within the past couple of decades Stockholm has become an important city for entertainment. The capital, which was once said to have a "cold beauty", is now a vibrant, trend-setting metropolis full of theatres, bars and music venues. International stars increasingly put Stockholm on their touring schedule, not least because of the magnificent indoor arena, Globen. Another factor is Swedish pop music's great position on the world stage which has made it an important export item. A wide range of entertainment is on offer and the short distance between venues is another benefit. The Royal Opera House, for instance, is only a few minutes' walk from the intimate clubs of Gamla Stan. Stockholm also has a rich cultural life with concerts, drama and exhibitions.

Jazz musician

Kungliga Operan (Royal Opera House), Gustav II Adolfs Torg *(see p64)*

ENTERTAINMENT LISTINGS

A reliable source of information about special events is the official guide *What's On Stockholm* which is available free of charge at most hotels, conference centres and tourist information offices. It is published 10 times a year in both English and Swedish. Daily newspapers also have detailed information on forthcoming events in a special section or in weekend supplements (but only in Swedish).

The Internet has several good sites with up-to-date information on special events. **Stockholm Visitors Board**, SVB *(see p190)* has an official "tourist site" (www.stock holmtown.com) which is constantly updated with detailed information and includes some useful links.

www. alltom stockholm.se gives a wealth of information about entertainment and events in Stockholm, including everything from museums and restaurants to concerts.

A third extremely useful and user-friendly site on entertainment in the capital is **www.ticnet.se**. Information on all three websites is partly in English.

Stampen, in Stora Nygatan, one of Stockholm's great jazz clubs *(see p179)*

BOOKING TICKETS

Tickets for events can usually be bought at the ticket office of the relevant theatre or sports arena. But to be sure of reserving a seat it is advisable to book in advance either with the help of your hotel or one of the Stockholm Information Service tourist offices, located at Sweden House adjoining Kungsträdgården and at the Hotellcentralen office in the Central Station. You can also use one of the city's ticket agencies, for example **Biljett Direkt TicNet**, which can make bookings by telephone for theatres, concerts, sporting events and excursions. A booking fee of 10–15 kr is charged. Tickets for various events can also be bought over the counter at the centrally located **Boxoffice**. Tickets booked direct can also be picked up here.

OUTDOOR CONCERTS AND FESTIVALS

Major outdoor events get under way in mid-May with the annual **Kungsträd-gården** programme. This includes a wide variety of music with regular lunchtime and evening concerts. In the second week of June the **Slottsgalorna** event takes place at Ulriksdals Slott with international stars and the country's top musicians. **Skansen** stages a wide range of music, especially in July, with jazz on Monday evenings. The **International Jazz & Blues Festival** is held on Skeppsholmen in mid-

A sea of people at the Royal Philharmonic Orchestra's outdoor concert

August, and attracts the big names in jazz and blues.

For classical music lovers, the **Royal Philharmonic Orchestra**'s outdoor concert at Sjöhistoriska (the National Maritime Museum) on the second Sunday in August is one of the summer's highlights. The concert is an annual tradition and attracts audiences of 25,000–30,000.

Other events include the **Restaurant Festival** at Kungsträdgården on the first weekend in June, the **American Festival** on the third weekend in June, and the **Boules Festival** on the first weekend in July.

NIGHT-TIME TRANSPORT

The Tunnelbana stops around 1am Sunday to Thursday nights, but on Friday and Saturday nights it runs until 4am. It is replaced by night buses. Several night buses depart from Sergels Torg, and most bus stops have maps showing the night routes. Taxis are usually not difficult to find, even on a Saturday evening *(see p201)*.

STOCKHOLM FOR CHILDREN

Compared with many major cities, Stockholm is an extremely child-friendly place and ideal for family visits.

It is easy to take prams and pushchairs on to the new buses, and there is plenty of space for them inside.

Most of the museums have children's corners with special activities. Museums and other important sights often have a cafeteria or restaurant with special menus or smaller portions for children. Toilets with a baby-changing table are frequently available.

Many of the favourite places for children are on Djurgården. **Junibacken** has an exciting journey through the fantastic world of the children's author Astrid Lindgren. The nearby **Vasamuseet** is also child-friendly as well as the **Aquaria** water museum only a short walk away. For decades the **Gröna Lund** funfair has been a mixture of traditional and exciting new attractions, making it an ideal excursion for families with

Gröna Lund's roller-coaster

DIRECTORY

EVENTS LISTINGS

Stockholm Visitors Board
Sweden House, Hamngatan.
Map 3 D4. **Tel** 508 28 508.
www.stockholmtown.com
Other good Internet sites:
www.alltomstockholm.se
www.ticket.se

TICKET BOOKINGS

Biljett Direkt TicNet
Tel 077-170 70 70.
www.ticnet.se

Boxoffice
Norrmalmstorg. **Map** 3 D4.
Tel 10 88 00.
www.boxoffice.se

STOCKHOLM FOR CHILDREN

Aquaria *p95*

Fjäderholmarna *p144*

Gröna Lund *p95*

Junibacken *p88*

Kulturhuset *p67*

Medeltidsmuseet *p59*

Skansen *pp96–7*

Naturhistoriska Riksmuseet/ Cosmonova *p124*

Leksaksmuseet *p131*

Vasamuseet *pp92–3*

both teenagers and younger children. The open-air museum **Skansen**, with all its animals and exciting activities, can keep a family happily occupied for a whole day.

Special children's weeks are organized on **Fjäderholmarna**, a group of islands which can be reached from the city centre in only 25 minutes.

Leksaksmuseet (the Toy Museum) on Söder is a safe bet for children. In the city centre **Kulturhuset** has a variety of children's activities with a cultural content.

Naturhistoriska Riksmuseet (the Swedish Museum of Natural History) is an interesting excursion in its own right. It houses the Cosmonova planetarium and IMAX cinema which is a big attraction for children and young people.

Drama and Classical Music

Stockholm's year as Cultural Capital of Europe in 1998 was a well-deserved honour, as all the city's various areas of culture reflect a high degree of dedication and talent. This applies particularly to the world of music, which has seen many top-class international artists emerge from the capital's stages. As a result opera, ballet and classical music is well supported by Stockholmers who have a wide home-grown repertoire to enjoy, which is complemented by a number of guest artists from all over the world.

BALLET AND DANCE

Classical ballet of the highest quality is mainly staged at the over 100-year-old **Kungliga Operan** (*see pp64–5*). Every season three of the best-known ballets, for example *The Nutcracker, Swan Lake*, and *Romeo and Juliet*, are performed to packed houses. Thanks to the choreographer Birgit Cullberg, now deceased, Stockholm has also become a noted centre for modern dance. Many established dance companies make guest appearances at **Dansens Hus** (*see p69*) which has taken over the previous home of Stadsteatern. **Moderna Dansteatern** in the old torpedo factory on Skeppsholmen is another important stage for modern dance.

OPERA

Traditional productions in their original language are staged mainly at **Kungliga Operan**. Lunchtime operas or concerts are sometimes performed in the Gustav III opera café. During the summer, major operas are presented at **Drottningholms Slottsteater** (*see pp146–49*). Dating from the 18th century, the theatre's stage settings and scene-shifting machinery are preserved in their original condition and are still in good working order. All the operas performed here are also from the 18th century, and over the years the theatre has revived several unknown works by Mozart, using instruments typical of that era. The theatre is open for guided tours.

Sweden's oldest Rococo theatre, **Confidencen**, is located near Ulriksdal (*see p125*). Between June and September weekly opera and ballet performances are held here. Another genre of classical opera is staged at **Folkoperan**, which performs the classics in Swedish and without elaborate scenery.

Regina-Stockholm Operamathus is a rebuilt cinema where audiences can dine in comfort while enjoying the opera.

THEATRES AND MUSICALS

Stockholm has a flourishing theatrical life, but performances are usually in Swedish. **Kungliga Dramatiska Teatern**, often known simply as "Dramaten" (*see pp72–3*), is Sweden's national theatre and has five stages. International and Swedish classics are regularly performed here, from Shakespeare to Strindberg, as well as modern foreign and Swedish productions. Ingmar Bergman was the theatre's director from 1963–6, and he has returned as an acclaimed guest director many times since then.

Södra Teatern (*see p128*) often presents modern productions despite having roots that go back to the 19th century. **Stockholms Stadsteater**, based in Kulturhuset (*see p67*), has a widely varied programme. A summer speciality is the popular series of **Parkteatern** productions in several of the city's parks with drama, dance and children's theatre. **Judiska Teatern** has a repertoire of new Jewish drama, as well as dance, poetry and film shows. **Teater Galeasen** is Stockholm's avant-garde stage for new Swedish and foreign drama.

Marionetteatern has puppet shows for both children and adults, along with a puppet museum on the same premises. **Pantomimteatern** is a theatre company which performs not only in Stockholm but tours rural areas, too.

Light-hearted plays are often staged at **China-Teatern**, and its programmes include some highly popular musicals and some much-loved plays for children. High quality musicals are also performed at **Oscars-Teatern**, **Göta Lejon** and **Cirkus**.

CLASSICAL MUSIC

World-standard classical music is regularly performed at **Berwaldhallen** (*see p106*). The hall is dedicated to the great Swedish composer Franz Berwald (1796–1868) and is home to the Swedish Radio Symphony Orchestra which has thrived under musical directors like Sergiu Celibidache and Esa-Pekka Salonen. The Swedish Radio Chorus, which is regarded as one of the world's great *a cappella* ensembles, is based here, too. Concerts are also given in the hall by other symphony orchestras and smaller ensembles.

Konserthuset (*see p68*) is the home of the Royal Philharmonic Orchestra, an internationally acclaimed 100-piece orchestra whose season runs from August to May. Its programme includes a couple of chamber music series and a jazz series, as well as performances for families on Saturdays. An annual composition festival is held every November.

Nybrokajen 11 (*see p83*) was formerly the home of the Musical Academy. Apart from July and August, its large hall is now used almost daily for concerts. In addition to classical music, you can hear performances of jazz, choral music and folk music. **Music at the Palace** is an annual summer series at the Royal Palace (*see pp50–53*) with two concerts every week, usually classical music but sometimes other styles. The concerts are normally staged in the Hall of

State or the Royal Chapel. The majestic staircase of **Nationalmuseum** *(see pp82–3)* is the setting for summer concerts. **Riddarhusmusik** at Riddarhuset *(see p58)* is a series by the Stockholm Sinfonietta .

FOLK AND CHURCH MUSIC

Rural folk music still flourishes in the capital, and this tradition is particularly

fostered at **Skansen** *(see pp96–7)*, where fiddlers and folk dance teams play a major role in the various festivals held there *(see pp26–7)*. Folk music is also on the programme at **Nybrokajen 11**.

Concerts are regularly given in the city's churches, for example visitors can relax and enjoy beautiful church music in the tranquil surroundings of **Jacobs Kyrka** in Kungsträdgården *(see p64)* every

Saturday at 3pm. Afternoon concerts usually take place in **Storkyrkan** *(see p49)* on Saturday and Sunday during spring and autumn.

BOOKING TICKETS

Tickets for Stockholm's theatres and concert halls can be booked through **Biljett Direkt TicNet**; directly at the relevant box office; or ordered by telephone *(see p166)*.

DIRECTORY

BALLET & DANCE

Dansens Hus
Barnhusgatan 12–14.
Map 2 C3.
Tel 508 990 90.
Fax 508 990 99.
www.dansenshus.se
@ biljett@dansenshus.se
Tickets on sale: noon–6pm Mon–Sat, noon–6pm Sun (during performances).

Kungliga Operan
Gustav Adolfs Torg.
Map 4 B1. **Tel** 24 82 40.
www.operan.se
Tickets on sale: noon–6pm Mon–Fri, noon–3pm Sat.

Moderna Dansteatern
Slupskjulsvägen 32,
Skeppsholmen.
Map 5 E2.
Tel 611 32 33.
www.modernadansteatern.
se
Tickets on sale: from Dansteatern/home page.

OPERA

Confidencen
Ulriksdals Slottsteater.
Tel 85 60 10.
www.confidencen.se

Drottningholms Slottsteater
Drottningholm Palace,
Lovön. **Tel** 660 82 25.

Folkoperan
Hornsgatan 72. **Map** 8 B2
Tel 616 07 50.
Fax 84 82 84.
www.folkoperan.se
Tickets on sale: noon–7pm Wed–Fri, noon–6pm Sat, noon–4pm Sun.

Kungliga Operan
Gustav Adolfs Torg.
Map 4 B1.
Tel 24 82 40.
www.operan.se
Tickets on sale: noon–6pm Mon–Fri, noon–3pm Sat.

Regina-Stockholm Operamathus
Drottninggatan 71 A.
Map 2 C3. **Tel** 411 63 20.
www.regina-
operamathus.com
Tickets on sale: noon–6pm Mon–Sat.

THEATRE

China-Teatern
Berzelii Park 9.
Map 3 D4.
Tel 566 323 50.
www.chinateatern.se
Tickets on sale: 11am–6pm Mon–Wed, 11am–7:30pm Thu–Fri.

Cirkus
Djurgårdsslätten.
Map 6 A4. **Tel** 660 10 20.
www.cirkus.se
Tickets on sale: 11am–6pm Mon, 11am–7:30pm Tue–Fri, noon–7:30pm Sat, noon–4pm Sun. Telephone bookings (not for same day): 10am–6pm weekdays.

Kungliga Dramatiska Teatern
Nybroplan.
Map 3 E4.
Tel 667 06 80
Fax 667 84 00
www.dramaten.se
Tickets on sale: 10am–6pm Mon, 10am–7pm Tue–Fri, 3:30–6pm Sat, 1:30–4pm Sun.

Drottningholms Slottsteater
Drottningholm Palace,
Lovön. **Tel** 660 82 25 / 556 931 00.

Göta Lejon
Götgatan 55.
Map 9 D3. **Tel** 643 67 00.
Tickets on sale: 11am–6pm Mon–Fri.

Judiska Teatern
Djurgårdsbrunnsvägen 59.
Map 7 E2. **Tel** 667 90 13.
www.judiskateatern.se

Marionetteatern
Brunnsgatan 6.
Map 3 D3.
Tel 411 71 12.

Oscars-Teatern
Kungsgatan. 63.
Map 2 B4. **Tel** 20 50 00.
www.oscarsteatern.se

Pantomimteatern
Gästrikegatan 14.
Map 2 A2. **Tel** 31 54 64.

Parkteatern
Tel 506 202 99.

Stockholms Stadsteater
Sergels Torg. **Map** 2 C4.
Tel 506 202 00.
www.stadsteatern.
stockholm.se
Tickets on sale: 11am–6pm Mon, 11am–7pm Tue–Fri, 11am–6pm Sat, noon–4pm Sun.

Södra Teatern
Mosebacke Torg 1–3.
Map 9 D2.
Tel 556 972 30.
www.sodrateatern.com
Tickets on sale: noon–6pm Mon–Fri, noon–4pm Sat.

Teater Galeasen
Slupskjulsvägen 32,
Skeppsholmen. **Map** 5 E2.
Tel 611 00 30.
www.galeasen.se

CLASSICAL MUSIC

Berwaldhallen
Dag Hammarshjolds Väg 3.
Map 6 A2.
Tel 784 18 00.
www.berwaldhallen.se

Konserthuset
Hötorget 8.
Map 2 C4.
Tel 506 677 88.
www.konserthuset.se

Music at the Palace
The Royal Palace,
Slottsbacken.
Map 4 C2.
Tel 10 22 47.

Nationalmuseum
Södra Blasieholmshamnen.
Map 5 D2.
Tel 519 543 00.
www.nationalmuseum.se

Nybrokajen 11
Nybrokajen 11
Map 4 C1.
Tel 407 17 00.

Riddarhusmusik
Riddarhuset,
Riddarhustorget 10.
Map 4 A3.
Tel 723 39 90.

CENTRAL TICKET AGENCY

Biljett Direkt TicNet
Tel 077 170 70 70.
www.ticnet.se

Nightlife and Entertainment

In common with most capitals, Stockholm has a rich variety of nightlife and entertainment, with something for everyone. Pop music is one of the country's biggest exports so there is no shortage of groups following in the footsteps of ABBA. Top-class musical entertainment is provided on a large scale in Globen or on a smaller more intimate basis in the pubs, clubs and bars. The Swedish jazz scene thrives in several venues where live music is played nightly.

ROCK AND POP

Stockholm's **Globen** is the city's biggest stage for rock and pop music. It attracts all the biggest international artists as well as leading Swedish groups. **Cirkus** and **Södra Teatern** *(see p176)* are other favourite venues for rock and pop, and they stage both musical and theatrical productions in beautiful settings. **Münchenbryggeriet**, a former brewery, also provides a great venue. Hard rock enthusiasts are well-catered for at **Anchor Pub** three or four times a week.

    Nalen is a traditional old-time music hall, built in the 1880s. Its heyday was between the 1920s and 1960s, and now it has been re-opened offering a variety of live music on several stages.

JAZZ MUSIC

A wide choice of jazz can be found in Stockholm. **Fasching Jazzklubb** has an international reputation for good music with performances virtually every day of the week. Another classic jazz spot is **Stampen** in Gamla Stan which attracts a rather older clientele. The bar at the **Lydmar Hotel** has one of the city's best stages, where top-class artists often give impromptu performances to a young and fashionable crowd. **Nalen** holds frequent jazz events, and usually provides live music to dance to on Sundays. **Glenn Miller Café** has a cosy atmosphere, with jazz nightly from Monday to Saturday. During the summer the vintage steamboat *SS Blidösund (see p143)* operates special jazz cruises around the archipelago four times a week.

MUSIC PUBS

Life in Stockholm's pubs and bars has changed in recent years as a number of establishments have introduced live music. Irish bands often play at **The Dubliner** *(see p172)*, and live music is also performed at the **Engelen** and **Akkurat** pubs. Engelen has a variety of music while the accent is on rock at Akkurat.

    Apart from these musical watering holes, there are plenty of traditional British and Irish pubs in the capital, generally with a wide choice of beer and whisky and snack meals *(see pp172–73)*.

BARS

The best bars are usually found in the hotels and restaurants, but those in the latter are often noisier and smokier. The most fashionable tend to have a long queue, supervised by a doorman, waiting to enter. For a quieter atmosphere with comfortable armchairs, hotel bars are the best bet. The minimum age for buying alcohol is 18, and young customers must be prepared to show proof of age.

    The **Cadier Bar** in the Grand Hôtel *(see pp79 & 156)* undoubtedly has the most elegant clientele because this is where the rich and famous stay. From the verandah there is a fine view of the Royal Palace and the archipelago boats and in the background gentle music is played on the white grand piano.

    Operabaren is a sight in itself with well-preserved Jugendstil decor, marble tables and leather sofas. The regulars often include authors, artists and intellectuals.

Gondolen at the top of Katarinahissen *(see p127)* offers arguably the most beautiful view of Stockholm and is a perfect place for a drink at sunset. It has comfortable leather armchairs, skilled bartenders and a relaxing atmosphere. **Sky Bar**, high up in the Royal Viking Hotel, has a panoramic view of the city, seen at its best after dark when the lights come on. The **Sheraton Living Room** is a classic international bar where business people from all over the world relax to the accompaniment of piano music while skilled bartenders fix their favourite cocktails.

    Lydmar Hotel has a bar in its lobby which has become a popular meeting place for artists, designers and musicians. Live bands play soft jazz, and the bartenders always know which drinks are in fashion. **Sturehof Bar** is a sophisticated and modern nightspot, particularly popular with people from the advertising and media worlds and other local night owls.

NIGHTCLUBS AND CASINOS

Most of Stockholm's best nightclubs are located around Stureplan *(see pp70–71)*. The traditional discotheque evenings are Friday and Saturday, and on other days of the week they are often hired by various clubs providing particular styles of music. The nightlife scene is changing all the time as new clubs come and go. **Café Opera**, Stockholm's most historic international-class nightclub, is located to the rear of Kungliga Operan *(see pp64–5)*. It has a mixed clientele of both the young and trendy and a more soberly dressed older generation.

    Sturecompagniet is a large disco on several floors which also has a rock bar at street level. **Fasching Jazzklubb** has soul from the 1960s and 1970s on Saturdays. **Spy Bar** is the place to rub shoulders with Swedish celebrities and international artists on tour. However, it is often crowded and a membership card may be necessary. **Blue Moon Bar**

is another "in" place with a fashion-conscious clientele. The younger generation enjoy dancing to a variety of music at **Mondo**. In the city centre is **Casino Cosmopol**, Stockholm's first casino.

CABARETS

Good food and top-class entertainment are on the menu at **Hamburger Börs**, which features cabaret shows performed by leading Swedish artists. **Wallmans Salonger** offers musical entertainment provided by the waiters and waitresses along with the food.

FILM

Films are not dubbed into Swedish, so non-Swedish speaking visitors can more often than not go to a cinema and enjoy a film that is in their own language. Films in languages other than English are usually screened at **Zita**, and **Sture** is also a good venue for cineasts. There are both classic cinemas like **Röda Kvarn**, showing quality international drama, and multi-screen complexes like **Filmstaden Sergel** which screens most of the current Hollywood repertoire.

DIRECTORY

ROCK AND POP

Anchor Pub
Sveavägen 90. **Map** 2 C2.
Tel 15 20 00.
⏲ *3pm–3am Mon–Fri, 1pm–3am Sat, 1pm–2.30am Sun.*

Cirkus
Djurgårdsslätten.
Map 6 A4.
Tel 587 987 00.

Globen
Globentorget 2.
Tel 0771 310 000.

Münchenbryggeriet
Torkel Knutssonsg 2.
Map 8 B1.
Tel 658 00 20;
for tickets: 0771 707070.

Södra Teatern
Mosebacke Torg 1–3.
Map 9 D2.
Tel 556 972 30.

Tre Backar
Tegnergatan 12–14.
Map 2 C3. *Tel 673 44 00.*
⏲ *1pm–midnight Mon–Thu, 6pm–1am Fri–Sat.*

JAZZ

Fasching Jazzklubb
Kungsgatan 63.
Map 2 B4.
Tel 534 829 60.
⏲ *7pm–midnight Mon–Fri, 7pm–4am Sat.*

Glenn Miller Café
Brunnsgatan 21 A.
Map 3 D3. *Tel 10 03 22.*
⏲ *5pm–1am Mon–Thu, 5pm–2am Fri–Sat;* 🎵 *from 8pm.*

Lydmar Hotel
Sturegatan 10.
Map 3 D3. *Tel 566 113 00.*
⏲ *11.30am–1am Mon–Thu, 11.30am–3am Fri, 1pm–2am Sat, 1pm–1am Sun.*

Nalen
Regeringsgatan 74.
Map 3 D3.
Tel 505 292 00.

Stampen
Stora Nygatan 5.
Map 4 B3. *Tel 20 57 93.*
⏲ *8pm–1am Mon–Thu, 8pm–2am Fri & Sat.*

SS Blidösund
Skeppsbron 10.
Map 4 C2. *Tel 24 30 90.*
⏲ *May–mid Sep: boat departing at 7pm Mon–Thu.*

MUSIC PUBS

Akkurat
Hornsgatan 18.
Map 8 C2. *Tel 644 00 15.*
⏲ *11am–1am Mon–Fri, 3pm–1am Sat & Sun.*

The Dubliner
Smålandsgatan 8.
Map 3 D4. *Tel 679 77 07.*
⏲ *4pm–3am Tue–Sat.*
🎵 *from 10pm daily.*

Engelen
Kornhamnstorg 59 B.
Map 4 B4. *Tel 20 10 92.*
⏲ *5pm–3am Mon–Sun.*

BARS

Cadier Bar
Grand Hôtel, Södra Blasieholmshamnen 8.
Map 4 C1. *Tel 679 35 00.*

Gondolen
Stadsgården 6.
Map 4 C5. *Tel 641 70 90.*

Lydmar Bar
Sturegatan 10.
Map 3 D3.
Tel 566 113 00.

Operabaren
Kungsträdgården.
Map 4 B1.
Tel 676 5808.

Sheraton Living Room
Tegelbacken 6.
Map 4 A1.
Tel 412 34 00.

Sky Bar
Vasagatan 1.
Map 2 B4.
Tel 506 540 00.

Sturehof Bar
Stureplan 2.
Map 3 D4. *Tel 440 57 30.*

NIGHT CLUBS AND CASINOS

Blue Moon Bar
Kungsgatan 18.
Map 3 D4. *Tel 24 47 00.*
⏲ *9pm–5am Tue, 7pm–3am Thu, 7pm–5am Fri–Sun.*

Café Opera
Operahuset, Kungsträdgården. **Map** 4 B2.
Tel 676 58 07.
⏲ *5pm–3am daily.*

Casino Cosmopol
Kungsgatan 65. **Map** 2 B4. *Tel 781 88 00.*
⏲ *1pm–5am daily.*

Fasching Jazzklubb
Kungsgatan 63.
Map 2 B4. *Tel 534 829 60.* ⏲ *Soul club: midnight–4am Sat.*

Mondo
Medborgarplatsen 8.
Map 9 D3. *Tel 642 22 69.*
⏲ *3pm–midnight.*

Spy Bar
Birger Jarlsgatan 20.
Map 3 D3. *Tel 545 037 01.*
⏲ *10pm–5am Wed–Sat.*

Sturecompagniet
Sturegatan 4. **Map** 3 D3.
Tel 545 034 48.
⏲ *10pm–3am Thu–Sat.*

CABARETS

Hamburger Börs
Jakobsgatan 6. **Map** 3 D5.
Tel 787 85 00.

Wallmans Salonger
Teatergatan 3. **Map** 3 E5.
Tel 505 560 00.

FILM

Filmstaden Sergel
Hötorget. **Map** 2 C4.
Tel 562 600 00.

Röda Kvarn
Biblioteksgatan 5.
Map 3 D4. *Tel 562 600 00.*

Sture
Birger Jarlsgatan 41.
Map 3 D3. *Tel 678 85 48.*

Zita
Birger Jarlsgatan 37.
Map 3 D3. *Tel 23 20 20.*

OUTDOOR ACTIVITIES

A s a city built around water and where the countryside reaches into the centre, Stockholm is ideally positioned for all kinds of open-air pursuits. The great outdoors plays an important role in the Swedish lifestyle, and the capital offers a plethora of activities throughout the year – for the energetic and not so energetic – from walking, cycling and ice-skating to fishing, skiing and hot-air ballooning. In spring, summer and

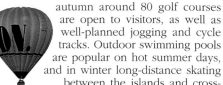

Hot-air balloon over Stockholm

autumn around 80 golf courses are open to visitors, as well as well-planned jogging and cycle tracks. Outdoor swimming pools are popular on hot summer days, and in winter long-distance skating between the islands and cross-country and downhill skiing are the things to do.

In many cases, it is simple to make your own contacts, but the Stockholm Visitors Board (SVB) will be able to advise you *(see p190)*.

Hagaparken, an inviting area for exercise and recreation *(see pp122–3)*

JOGGING, WALKS AND CYCLING

It can be both practical and rewarding to take some exercise while exploring the capital. Everything in the city centre is within easy walking distance, including major sights, beautiful parks and

Fishing at Blasieholmskajen in the centre of the city

modern shopping malls. A walk in Stockholm always takes you close to the water or some unusual sight. The organized walks in the city are usually conducted in Swedish but there are also tours of Gamla Stan with English-speaking guides. Contact Stockholm Information Service (SIS) for advice on a route.

Even if you want to head out of the city centre, there is no need to travel far. The No. 47 bus goes out to Djurgården, where you can have a walk or jog along the shores, through the avenues under the oak trees, or over green fields. Walking paths along the city's waterfronts *(see pp40–41)* provide both good routes and stunning views. There are many floodlit jogging tracks, and plenty of fun-run events to choose from *(see pp26–9)*.

Those who prefer to move at a gentler pace can head for **Skansen** open-air museum

(see pp96–7) or the **Gröna Lund** amusement park *(see p95)*, both suitable for the whole family, providing a day out in the open air.

Djurgården has plenty of cycle paths and bicycles can be hired from **Cykel Mopeduthyrningen** or **Skepp & Hoj** *(see p205)*, near Djurgårdsbron *(see p98)*. Roller-blades can also be hired near the bridge.

Cyclists planning to take a longer tour should visit SIS and ask to be put in touch with the Cykelfrämjandet cycling organization.

HORSE RIDING

Several riding schools near the city centre, such as **Stockholms Ridhus**, offer lessons. For those who prefer to discover Stockholm's surrounding areas, tours on Icelandic ponies are operated from quite a few stables.

Rundemars Gård hires out horses to experienced riders to explore the Tyresö nature reserve, southeast of the city, after an initial briefing.

WATER SPORTS

There are excellent opportunities for water sports. Canoes, rowing boats, pedalos and larger boats for longer tours, can be hired from **Tvillingarnas Båtuthyrning** and **Skepp & Hoj** *(see p205)*, both near Djurgårdsbron. A good area for canoeing is the canal near Djurgården *(see pp85–99)*, where **Djurgårdsbrons Sjöcafé** hires out canoes.

SWIMMING

During the summer there are plenty of outdoor swimming pools to choose from. They include **Eriksdalsbadet** in Södermalm, **Kampements-badet** at Gärdet and **Vanadis-badet** in Vasastan. There are several good places for a swim along the Kungsholmen shores of Riddarfjärden. And on Långholmen there are both sandy beaches or rocks to swim from (see p132).

For a completely different bathing experience, try the Japanese **Yasuragi** at Hassel-udden. For indoor pools, try Centralbadet (see p69) or Sturebadet (see p71).

GOLF

Golfers will find about 80 golf courses within easy reach of the city centre. The closest, such as **Djurs-holms Golfklubb**, are in delightful settings.

The courses are popular and advance bookings are recommended. Golf information is available on Stockholm's official website (www.stockholmtown.com).

OTHER ACTIVITIES

Brightly coloured hot-air balloons hovering over the city are a common sight in the evening. Several companies operate charter trips in balloons. You can book via SIS or directly with a company such as **Far & Flyg**.

Game fishing for salmon and trout is possible right in

Vanadisbadet in Vasastan

the city centre near the Royal Palace. Suitable tackle can be hired at **Fiskarnas Redskaps-handel.** The **Anglers' Association** can provide information on fishing in and around Stockholm.

Outdoor tennis courts are available at several places, including **Kungliga Tennis-hallen**, where the Stockholm Open ATP indoor tournament is held every November.

You can go scuba-diving around Stockholm too. Contact SIS for details of diving schools and equipment hire.

Ice-skaters are in their element once the open waters of the archipelago have frozen over. Meanwhile, the artificial rink at Kungsträdgården is open throughout the winter, and hires out skates.

The outdoor activities organization **Friluftsfrämjandet** provides information on skating and skiing in the area.

Visitors with disablities can find out more about the availability of outdoor pursuits by contacting **De Handikappades Riksförbund** (see p191).

(see p191).

DIRECTORY

HORSE RIDING

Rundmars Gård
Rundmars Gård, Tyresö.
Tel 770 23 29.

Stockholms Ridhus
Storängsvägen 29. **Map** 3 F1.
Tel 664 61 79.

WATER SPORTS AND FISHING

Anglers' Association
Tel 19 78 20 (10am–1pm).

Djurgårdsbrons Sjöcafé
Galävarvsvägen 2. *Tel* 660 57 57.

Fiskarnas Redskapshandel
S:t Paulsgatan 2–4.
Map 8 C2. *Tel* 556 096 50.

SWIMMING

Eriksdalsbadet
Hammarby Slussv. 8.
Map 9 D5. *Tel* 508 402 50.

Kampementsbadet
Sandhamnsgatan (Gärdet).
Tel 661 62 16.
⏱ 25 May–25 Aug.

Vanadisbadet
Vanadislunden. **Map** 2 B1.
Tel 34 33 00. ⏱ 25 May–31 Aug.

Yasuragi
Hasseludden Konferens & Yasuragi.
🚆 35-min journey from Slussen.
Tel 747 61 00. ⏱ 7am–11pm.

GOLF

Djursholms Golfklubb
Hagbardsvägen, Djursholm.
Tel 544 964 50.

OTHER ACTIVITIES

Far & Flyg
Gröndasvägen 38nb.
Tel 645 77 00.
www.farochflyg.se

Kungliga Tennishallen
Lidingövägen. *Tel* 459 15 00.
www.kungl.tennishallen.se

Friluftsfrämjandet
Tel 447 44 40.
www.frilufts.se

One of Stockholm's many golf courses

SHOPPING IN STOCKHOLM

Stockholm is worth visiting for the shopping alone. All the best shops in the central area are within easy walking distance and they stock virtually everything anyone could want. There are plenty of small boutiques for fashion and interiors, as well as antique shops, luxury international designer outlets and well-stocked department stores.

Shopping is good all over the city. Exclusive shops can be found in fashionable Östermalm. Gamla Stan is a good place for handicrafts and unusual knick-knacks. Södermalm and Vasastan have antique and second-hand shops. Cameras, mobile telephones, furs, children's clothing, toys and Swedish glass are cheaper in Sweden than in most other countries. No expedition is complete without a visit to one of the city's splendid market halls which sell Swedish delicacies like reindeer and elk meat, caviar and cloudberries.

Dala horse
(see p184)

OPENING TIMES

Most shops usually open at 10am and close at 6pm, although many in the city centre remain open until 7pm. Most shops are open until 2pm on Saturdays, and the major department stores stay open until 5pm. Large stores, shopping malls and a number of shops in central Stockholm are open on Sundays. Market halls are closed on Sundays and public holidays. Larger supermarkets are open daily until 8pm.

PAYMENT

All the main credit cards and travellers' cheques are accepted at most Stockholm shops. If you are paying by card you may be asked for proof of identity. Goods can be exchanged if you produce the receipt. Purchases can usually be made on a sale-or-return basis, providing this is noted on the receipt.

VALUE ADDED TAX

Value added tax ("moms" in Swedish) is charged on all items except daily newspapers. The VAT rate is 25%, except on food, for which the rate is only 12%. VAT is always included in the total price.

TAX-FREE SHOPPING

Residents of countries out side the European Union are entitled to a refund of the VAT they have paid on their purchases. Tax-free shopping with Global Refund gives visitors a cash refund of 15–18 per cent on their departure from the EU. Look for the "Tax-free shopping" sign. Global Refund is at all departure points, including Arlanda Airport.

Biblioteksgatan, an attractive shopping street in Stockholm

SALES

Twice a year Stockholm's shops and department stores have sales with reduced prices on clothing, shoes and other fashion goods. Sales are indicated by the *rea* sign. The year's first sales start after Christmas and continue throughout January. The second sales period lasts from late June to the end of July.

SHOPPING CENTRES AND DEPARTMENT STORES

Stockholm's best-known superstore is **IKEA**, which has become a popular tourist attraction in its own right. It sells not just furniture but also everything else for the home, and all at attractive prices. The textiles section is particularly good, as well as the kitchenware and porcelain departments. IKEA's store is located outside the city but is

NK, Stockholm's most exclusive department store

Nordiska Kristall, a major outlet for Swedish glass in Stockholm

easy to reach by a free shuttle bus from Regeringsgatan 13 to Kungens Kurva, hourly on weekdays from 10am to 5pm.

Another well-known store is the fashion house **H&M** (Hennes & Mauritz), which has branches in many European cities and several outlets in Stockholm. H&M stocks the latest fashions at low prices. It has its own designers and makes clothing for women, men, teenagers and children. The shops also sell accessories, jewellery, underwear, perfume and cosmetics.

Nordiska Kompaniet (NK) on Hamngatan is Stockholm's leading department store, where many well-known names in fashion and cosmetics have their own shops. NK also stocks Swedish-designed products, jewellery, handicrafts and souvenirs as well as cameras, films, books and CDs.

PUB on Hötorget is another established department store with a wide selection of goods.

One of Arsenalsgatan's fine antique shops

The **Duka** boutique chain has a good choice of table coverings and decorations, both classic and modern.

Most shopping items can be bought inexpensively at **Åhlens** department store in City, Vasastaden, Kungsholmen and Östermalm, as well as some suburbs.

There are several indoor shopping malls. **Gallerian** on Hamngatan is the largest and the prices are lower than in the elegant **Sturegallerian** near Stureplan with its many trendy boutiques. Also there are shopping centres in most suburbs where nearly all the retail chains are represented.

MARKETS

A traditional Christmas market is held at Skansen *(see p96)* every Sunday in December. Stortorget in Gamla Stan *(see p54)* also has a delightful market at Christmas.

Vegetables, fruit and flowers are sold from Monday to Friday at Hötorget *(see p68)*, Östermalmstorg *(see p71)* and Medborgarplatsen *(see p131)*. Street stalls along Drottninggatan and around Sergels Torg sell watches, clocks, toys and other knick-knacks.

Stockholm's flea market, **Skärholmens Loppmarknad**, offers a wide variety of clothes, practical objects and bric-a-brac for sale.

WINES AND SPIRITS

The only shops selling alcohol in Sweden are run by Systembolaget, the State monopoly chain. They are open Monday to Friday 10am–6pm (some open on

DIRECTORY

SHOPPING CENTRES & DEPARTMENT STORES

Duka
Konserthuset, Kungsgatan 41.
Map 2 C4. *Tel 20 60 41.*
www.duka.se

Fältöversten
Karlaplan 13.
Map 3 F3. *Tel 528 098 11.*

Gallerian
Hamngatan 37.
Map 3 D4. *Tel 791 24 45.*
www.gallerian.se

H&M
Hamngatan 22. **Map** 3 D4.
Tel 524 635 30.
Sergels Torg 12. **Map** 2 C4.
Tel 796 54 46.
www.hm.com

IKEA
Kungens Kurva, Skärholmen.
Tel 020 439 050.
Barkarby, Järfälla.
Tel 795 40 00. www.ikea.se

NK
Hamngatan 18–20. **Map** 3 D4.
Tel 762 80 00. www.nk.se

PUB
Hötorget. **Map** 3 C4.
Tel 402 16 12. www.pub.se

Sturegallerian
Grev Turegatan 9.
Map 3 D4. *Tel 611 46 06.*
www.sturegallerian.se

Åhléns
Klarabergsgatan 50. **Map** 2 C4.
Tel 676 60 00.
Fridhemsplan. **Map** 1 B2.
Tel 617 97 00.
Odenplan. **Map** 2 B2.
Tel 728 53 00.
www.ahlens.com

MARKETS

**Skärholmens
Loppmarknad**
P-huset. Skärholmen.
Tel 710 00 60.
☐ 11am–6pm Mon–Fri,
9am–3pm Sat, 10am–3pm Sun.

Saturdays 10am–2pm, but not on a public holiday weekend). The minimum age for buying alcohol at Systembolaget shops is 20 *(see also p191)*.

What to Buy in Stockholm

Elk candlestick

The Dala wooden horse must be the most typical Swedish souvenir. But it is facing strong competition from the elk, which has become a symbol for a country with vast tracts of unspoilt countryside. The Swedes love the great outdoors, so there are plenty of shops selling top-class sporting equipment. Swedish glass and crystal are renowned around the world. Orrefors and Kosta are just two of several glassworks producing both classic and modern glassware. Educational toys in natural materials are a Swedish speciality and so are clogs, which can be found in many shoe shops.

Hand-painted clogs

HANDICRAFTS & DESIGN

Modern Swedish design is a familiar concept in many households worldwide, even for simple everyday items *(see pp38–9)*. Handicrafts have a long tradition in Sweden and contemporary designers often use wrought-iron work, weaving, pottery and woodcarving.

Dala Horse and Cockerel
Originally the brightly painted Dala horses and cockerels were toys carved from left-over fragments of wood. Later the horse became a national symbol and is sold in many variants.

Swedish Glass
Hand-blown sets of glassware are made in Sweden's glassworks, as well as artistic crystal creations and beautiful objects for everyday use.

Tray with design by Josef Frank, Svenskt Tenn

Cheese slicer and knife by Michael Björnstierna

Nobel glass carafe from Orrefors by Gunnar Cyrén

Traditional schnapps glasses

Designer Objects
The larger department stores often commission well-known designers for porcelain, glass, textiles and household items which make highly desirable gifts.

***Mama*, a humorous clothes hanger**

***Crux* rug by Pia Wallén**

Children's Toys
Colourful wooden children's toys from Brio are worldwide favourites. Educational picture books, games and puzzles are all excellent gifts for children.

OUTDOOR GEAR

Many Swedes enjoy outdoor pursuits like fishing, hunting, sailing, golf, camping and all types of winter sports, so there are many well-equipped sports shops around. Unique items include Lapp handicrafts beautifully made from reindeer horn or skin.

Hand Knits
Caps and gloves with attractive designs, known as lovikka, *are made from a special wool which gives good protection in cold or wet conditions.*

Drinking vessel in carved wood

Reindeer Skin Rucksack
Rucksacks are popular for both adults and children. This exclusive model is made in Lapland.

Lapp Handicrafts
A hunting knife with a sheath of reindeer horn, or a kåsa, *a drinking vessel carved in birch, are not only attractive but useful when out walking in the wild.*

Spinning Reel and Lures
ABU-Garcia makes top-quality fishing tackle perfect for Sweden's long coastline, countless lakes and rivers with their rich and varied fishing.

SWEDISH DELICACIES

Popular preserves are made from wild berries such as bitter lingonberries (for meatballs) or sweet cloudberries (served with whipped cream). Herring, crispbread and ginger biscuits can be bought in all groceries, and sweets are sold loose. Schnapps miniatures come in gift packs.

Lingonberry preserve   **Cloudberry jam**

Pickled Herring
Pickled herring should be enjoyed with new potatoes cooked with dill, chopped chives and crème fraîche. Versions flavoured with mustard, dill or other herbs or spices are also available.

Swedish schnapps gift-pack miniatures

"Raspberry boat" candy   **Salt liquorice**   **Crispbread**   **Box of ginger biscuits**

Where to Shop in Stockholm

Clothing from all the well-known international fashion houses can be found in Stockholm, and many have their own shops. If you want something rather different it is worth seeking out the creations of younger Swedish fashion designers. Swedish interior design is famous for its clean lines, functionalism and the use of pale wood, and Stockholm is a paradise for anyone interested in design. Handicrafts are of a high quality. Leisurewear and sports goods offer excellent value for money.

FASHION

Stockholm's top places for fashion are in the "golden triangle" bounded by Stureplan, Nybroplan and Norrmalmstorg. Clothing at more moderate prices can be bought around Sergels Torg.

If you are looking for Swedish designers, **NK** has a selection of clothing created by younger designers as well as mainstream local products. Classic men's clothing of high quality is designed by Oscar Jacobsson, while Stenström shirts are sold in department stores and the more elegant menswear boutiques. **Björn Borg** has his own shops selling men's and women's clothing and underwear, perfume and accessories. **Johan Lindeberg** produces unusual fashions for the daring man, while fashion-conscious young people shop at **Sneakersnstuff**. The designer **Filippa K** produces smart clothing for trendy women. **Anna Holtblad** has a good selection of stylish women's garments, while **Thalia** in Östermalm has a good range of exclusive party outfits.

DESIGN AND INTERIOR DECORATION

The city centre, Östermalm and Hornsgatan in Södermalm have a number of interior decoration shops selling the products of young designers and artists. To see the latest on offer, visit **DesignTorget**, where young designers display their work. **R.O.O.M** on Kungsholmen, **Asplund** in Östermalm and **Norrgavel** in City are just a few of the most up-to-date shops and they all have a good selection of products.

Svenskt Tenn is the city's oldest shop for interior decoration, with both new and classic designs. **Nordiska Galleriet** has exclusive modern furniture and decoration items while **Georg Jensen** specializes in silver. **Kao-Lin, Nutida Svenskt Silver, Blås&Knåda** and **Galleri Metallum** stage exhibitions and sell Swedish-designed products. Modern printed textiles can be found at **Tio-Gruppen** in Södermalm. **Orrefos Kosta Boda** and **Nordiska Kristall** both have a wide choice of Swedish glassware, which can also be found at the various department stores.

ANTIQUES

A large number of antique shops can be found along Odengatan, Upplandsgatan and Roslagsgatan in Vasastan. Gamla Stan also has many shops offering collectables. Shops selling art, silver and porcelain of a more exclusive variety are on Arsenalsgatan on Blasieholmen, and also around Östermalmstorg. Södermalm has small shops selling bric-a-brac.

MUSIC AND MULTIMEDIA

Many Swedish pop bands now have an international reputation. Exciting new talents continue to find their way into the charts, and the latest products can often be bought in the record shops before they become available outside Sweden. Apart from pop and rock, Sweden has a long folk-music tradition, as well as many skilled jazz musicians and opera singers. **ROCKS** has a wide selection of CDs, as do the large department stores.

SPORT AND LEISURE

The Swedes devote a lot of time to outdoor sports and activities. **Naturkompaniet** and **Peak Performance** have an exclusive selection of sportswear and equipment. **Stadium** and **Alewalds** have a varied choice of sports clothing and equipment at attractive prices. Equipment and exclusive clothing for hunting or fishing can be bought at **Walter Borg**.

SOUVENIRS AND HANDICRAFTS

Glasses for schnapps, silver jewellery, hand-painted clogs, Lapp *(Same)* crafts, hand-knitted woollen gloves and caps, hand-made candles, traditional Christmas decorations and wrought-iron products can all be bought in the main department stores. Alternatively you can go to the Gamla Stan shops like **Carl Wennberg Sameslöjd** and **Handkraft Swea. Svensk Hemslöjd** and the various museum gift shops are also good places to shop. Visitors to Skansen *(see pp96–7)* can buy handicrafts made in its shops. **Sweden Shop** sells Swedish hand-icrafts and quality souvenirs.

BOOKS

Photography books, cookery books, books on Swedish design and children's books make good souvenirs to take home. Apart from the **NK Bookshop** and at other department stores, **Hedengrens Bokhandel** has a large foreign-languages department. The **Sweden Bookshop** has a good selection of books on Stockholm and Sweden in English.

TOYS AND BABY EQUIPMENT

It is worth buying high-quality baby prams and pushchairs produced by Emmaljunga and baby equipment by Babybjörn. **Babyland** and **Bonti** have a wide selection of these and other well-made products for children. Brio's wooden toys and other attractive toys are also favourite presents. **Bulleribock** and **BR Leksaker** offer a wide choice. Practical children's clothing can be found at **Polarn och Pyret** or at the larger department stores.

SWEDISH DELICACIES

The capital has three superb market halls: **Östermalmshallen**, **Hötorgshallen** and **Söderhallarna**. Delicacies on sale include salmon, bleak roe, smoked eel and smoked reindeer meat, which are all delicious culinary souvenirs. The food sections of the major department stores sell tinned herrings, lingonberry or cloudberry jam, crispbread, gingerbread and sweets, which make good presents.

DIRECTORY

FASHIONS

Anna Holtblad
Grev Turegatan 13.
Map 3 E4.
Tel 545 022 20.

Björn Borg
Sergelg 12.
Map 2 C4.
Tel 21 70 40.

Filippa K
Grev Turegatan 18.
Map 3 E4.
Tel 545 882 56.

Johan Lindeberg
Grev Turegatan 9.
Map 3 D4.
Tel 678 61 65.

NK
Hamngatan 18–20.
Map 3 D4.
Tel 762 80 00.

Sneakersnstuff
Åsögatan 124.
Tel 743 03 22.

Thalia
Karlavägen 62.
Map 3 E3.
Tel 660 54 30.

DESIGN AND DECORATION

Asplund
Sibyllegatan 31.**Map** 3 E3.
Tel 662 52 84.

Blås&Knåda
Hornsgatan 26.
Map 4 B5.
Tel 642 77 67.

DesignTorget
Kulturhuset, Sergels
Torg 3. **Map** 2 C4.
Tel 219 150.
Götgatan 31.
Map 9 D2.
Tel 462 35 20.

Galleri Metallum
Hornsgatan 30.
Map 4 B5. *Tel 640 13 23.*

Georg Jensen
Birger Jarlsgatan 13.
Map 3 D4.
Tel 545 040 80.

Kao-Lin
Hornsgatan 50.
Map 8 C2.
Tel 644 46 00.

Konsthantverkarna
Södermalmstorg 4.
Map 9 D2, 4 B5.
Tel 611 03 70.

Nordiska Galleriet
Nybrogatan 11.
Map 3 E4.
Tel 442 83 60.

Nordiska Kristall
Kungsgatan 9.
Map 3 D4.
Tel 10 43 72.

Norrgavel
Birger Jarlsgatan 27.
Map 3 D3.
Tel 545 220 50.

Nutida Svenskt Silver
Arsenalsgatan 3.
Map 3 D4.
Tel 611 67 18.

Orrefors Kosta Boda
Birger Jarlsgatan 15.
Map 2 C2.
Tel 545 040 84.

R.O.O.M
Alströmergatan 20.
Map 1 C2.
Tel 692 50 00.

Svenskt Tenn
Strandvägen 5.
Map 3 E4.
Tel 670 16 00.

Tio-Gruppen
Götgatan 25.
Map 9 D2.
Tel 643 25 04.

MUSIC AND MULTIMEDIA

ROCKS
Sankt Eriksgatan 45.
Map 1 C1.
Tel 651 01 10.

SPORT AND LEISURE

Alewalds
Kungsgatan 32.
Map 6 D3. *Tel 21 90 00.*

Naturkompaniet
Sveavägen 62.
Map 2 C3.
Tel 24 30 02.
Kungsgatan 26.
Map 3 D4.
Tel 24 19 96.

Peak Performance
Biblioteksgatan 18.
Map 3 D4.
Tel 611 34 00.

Stadium
Sergelgatan 8.
Map 2 C4. *Tel 14 09 90.*

Walter Borg
Klara Norra Kyrkogata 26.
Map 2 C4.
Tel 14 38 65.

SOUVENIRS AND HANDICRAFTS

Carl Wennberg Sameslöjd
Svartmangatan 11.
Map 4 B3.
Tel 20 17 21.

Handkraft Swea
Västerlånggatan 24.
Map 9 D1, 4 B3.
Tel 20 06 36.

Svensk Hemslöjd
Sveavägen 44.
Map 2 C3.
Tel 23 21 15.

Sweden Shop
Sverigehuset. Hamngatan
27. **Map** 3 D4.
Tel 508 285 46.

BOOKS

Hedengrens Bokhandel
Stureplan 4. **Map** 3 D4.
Tel 611 51 28.

NK Bookshop
Hamngatan 18–20.
Map 3 D4.
Tel 762 83 39.

Sweden Bookshop
Slottsbacken 10,
Map 4 C2. *Tel 453 78 00.*

TOYS AND BABY EQUIPMENT

Babyland
Karlbergsvägen 40.
Map 2 A2. *Tel 31 58 00.*

Bonti
Norrtullsgatan 33.
Map 2 B2. *Tel 30 69 16.*

BR Leksaker
Gallerian, Hamngatan 37.
Map 3 D4.
Tel 545 154 40.

Bulleribock
Sveavägen 104.
Map 2 C2.
Tel 673 61 21.

Polarn och Pyret
Gallerian, Hamngatan 35.
Map 3 D4. *Tel 411 22 47.*

SWEDISH DELICACIES

Östermalmshallen
Östermalmstorg.
Map 3 E4.

Hötorgshallen
Hötorget. **Map** 2 C4.

Söderhallarna
Medborgarplatsen.
Map 9 D3.

SURVIVAL
GUIDE

PRACTICAL INFORMATION

Tourist office symbol

With Stockholm growing rapidly as an important destination for tourism and special events in recent years, service standards in the tourist industry and in shops have improved greatly. It is easy to be a foreign visitor in the city, not least because most people speak English. The city's official tourism organization, Stockholm Visitors Board (SVB), provides an excellent range of services and its printed and Internet information material, as well as that of most attractions, is nearly always available in English and often in other languages, too. Stockholm is a small capital and is generally safe, but it still has its share of pickpockets, and it's wise to take care at night in the deserted business and shopping area in the centre.

TOURIST INFORMATION

Stockholm's official tourist information organization is **Stockholm Visitors Board** (SVB). It offers a year-round service at its main office in Sweden House on Hamngatan *(see pp63–4)*, as well as its office at Centralstationen. The green "i" sign indicates an authorized tourist information office. Hotel staff are often well informed. Most hotels, as well as many department stores and museums, stock the brochure *What's On Stockholm*, which is distributed every month free of charge.

The Stockholm police are always pleased to help visitors, as are most Stockholmers who are familiar with their city. Swedes usually speak English reasonably fluently.

Visitors can obtain the latest information about Stockholm on the Internet before travelling to Sweden. The city's official tourism website, www.stockholmtown.com, can probably answer the most common questions. Visitors can frequently book hotel accommodation on the Inter-

net, check the city's calendar of special events, and book tickets. This guide quotes web addresses for all the most important sights. The majority of museums also have their own excellent websites, and www. stockholmsmuseer. com is a useful site with a large number of links that give an excellent overview of the city's museums.

The logo of Stockholm Visitors Board (SVB)

PASSPORTS & CUSTOMS

Citizens of virtually all countries can enter Sweden without a visa. Since 2001, passports are not needed by visitors from European countries which have signed the Schengen agreement. All visitors should check their requirements prior to travelling.

Differing rules often apply between travellers from the European Union (EU) and those from other countries. Travellers from within the EU are able to bring for their private consumption 10 litres of spirits

or 20 litres of fortified wine, 90 litres of wine, 110 litres of strong beer and 800 cigarettes. Travellers from outside the EU may only bring (again, for private use) 1 litre of spirits or 2 litres of fortified wine, 2 litres of wine and 200 cigarettes.

The rules governing the importing of food also differ. All visitors can take in canned foods, but EU citizens can also take in a maximum of 15 kg (33 lb) of fresh food per person, while visitors from other areas must have a certificate from a recognized exporter. Visitors from non-EU countries can take in goods, including beer, up to a value of 1,700 kr in addition to normal travel-related items.

Dogs and cats from other EU countries are allowed to be taken into Sweden, so long as they have a veterinary certificate from the animal's home country. The animal must also have a recognised identification marking, as well as an import permit issued by the Swedish Agricultural Authority (which is available from Swedish embassies).

Tax-free sales in Sweden are permitted only for travellers with a final destination outside the EU.

OPENING HOURS

Most museums and other sights are open between 10am or 11am and 5pm or 6pm all year, and they often have longer opening hours in the summer. They are usually

The tourist information office at Sweden House on Hamngatan

◁ **The ice-covered waters of Riddarfjärden, transformed into walking grounds**

Toilet for handicapped, parents of small children, women and men

closed on Monday. Information on current activities is available in the brochure *What's On Stockholm*, available at tourist information offices, hotels and department stores.

DISABLED VISITORS

Under Swedish law, public areas have to be accessible by physically or visually disabled people, as well as those suffering from allergies. Stockholm is a long away ahead of many other big cities in this respect. Disabled visitors from abroad can obtain information in English before their stay from **De Handikappades Riksförbund**.

The Tunnelbana underground network is adapted for disabled passengers, and most buses "kneel" at bus stops to give a reasonable height for passengers to get on or off. Disabled car drivers with a disability permit from their home country can park in special areas. Some useful brochures with detailed information about facilities for disabled visitors at theatres, cinemas, museums and libraries can be found at tourist information offices.

ADMISSION CHARGES

Entrance fees to Stockholm's museums are generally between 50 and 70 kr. Discount prices are usually available for students, children and senior citizens. The Stockholm Card (*Stockholmskortet*) gives free admission to more than 70 museums and other attractions along with free travel on local buses, Tunnelbana trains and local trains. It also offers

The Stockholm Card, giving free admission to museums

free parking at official city parking areas, as well as seasonal special offers.

Tickets for theatres, concerts and sports events can be bought at the venue or on the Internet. Tickets can also be bought in the Excursion Shop at **Sweden House**. Ticket agencies such as **Box Office** and **Biljett Direkt TicNet** also sell tickets *(see p175)*.

ETIQUETTE

Bans on smoking are increasingly common throughout Sweden. Smoking is generally not permitted in public places, including all local transport and queues at bus stops and railway stations. Restaurants are obliged to provide no-smoking areas.

The Swedes queue patiently, but guard their place jealously. They are usually friendly and glad to help foreign tourists. The use of first names is the norm and a friendly "Hej!" is a familiar greeting.

Casual clothing is acceptable almost everywhere, including restaurants, particularly in the summer. Tips are always included in restaurant prices, but it is usual to round up the bill by up to 10 per cent for good service.

The logo of Systembolaget, the State-owned liquor store

ALCOHOL

Swedish policy towards alcohol is restrictive. Wines and spirits can be bought only in the relatively few shops of the State monopoly Systembolaget. They are open Monday–Friday from 10am to 6pm, and also at a limited number of shops from 10am to 3pm on Saturday. Queues tend to be long, particularly on Friday. The minimum age for buying liquor in these shops is 20, and young people may be asked to produce proof of their age. In restaurants the minimum age for

DIRECTORY

TOURIST INFORMATION

Sweden House/Sverigehuset
Hamngatan 27 (Kungsträdgården).
Box 7542, 103 93 Stockholm.
Map 4 E1. ◻ 9am–7pm Mon–Fri, 10am–5pm Sat, 10am–4pm Sun. ◼ 24 & 25 Dec, 1 Jan. **Tel** 508 285 08. **Fax** 508 285 09.
www.stockholmtown.com

Hotellcentralen
(hotel bookings)
Centralstation, 111 20 Stockholm.
Map 4 E1. ◻ 24 hours.
Tel 508 285 68. **Fax** 791 86 66.

De Handikappades Riksförbund
(information for disabled visitors)
Tel 685 8000. **www**.dhr.se

SIGHTSEEING

City Sightseeing
(guided tours by bus) Gustav Adolfs Torg, **Map** 4 F1. **Tel** 587 140 20. **www**.citysightseeing.com

Stockholm Sightseeing
(guided tours by boat)
Strömkajen, Grand Hôtel.
Map 2 D5. **Tel** 587 140 20.
www.stockholmsightseeing.com

Guided Tours
Tel 508 285 08.

EMBASSIES AND CONSULATES

United Kingdom
Skarpögatan 6–8. **Tel** 671 30 00.
www.britishembassy.com

United States
Dag Hammarskjölds väg 31.
Tel 783 53 00. **www**.usemb.se

buying liquor is 18. Most restaurants and pubs stop selling alcohol at 1am, but some city centre bars stay open till 5am.

With the maximum permitted blood alcohol level of only 0.2 per mil, drinking is effectively totally banned for car drivers.

The Swedish custom of "skåling" confounds many visitors. To "skål", look the person straight in the eye, raise your glass, drink, then repeat the eye contact before putting your glass down.

Personal Security and Health

Police symbol

Stockholm is outstandingly safe compared with virtually any other major city. To a great extent the city has been spared the scourges of violence and terrorism, and natural disasters like earthquakes and severe storms do not occur. But it is worth noting that in recent decades the city centre has been given over mainly to offices and public buildings, so the area tends to be deserted at night, with all the risks that entails. Sweden has a well-developed network of emergency services which visitors can naturally call on. Rescue services and hospital emergency clinics are highly efficient.

Policeman   **Security guard**

Police car

PROTECTING PROPERTY

Although Stockholm is basically a safe city, tourists can naturally run into trouble at times. Especially in the summer months, the many popular events attract bag-snatchers and pickpockets. Visitors should be particularly careful to keep an eye on their property in crowded public areas, especially handbags and cameras.

It is advisable to leave your passport and travel documents at the hotel when going out. Valuables and personal documents should always be locked in your room safe or in the hotel strongbox. There is no need to carry large amounts of cash when exploring the city. All the main credit and debit cards are accepted in virtually all shops and restaurants, and cash-card machines can be used for any amounts.

It is equally important not to leave any valuables in your car;

ideally, choose a hotel with its own parking facilities.

Visitors to Stockholm with their own car should ensure they have an international Green Card for insurance.

PERSONAL SAFETY

Police in Stockholm are generally extremely helpful and speak good English. Police patrolling on foot or in cars are a routine sight in the city centre, and mounted police are often used at special events. There are police stations in every part of the city, and also at the

Mounted police officers

Central Station/T-Centralen. In addition to the police, uniformed security guards are a common feature at central Tunnelbana stations and in department stores, as well as in office reception areas.

Stockholm is a good city for tourists because of the compact size of the central area and the fact that it is easy to explore on foot. In addition, the Tunnelbana (underground railway) is efficient and comfortable as well as being safe at most times, but avoid empty carriages. TV security systems are installed at some Tunnelbana stations, the Central Station, main squares, department stores and many shops.

Visitors need to be careful about using unauthorized taxis, particularly when arriving at Arlanda Airport or at night in the city centre.

For some years it has been illegal to buy sexual services in Sweden so it is the buyer, not the prostitute, who is prosecuted. As a result of this law and increased police activity, street prostitutes are now a very rare sight indeed in the inner city.

LOST PROPERTY

Lost or stolen property should be reported to the nearest police station. The **Police Lost Property Office** (Polisens Hittegodsexpedition) is open Monday–Friday from 9am to noon. Telephone enquiries can be made during the same hours. **Swedish State Railways** (Statens Järnvägar) has its own lost property office at the Central

Station for items lost on long-distance or local trains. For property lost on a bus or a Tunnelbana train, check with the **SL Lost Property Office** (Hittegodsavdelning), open Monday–Friday between 10am and 5pm.

EMERGENCIES

The emergency telephone number for police, fire or ambulance is 112. It can be dialled free of charge from all public telephones, but should be used only in emergencies. For minor illnesses or concerns, ring the **Healthcare Information Service** (Sjukvårdsupplysningen).

HEALTHCARE

No special vaccinations are needed by anyone planning a visit to Sweden. Several city hospitals have accident and emergency clinics, including **Karolinska Sjukhuset**, **Astrid Lindgrens Barnsjukhus** (children), **Danderyds Sjukhus**, **S:t Eriks Sjukhus** (eye and dental emergencies), **S:t Görans Sjukhus** (privately owned) and **Södersjukhuset**.

Patients should not report to individual emergency clinics without contacting the **Healthcare Information Service** beforehand.

The information service can provide advice in English. Its staff have up-to-date knowledge about the current situation in the city's hospitals and can assign patients to a suitable hospital or duty doctor. It is always advisable to make use of this central information service, otherwise there can be long waiting times for those with minor ailments who go direct to a hospital emergency clinic.

For severe tooth-ache, patients should report to **S:t Eriks Sjukhus** between 7:45am and 8:30pm, or to the **Emergency Dental Clinic** after 8:30pm.

Foreign visitors are advised to take out medical insurance before departure to cover medical care or hospital in-patient treatment.

Citizens of other EU countries are entitled to free

Pharmacy sign

medical care on production of a European Health Insurance Card and a valid passport or other form of identification. Not all treatment is covered by the card though, so it is advisable to also take out separate medical insurance.

MEDICINES

Pharmacies can dispense medicines for most minor ailments without a prescription, and the staff can usually give good advice on suitable medication. Pharmacies are normally open Monday–Friday from 8:30am to 4pm or 6pm. Some also open on Saturday. The **C W Scheele** pharmacy near the Central Station is open 24 hours.

MOSQUITOES AND TICKS

Mosquitoes can be a nuisance between June and late September, especially at dusk. This is particularly the case in parks, along waterways and, above all, in the archipelago. Ticks can also give a nasty bite. Pharmacies can supply mosquito repellent. Ticks should be removed from the skin with tweezers as quickly as possible. If the redness around the bite area persists a doctor should be consulted.

Ambulance

DIRECTORY

EMERGENCIES	S:t Eriks Sjukhus	24-hour Pharmacy	LOST PROPERTY
Ambulance, Police, Fire Brigade	Map 1 C2.	**C W Scheele**	**Police Lost Property**
Tel 112.	*Tel 672 31 00.*	Klarabergsgatan 64.	**Office**
	Södersjukhuset	Map 2 C4.	Bergsgatan 39. **Map** 1 C3.
HEALTHCARE	Map 8 B4.	*Tel 454 81 30 (24-h).*	*Tel 401 07 88.*
	Tel 616 10 00.		
Danderyds Sjukhus	**Astrid Lindgrens**	**24-HOUR**	**Swedish State**
Tel 655 50 00 (24 h).	**Barnsjukhus**	**HEALTHCARE**	**Railways Lost**
	Map 2 A1.	**INFORMATION**	**Property Office**
Karolinska	*Tel 517 771 02.*		Central Station,
Sjukhuset		**Healthcare Infor-**	Vasagatan.
Map 2 A1.	**Emergency Dental**	**mation Service**	Map 2 C4.
Tel 517 700 00 (24 h).	**Clinic**	*Tel 32 01 00 (24-h).*	*Tel 762 25 50.*
	S:t Eriks sjukhus		
S:t Görans Sjukhus	Map 1 C2.	**Poisons Informa-**	**SL Lost Property**
Map 1 A2.	⏰ 7:45–8:30pm:	**tion Service**	**Office**
Tel 587 010 00.	*Tel 545 512 20.*	*Tel 33 12 31 (24-h).*	Klara Östra Kyrkogata 4.
	After hours: 24-h dentist		Map 2 C5.
	Tel 32 01 00.	**Pharmaceutical**	*Tel 600 10 00.*
		Information	
		Tel 0771 450 450 (24-h).	

Banking and Local Currency

While Sweden remains outside the European Monetary Union (EMU), goods are priced only in Swedish kronor and not in euros. Visitors can change currency in banks, which provide an efficient service, but better rates can often be obtained at bureaux de change, which have longer opening hours and are strategically sited in the city centre. Automatic cash machines can be found outside most banks and in larger shopping centres. Credit and debit cards are accepted virtually everywhere, and the larger stores will accept traveller's cheques and sometimes also the most important foreign currencies.

The logo of Forex, a bureau de change with many branches

Bankomat, the joint cash-machine system of the business banks

BANKS

There are plenty of banks in the city centre, all providing a good service. Their opening times vary, but the normal hours are 9:30am– 3pm. Some banks stay open until 6pm at least once a week. All banks are closed at weekends and on public holidays, as well as the day before a public holiday.

Automatic cash machines operate efficiently. There are two types: *Bankomat* machines are the joint system of the business banks, while *Uttag* machines belong to

Föreningssparbanken. Foreign visitors can use all the city's cash machines provided that they have a bank card with a PIN code that is linked to, for example, Visa or MasterCard. Machines usually have instructions in several languages. The charge for withdrawing cash varies according to the type of card.

CURRENCY EXCHANGE

Various bureaux de change chains are represented in Stockholm. Generally they provide a better exchange rate than the banks.

Changing money in your hotel is the most expensive option. It is always worth checking exchange rates and commission charges because the differences can be significant. An advantage of the specialist bureaux de change is that they are easily accessible. In the city centre there is always an office close at hand.

Currency can be changed at Arlanda Airport from 5:30am, and from 7am at the Central Station, and both these outlets are open for more than 12

DIRECTORY

BANKS

Handelsbanken
Kungsträdgårdsgatan 2.
Map 4 C1. **Tel** 701 10 00.

Nordea
Hamngatan 10. **Map** 3 D4.
Tel 614 70 00.

S-E-Banken
Sergels Torg 2. **Map** 2 C4.
Tel 785 10 00.

CREDIT CARDS

Diners Club
Tel 14 68 78 (lost foreign cards).
MasterCard Global Service
Tel 020 791 324 (emergency assistance for international visitors).

Visa
Tel 020 793 146
(lost foreign cards).

American Express
Magnus Ladulåsg. 5. **Map** 8 B3.
Tel 429 54 29 (lost cards).
Tel 0200 110 453 (trav. cheques).

BUREAUX DE CHANGE

Forex
Sweden House, Hamngatan 27.
Map 3 D4. **Tel** 20 03 89.
NK. **Map** 3 D4. **Tel** 762 83 40.
Central Station.
Map 2 C5. **Tel** 411 67 34.
Cityterminalen.
Map 2 B4. **Tel** 21 42 80.
Vasagatan 14.
Map 2 C5. **Tel** 10 49 90.
Arlanda Airport, Terminal 2.
Tel 593 622 71.
www.forex.se

X-change
Kungsgatan 30.
Map 3 D4. **Tel** 506 107 00.
PUB Department Store, Hötorget
Map 2 C4. **Tel** 10 30 00.
Arlanda Airport, Terminal 5.
Tel 797 85 57.
www.x-change.se

The head office of Handelsbanken at Kungsträdgårdsgatan, City

hours daily. At the Central Station there are foreign-exchange offices both in the main entrance hall and on the underground train level.

There is a Forex branch at the tourist information office in Sweden House *(see p191)*, so visitors can change money while checking on current events in the city.

CREDIT CARDS

All the well-known credit cards like **Visa**, **Master-Card**, **American Express** and **Diners Club** are accepted not just by the larger hotels and restaurants but by virtually all shops and services. One notable exception is the State-owned chain of liquor stores, Systembolaget, where only Swedish debit cards or cash are accepted. If you pay by

credit card, you may sometimes be asked to produce proof of identity.

Cash machines can be used to make withdrawals using an internationally accepted credit card with a PIN code.

TRAVELLER'S CHEQUES

If you are planning any large purchases, traveller's cheques are a useful method of payment. They are not accepted in all shops but can be changed at banks. When buying cheques in your home country, it is worth checking the procedure if you lose any of your cheques. It is sensible to keep a receipt showing the serial numbers of the cheques in a separate place.

CURRENCY

Sweden's currency is the krona (plural kronor). The krona (abbreviated as SEK or kr) is divided into 100 öre. The smallest coin is 50 öre, available in two versions, and the largest note is 1,000 kronor, which is not used much. If possible, it is advisable not to carry notes of more than 500 kr.

Most of the larger shops and department stores will accept euros as payment, but it is advisable to check this before trying to pay for your goods.

20 kronor

Notes
Swedish currency notes are issued in denominations of 20, 50, 100, 500 and 1,000 kronor. They depict historic Swedish artists, authors, scientists and monarchs.

50 kronor

500 kronor

100 kronor

1,000 kronor

Coins
Coins are issued in values of 50 öre, and 1, 5 and 10 kronor. The 1 kr coin depicts Sweden's monarch on the obverse side while the 5 kr has his monogram on the reverse side. The 50 öre piece incorporates the State "three crowns" symbol.

50 öre   1 krona   5 kronor   10 kronor

Telecommunications, Post and Media

Sweden has a first-class public telephone system. A top-ranking telecommunications industry, one of the most successful and innovative in the world, and high living standards have placed the Swedes among the world's biggest users of mobile telephones, and there is a very high level of Internet usage. The "Inform@fon" system, for example, can be used not just to make a phone call but also as a text telephone, to send a fax or e-mail, or even to surf the Internet. Telephone cards – and usually credit or debit cards as well – can be used to make a call from a public kiosk. There is no risk of being cut off from the world when you visit Stockholm.

A typical Swedish telephone kiosk

MAKING A PHONE CALL

Public telephone kiosks are usually operated by card only and owned by the State-owned Telia company. The cards can be bought at newspaper kiosks and in shops and are available for 30, 60, or 120 units. For a local call, one unit buys one minute while other calls cost two units per minute. Normal credit cards or international telephone cards like Access can also be used. It is possible to make reverse-charge (collect) calls from all public phones, as well as calls to the emergency number 112 (free of charge).

Instructions on how to use public telephones are shown in English, but phone directories are not often available. Numbers can be obtained by ringing Telia directory enquiries on 118 118.

The prefix for international calls from Sweden is 00, after which one dials the country code, the area code (omitting the initial 0), followed by the local number.

Coin-operated phones are very rare but have instructions in English. Coins accepted are 1 kr, 5 kr and 10 kr.

MOBILE PHONES

The number of telephone kiosks in Sweden has shown a marked decline in recent years because virtually every Swede now has a mobile phone. In most cases foreign visitors can use their GSM phone in Sweden. Within the Stockholm area you dial the area code 08 before the local number – the country code is not needed. The GSM network also has good coverage outside the cities.

FAX, TELEGRAMS AND E-MAIL

An advanced new telecommunications system, "Inform@fon", has been introduced in Stockholm. It is located indoors at more than 100 points including airports, railway stations, shopping centres and other public areas. The system can be used as a normal telephone, text telephone and fax, or to send e-mails, surf the Net and leave a message on a GSM-connected mobile phone. The system is particularly useful for the hard of hearing: one simply writes a message via the keyboard. Payment can be made by a normal phone card or credit/debit card.

The larger hotels offer guests fax, telegram and e-mail services.

E-mail messages can be sent or picked up at **Café Access** in Kulturhuset in Sergels Torg (see p67).

USING A CARD TELEPHONE

1 Select instructions in the language of your choice.

2 Lift the receiver.

3 Insert the card and wait for the dialing tone.

4 Dial the number and wait to be connected. If your phonecard credit is running out you will hear a signal. Press the cardswitch button and insert a new card to continue the call.

5 Remove the card. If you forget, you will hear a signal.

Telephone cards
for 30 units.

Swedish postage stamps

POST

In 2003 the Swedish postal service was restructured, away from dedicated post offices to small postal kiosks located in local grocery stores. These kiosks offer most common services and are open during normal shop hours. Look for the blue and gold postal symbol. For more specialist services some main offices remain, such as the one at the Central Station, which is open on weekdays from 7am to 10pm and from 10am to 7pm on Saturdays and Sundays. Stamps can be bought at post offices and kiosks, as well as at Pressbyrån kiosks and tourist information offices. It costs 5.50 kr to send a postcard or letter under 20 g (0.04 lb) within Sweden and 10 kr to the rest of the world. Postboxes are painted in different colours. The yellow boxes should be used for mail going abroad, and the blue boxes for letters within the Stockholm area (post codes starting with "1"). There are also red boxes for

Yellow postbox for national and international, blue for local mail

local post, but these need a special stamp which can be bought at Pressbyrån kiosks. White boxes are used only for giro payments. Collection times vary and are always shown on the postbox.

Most international courier services are represented in Stockholm. In addition, special services are also operated by the Swedish post office.

TV AND RADIO

Virtually all hotels provide television in their rooms with both national and foreign channels. The most commonly used are the Swedish SVT1, SVT2, TV3, TV4 and Channel 5, as well as the international CNN, Sky News, MTV and Eurosport. SVT1 and 2 are State-run public-service channels. SVT2 and TV4 broadcast local programmes in the morning and evening which include weather forecasts.

There are a number of local radio stations in Stockholm, broadcasting a selection of mainly international and Swedish music. P6, Stockholm International, broadcasts a variety of English- and German-language programmes on 89.6 MHz.

Post office logo

NEWSPAPERS AND MAGAZINES

Most of the important foreign newspapers and magazines can be bought in Stockholm. For the widest choice available you will need to visit Press Point, Press Center and Press Specialisten. Alternatively, the many Pressbyrån kiosks and tourist information offices around the city do stock foreign publications. However, they usually offer only a limited selection of titles amongst the many Swedish publications.

Pressbyrån kiosks, newsagent selling stamps

DIRECTORY

TELECOMMUNICATIONS

International Operator
Tel 11 81 19.

Sending Telegrams
Tel 020-999 777 (Telia).

Directory Enquiries
Tel 118 118 (Telia).

International Directory Enquiries
Tel 118 119 (Telia).

Wake-up Call
Tel 90 180 (50 kr per call).

E-MAIL SERVICES

Café Access
Kulturhuset, Sergels Torg.
Map 2 C4. *Tel* 508 314 88.

COURIER SERVICES

DHL
Tel 020-345 345.

Federal Express
Tel 0200 252 252.

TNT
Tel 020-960 960.

FOREIGN NEWSPAPERS

Pressbyrån Centrallen
Stora Hallen, Centralplan 15.
Map 2 C4. *Tel* 20 56 08.

Press Stop
Gallerian, Hamngatan 37.
Map 3 D4. *Tel* 723 01 91.

Press Stop
Götgatan 31. **Map** 9 D2.
Tel 644 35 10.
www.press-stop.se

GETTING TO STOCKHOLM

Stockholm's position at the centre of the Baltic region has made it an important transport interchange. The capital now has daily direct flights to and from most major European and North American cities. Arlanda Airport is one of the most efficient in the world. It is served by about 60 international and domestic airlines. Sweden's infrastructure is constantly being improved, with new motorways

Aircraft of Scandinavian Airlines (SAS)

being built and the railway system being upgraded for high-speed trains. Car ferries operate to Stockholm from Finland and other points in the Baltic in about 11–15 hours. From Sweden's west and south coasts the capital can be reached by high-speed trains and motorways in no more than six hours. Sweden has a direct link to the Continent via the new Öresund road and rail bridge to Denmark in the south.

ARRIVING BY AIR

Most major European cities have direct flights to the Swedish capital. Many of the world's leading airlines and Swedish domestic flights serve Arlanda Airport, located about 40 km (25 miles) north of the city centre.

Stockholm is served by two other airports. Bromma, close to the city centre, is used by a few of the smaller domestic airlines. Passengers flying with **Malmö Aviation** from London via Malmö also arrive here. Skavsta, about 100 km (62 miles) south of Stockholm near Nyköping, is used by **Ryanair** for budget-price flights to and from London Stansted Airport. A bus takes travellers into Stockholm.

Services between Stockholm and North America are operated by **SAS** (Scandinavian Airlines) and **Finnair** and by the US airlines Delta and American. The charter airline Premiair has frequent flights across the North Atlantic.

The Arlanda Express, linking Arlanda Airport with the city

GETTING FROM AND TO ARLANDA AIRPORT

There are several ways of getting to the city centre from Arlanda Airport. The "Flygbussarna" bus service which operates every five minutes at peak times takes 45 minutes to the City Terminal at Central Station and costs about 80 kr (100 kr between midnight and 5am). An

SAS logo

onward journey by taxi can be booked on the bus. The taxi journey into town from the airport is quicker but more expensive. Most taxi firms have a fixed charge of about 390 kr to the city centre. Avoid the so-called "black taxis" and check the fare before departure. The shortest journey time is by the Arlanda Express train, which costs about 180 kr for the 20-minute trip to Central Station. There are two stations at the airport: one for terminals 2, 3, 4 and the other for terminal 5. Arlanda's Sky City station is served by long-distance trains.

AIR FARES

Fare options are varied, particularly if you are flexible about departure and arrival dates, or can book well in advance. SAS, for example, has low-cost fares which must be booked at least seven days before departure and require a Saturday night stay at the destination. Bookings using this type of ticket cannot usually be changed.

Increased competition has meant that it is sometimes possible to fly to Stockholm from London for a return fare of less than £100.

Scheduled airlines generally maintain their basic fare structure throughout the year, but special offers are frequently available. Newspaper advertisements and travel companies' websites often have details of last-minute deals.

Terminal 5 (International) at Stockholm's Arlanda Airport

Ferry from Finland on the way to its terminal at Stadsgården

TRAVEL BY TRAIN OR COACH

Rail or coach travel from the Continent to Stockholm is relatively quick, inexpensive and comfortable. Journey times have been speeded up with the opening of the Öresund bridge between Denmark and Sweden which carries both rail and road traffic. Travel agencies can give more information on the options available.

Within Sweden the State-owned railway company **Statens Järnvägar** operates many of the long-distance trains. Some routes are run by private companies, notably **Tågkompaniet** (Stockholm–northern Sweden). In recent years air travel between Stockholm and Malmö or Gothenburg has faced strong competition from the X 2000 high-speed train. The journey time by train from Malmö to Stockholm is about 5 hours and from Gothenburg it takes about 3 hours.

The same routes are served by express coaches such as **Swebus**. Journey times are naturally longer (about 7 hours from Gothenburg and about 9 hours from Malmö), but fares are generally much lower and advance booking is not required.

TRAVEL BY FERRY

Large passenger/car ferries sail to Stockholm from Finland. Both **Viking Line** and **Silja Line** operate daily services and have their own terminals at Stadsgården near the city centre and Värtahamnen respectively. The journey from Helsinki takes about 15 hours and from Turku 11 hours. Both shipping lines offer excellent passenger facilities, including good food, entertainment and shopping. From Tallinn in Estonia **Tallink** operates daily to the Värtahamnen terminal.

TRAVEL BY CAR

Visitors driving from Denmark can use the spectacular new Öresund toll bridge between Copenhagen and Malmö. On the Swedish side the bridge connects with the E4, a 550-km (340-mile) motorway to Stockholm. Another option is the 20-minute car ferry from Helsingør in Denmark to Helsingborg in Sweden.

Car ferries to Gothenburg operate from Denmark (Frederikshavn) and Germany (Kiel), with an onward journey on the E3 to Stockholm, about 450 km (280 miles). The fastest route from Germany to Sweden is the catamaran ferry from Rostock to Trelleborg in southern Sweden, then the E6 to Malmö and E4 to Stockholm. Speed limits on Swedish motorways are 110 km/h (68 mph), and 90 km/h (56 mph) on other main roads. The limit in built-up areas is 50–70 km/h (31–43 mph). When driving in the countryside, take care at dawn and dusk especially, since elk and deer can then suddenly appear on the road.

SJ
Swedish Railways logo

Warning, elk on the road

Arrival hall at Stockholm Central Station

DIRECTORY

AIRLINES

SAS
Tel 020 727 727.
Tel 0845 607 27 727 (UK).
www.scandinavian.net

British Airways
Tel 0770 110 020.
Tel 0870 850 9850 (UK).
www.britishairway.se

Malmö Aviation
Tel 0771 55 00 10.
www.malmoaviation.se

Finnair
Tel 020-78 11 00.
Tel 0870 241 4411 (UK).
www.finnair.com

Ryanair
Tel 0900 200 4040.
Tel 0906 270 5656 (UK).
www.ryanair.com

RAILWAYS

Statens Järnvägar (SJ)
Tel 0771 757 575.

Tågkompaniet (Svenska)
Tel 0771 444 111.

FERRY LINES

Silja Line
Tel 22 21 40.

Tallink
Tel 666 60 00.

Viking Line
Tel 452 40 00.

EXPRESS COACHES

Swebus
Tel 0200-21 82 18.
www.swebus.express.se

GETTING AROUND STOCKHOLM

Pedestrian and cycle route

Stockholm is a perfect city for pedestrians. Distances between sights are usually short, and around every corner there is always something interesting to discover. The capital extends across a large number of islands, offering eye-catching vistas and waterfront scenes. There are many cycle lanes, although not everywhere in the busy city centre, and for inexperienced visitors it might be safer to stick to green areas like Djurgården. Public transport on buses, underground trains, trams and local trains is efficient and covers the entire city and surrounding region. Apart from the area of Gamla Stan, and during the rush hours, driving a car in Stockholm is relatively easy and indoor parking facilities are adequate. But the best way of exploring the city centre is on foot.

STOCKHOLM ON FOOT

In large parts of central Stockholm, walking is the best way to see the sights, but one needs to be aware of the regulations. Pedestrians are not allowed to cross a road against a red light, but motorists must stop and give way to pedestrians at zebra crossings without traffic lights (always look carefully). If you are waiting at a crossing with lights press the button, otherwise you are likely to wait a long time before the light changes to green.

The clear street signs make it easy to find one's way around, and Stockholmers are always glad to help visitors. There are walking and cycling routes everywhere in the city, as well as plenty of pedestrian precincts and parks.

Gamla Stan is a popular area for exploring on foot, and there is always something to see around Kungsträdgården as well. A stroll along the quayside opposite the Grand Hôtel and Nationalmuseum, followed by a walk around Skeppsholmen, makes

Taking a waterfront stroll along Djurgårdsbrunnsviken

an interesting route. Another delightful area is Djurgården, with a host of attractions set in parkland only a short distance from the centre.

Those who like to walk along the waterfront can follow the quaysides, for example from Stadshuset along Norr Mälarstrand and the Riddarfjärden bay. You will not lack company – jogging is a popular pastime in Stockholm. Fjällgatan (see p129) is also recommended, not least for its magnificent view of the city.

Guided walks are organized regularly, often with a special theme – history, architecture or parks, for example. Sometimes they are available in different languages, especially during the summer months. Most walks take in the Old Town, but there are a number of other routes – tourist information offices will have details (see Directory, p191).

Pedestrians crossing signals: red for wait and green for go

DRIVING IN STOCKHOLM

Anyone familiar with driving in large cities will have no problems in Stockholm. It is relatively easy to find one's way around by car, except during the rush hours (7.30–9.30am, 12 noon to 1pm, and 3.30–6pm). Cars are not really necessary in the city centre because of the short distances between sights and excellent public transport. However, a car is an advantage if you want to explore further afield.

The speed limit is usually 50 km/h (31 mph), but near schools, for example, it is 30 km/h (19 mph). Speeds up to 70 km/h (43 mph) are permitted only on the main roads in and out of the city. Fines for speeding are high, and even if the limit is only slightly exceeded, you can lose your driving licence. Drivers and passengers must always wear seat belts. Drink-drive laws are zero-tolerance: the maximum permitted blood alcohol level is 0.2 mg per mil. Motorists must give way to pedestrians at crossings without traffic lights. The yellow light means "Stop".

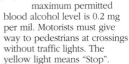

Pedestrian crossing sign

READING STREET SIGNS

Street name

Roslagsgatan

kv. Ingemar **46–34**

Block

Street number range in block

CAR RENTAL

Most of the international car-rental firms have offices in Stockholm, as well as several local operators. The larger hotels and the tourist information office at Sweden House *(see p191)* can arrange a car which can be delivered at your convenience. The only documentation needed is a national driving licence which must be shown when you sign the rental contract.

PARKING

There are plenty of parking spaces on the streets and in multistorey car parks, but it can sometimes be difficult to find a vacant spot, particularly in summer. If you plan to park on the street you need to familiarize yourself with the various road signs. In the city centre it often costs 10 kr or more per hour to park. Parking in many areas is free, particularly at week-ends, or between 5pm and 9am except on street-cleaning nights as indicated on road signs. Major attrac-

No parking sign permits short stop to set down or pick up (5–10 min).

No stopping zone, indicated by yellow line by pavement.

Parking zone

Parking charge 9am–5pm; free at other times

No parking on weekday night indicated, midnight–6am

tions like museums often have their own car parks, which are subject to a charge throughout the week.

The city's parking wardens are diligent. Any breach of regulations can involve a fine of 400 kr or more, and it costs 700 kr if one parks within 10 m (33 ft) of a crossing. Do not leave valuables in the car, even in multistorey car parks.

Parking warden

PARKING METER

Rates & Times

Coin slot

Green button: non residential parking

Yellow button: residential parking

Day and date

Time of expiry

Parking ticket for non-residents

GETTING AROUND BY TAXI

With the short distances between places in the city centre, the need for a taxi is not so important, but it is convenient and for brief journeys relatively cheap.

There are usually plenty of taxis available, particularly at stations and sights, with the exception of the rush hours. One can also hail an empty taxi, indicated by the illuminated sign on the car roof. The best method is to order a taxi by telephone or book one in

Taxi sign lights up when available

Taxi sign

advance. The initial charge is usually 30 kr, with an additional 70–120 kr for a journey within the central area. It is always worth enquiring what the fare is likely to be.

One should be careful about using the unauthorized so-called "black taxis", especially at night.

A Stockholm taxi

DIRECTORY

TAXI

Taxi Kurir
Tel 30 00 00. www.taxikurir.se

Taxi Stockholm
Tel 15 00 00.
www.taxistockholm.se

Taxi 020
Tel 020 20 20 20.
www.taxi020.se

CAR RENTAL

Avis
Tel 0770 820 082.
www.avis-se.com

Europcar
Tel 020 78 11 80.
www.europcar.se

Hertz
Tel 0771 21 12 12. www.hertz.se

Statoil
Tel 0770 25 25 25.
www.statoil.se

Getting Around by Tunnelbana and Bus

Stockholm Tunnelbana logo

Virtually all Stockholm's sights and attractions can be reached easily by Tunnelbana (underground train) or bus. The map below shows the Tunnelbana network, and a map of inner-city bus routes is on the inside back cover. Along with other operators, SL is responsible for public transport by Tunnelbana, bus and local shuttle train. The various types of transport complement each other and cover Greater Stockholm.

Full-price Tunnelbana coupon (top) and SL's one-day ticket

TUNNELBANA

In the late 1940s work started on the building of Stockholm's first underground railway. Since then the network has been extended and now has 100 stations on three main routes – the green, red and blue lines. These link up at T-Centralen adjoining Central Station.

Of the 100 stations, 19 are located in the inner city, and nearly all the sights described in this guide can be reached by Tunnelbana or the main bus routes. The Tunnelbana system has four zones, with the inner zone covering a large part of the city centre. This means that one can travel direct to many of the sights for 20 kr. Most ticket barriers are manned.

A modern SL Tunnelbana train

Apart from single tickets, there are travelcards for one day, three days or a month. Cards are valid for all zones. You can also use the Stockholm Card (see p191). It can pay to buy a book of discount coupons valid for 10 journeys in the inner-city zone for about 145 kr. Tickets can be bought at Pressbyrån kiosks, the SL central ticket office, or at stations. Tickets for a single journey can be bought at Tunnelbana stations or on buses.

Sunday to Thursday nights the Tunnelbana operates until 3:30am while on Friday and Saturday nights it runs until 4am. At other times there are night bus services.

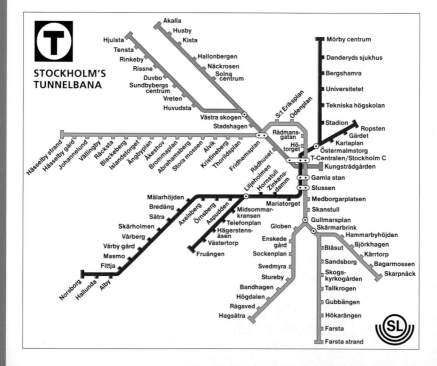

STOCKHOLM'S TUNNELBANA

GETTING AROUND BY BUS

The network of "red" city buses is built up around a number of "blue" feeder routes which complement the Tunnelbana network. Many streets in the city centre have special bus lanes which speed up the traffic. The buses are all modern and comfortable, with easy access for prams, and frequently use environmentally friendly fuels like ethanol and gas.

Travelling by bus is a pleasant and economical way of seeing the city. A two-coupon single ticket gives two hours' travel, with an unlimited number of changes. The best routes for sightseeing are 2, 3, 4, 47, 62 and 69. These cover most of the central area and

Restored vintage tram, a popular way of getting to Djurgården

stop near many sights. Routes 47 and 69 from, for instance, Norrmalmstorg are particularly useful for reaching sights not served by Tunnel-bana. Route 47 takes visitors to Djurgården with its attractions including Skansen, Gröna Lund, Vasamuseet and Nordiska Museet, continuing to Waldemarsudde. Route 69 goes to southern Gärdet with its four important museums and Kaknästornet, continuing via Thielska Galleriet to Blockhusudden at the easternmost tip of Djurgården.

Red city bus and blue "feeder" bus

VINTAGE TRAMS

A charming way of travelling to Djurgården, particularly in the summer, is to take one of the lovingly restored vintage trams. Trams ceased to operate in Stockholm in 1967, when Sweden switched over to right-hand driving, but since 1991 a voluntary organization of tram enthusiasts has operated services on the former route 7 between Norrmalmstorg and Djurgården, where 14 trams are stabled.

Every year more than 300,000 passengers enjoy a trip using this popular method of travel. Refreshments are served on some services.

ART ON THE TUNNELBANA

Stockholm's Tunnelbana network is an attraction in itself. From the start, time and money were invested in decorating the stations artistically. Today about 130 artists are represented by sculptures, mosaics and paintings. SL has an artistic advisory board which is responsible for choosing new works of art and has an annual budget of 3 million kronor. Some stations are particularly worth seeing, including the following:

Kungsträdgården
Sculptures, waterfall, arch paintings, etc (Ulrik Samuelson, 1977–87.)

Fridhemsplan *Homage to Carl von Linné* glazed wall and terracotta sculpture (Dimas Macedo, 1997).

Zenith, a painted steel sculpture by Leif Tjerned at Gullmarsplan station

Östermalmstorg Reliefs on the theme *Women's rights, and the peace and environmental movements* (Siri Derkert, 1965).

Stadion Wooden sculptures linked to the 1912 Olympic Games, Stockholm Stadium, and the Royal Musical Academy (Enno Hallek, Åke Pallarp, 1973).

Universitetet *The United Nations Declaration of*

Human Rights, wall decoration in ceramics (Françoise Schein, 1998), video installation (Fredrik Wretman, 1998).

Rissne *Time axis from the pyramids to the present day* (Madeleine Dranger, Rolf H Reimers, 1985).

A guide in English to art on the Tunnelbana is available at the SL central ticket office or tourist information offices.

Getting Around by Ferry and Boat

Stockholm's location between Lake Mäla-ren and the Baltic archipelago means that its waterways play an important role in city life. Boats and ferries are a familiar feature of the Stockholm scene and provide a delightful way of getting to know the city and its surroundings. A large number of scheduled boat services, ferries and sightseeing tours offer visitors almost end-less opportunities to enjoy Stockholm from the water. Note that from mid-August transport schedules are adjusted for winter, so always check the times.

Waxholms-bolaget's logo

Sightseeing boat crossing Stockholms Ström

GETTING AROUND BY FERRY

For many decades it has been a tradition to visit the attractions of Djurgården by ferry from the city centre. This pleasant service links with bus and Tunnelbana routes, and can be used free of charge by holders of SL's 1-day or 3-day card (the Stockholm Card is not valid).

There is a year-round ferry service from Slussen via Skeppsholmen to Allmänna Gränd near Gröna Lund from 7.30am until after midnight. From May to August there is a route from Nybroplan to Vasamuseet, Skeppsholmen and Gröna Lund from 9am–6pm. Both these ferries operate at frequent intervals. During the summer **Strömma Kanalbolaget**'s neat little

ferries ply between the jetties around Brunnsviken alongside the Haga Park *(see p121)*.

SIGHTSEEING BY BOAT

A pleasant way of enjoying Stockholm from the water is to take an excursion run by Stockholm Sightseeing (**Strömma Kanalbolaget**). A "Round Kungsholmen" tour departs hourly from the quay-side near the City Hall from

Djurgården ferry in front of Nordiska Museet

10.30am to 4.30pm. Tickets costing about 100 kr can be bought on the quay. Guides speak English and Swedish and often a third language.

The "Under Stockholm's Bridges" and "Round Djur-gården" tours depart hourly from Strömkajen near the Grand Hôtel, and passengers are also picked up from Nybroplan. Tickets can be bought at both these points. The former tour operates between 10am and 8pm and costs about 160 kr, the latter between 10.30am and 6pm for about 100 kr. A comment-ary is provided on headsets in a variety of lan-guages. Tours are available during summer until the end of August apart from "Round Djurgården" which runs to De-cember. Go to www.stockholm sightseeing.com or contact a tourist information office.

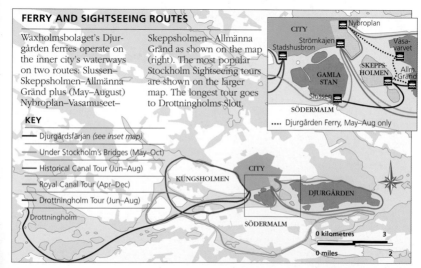

FERRY AND SIGHTSEEING ROUTES

Waxholmsbolaget's Djur-gården ferries operate on the inner city's waterways on two routes: Slussen–Skeppsholmen–Allmänna Gränd plus (May–August) Nybroplan–Vasamuseet–

Skeppsholmen–Allmänna Gränd as shown on the map (right). The most popular Stockholm Sightseeing tours are shown on the larger map. The longest tour goes to Drottningholms Slott.

CITY — Nybroplan
Strömkajen
Stadshusbron
Vasa-varvet
SKEPPS-HOLMEN
GAMLA STAN
Allm. Gränd
Slussen
SÖDERMALM
···· Djurgården Ferry, May–Aug only

KEY

— Djurgårdsfärjan *(see inset map)*

— Under Stockholm's Bridges (May–Oct)

— Historical Canal Tour (Jun–Aug)

— Royal Canal Tour (Apr–Dec)

— Drottningholm Tour (Jun–Aug)

Drottningholm

KUNGSHOLMEN

CITY

DJURGÅRDEN

SÖDERMALM

0 kilometres   3

0 miles   2

HIRING BOATS AND CANOES

Enjoying the city from the water on one's own is an exciting experience. Rowing boats, canoes, kayaks, pedalos and small boats with an outboard motor can be hired near the Djurgården bridge at **Tvillingarnas Båthyrning** and **Skepp & Hoj**. The gentle waters of the Djurgården Canal are ideal for rowing or canoeing. A motor-boat trip round Djurgården takes about an hour. Larger boats for exploring the archipelago can be rented by the hour or day.

EXCURSIONS BY BOAT

The many scheduled public transport boat services operated by **Waxholmsbolaget** generally sail year-round, but most frequently between June and mid-August. An excellent way of exploring the archipelago independently is to take one of the regular services from Strömkajen which call at countless picturesque jetties along the way. The ferry company and tourist information offices can suggest suitable itineraries.

Organized excursions both in the archipelago and on Lake Mälaren are run by **Strömma Kanalbolaget** and other operators. You can, for instance, take a gastronomic evening cruise to Vaxholm, departing at 7pm and returning at 9.45pm, and other attractive options are available.

Gourmet steamer cruise in the archipelago with top-class Swedish cuisine

A number of sights which can be reached by fast passenger boats or traditional steamers are listed on pages 140–151.

Getting Around by Bicycle

Suggested bicycle tour

The capital's network of bicycle tracks is increasing all the time, but you need to be an experienced city cyclist if you want to explore the central area from the saddle. Otherwise Stockholm and its surrounding area are tailor-made for cycling. Anyone wanting to go out into the countryside and enjoy the fresh air and beautiful surroundings does not need to travel far from the city centre.

Visitors who want to find out more about hiring bicycles in Stockholm, and throughout Sweden, should contact **Cykelfrämjandet**. Otherwise the SVB tourist information office at Sweden House (see p191) can put cyclists in touch with a local cycling organization which will be pleased to give some useful suggestions.

Two bicycle-hire firms, **Djungårdsbrons Sjöcafé** and **Cykel & Mopeduthyrningen**, are located on Strandvägen near the Djurgården bridge. From there it is only a short ride to Djurgården with its gently graded cycle tracks and roads which are mostly free of cars.

Gärdet, Lilljanskogen and Haga are other good areas for biking, and there are also marked routes which stretch further out from the city centre. It is also possible to cycle in parts of Ekoparken (see p121) which are virtually traffic-free.

Rollerblades can be hired at the same outlets as bikes, while **Cykelstallet** is the best place to go for mountain bike rental.

Maps can be bought from, among others, **Kartcentrum** and **Kartbutiken**.

Cycling on the peaceful Djurgården

STOCKHOLM STREET FINDER

T he map below shows the areas of Stockholm covered by the street map. Gamla Stan (Old Town) is shown on a larger scale than the rest of the city. The map references listed in the guide for many sights, restaurants, hotels, shops and entertainment spots refer to the maps in this section. The first figure of the refer-

Japanese visitors

ence indicates the map page, while the letter and following figure shows its location on the map grid. All the more important sights are marked so that they are easier to find. The key below explains other symbols on the map, including post offices, tunnelbana stations and churches. An overview map of Stockholm is on pp12–13.

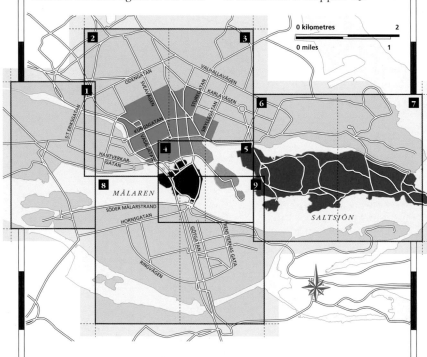

0 kilometres 2

0 miles 1

KEY TO STREET FINDER

■	Major sight	ℹ	Tourist information office
■	Place of interest	✚	Hospital
□	Other building	🚓	Police station
🚆	Train station	✝	Church
Ⓣ	Tunnelbana station	✡	Synagogue
🚌	Main bus stop	☪	Mosque
🚏	Coach station	⊠	Post office
⛴	Ferry boarding point	�	Viewpoint
🚋	Tram stop	═	Railway line
P	Car park	▬	Pedestrian street

SCALE OF MAP PAGES
1–3 AND 6–9

0 metres 200

0 yards 200

SCALE OF MAP PAGES
4–5

0 metres 200

0 yards 200

Street name index on pp216–18

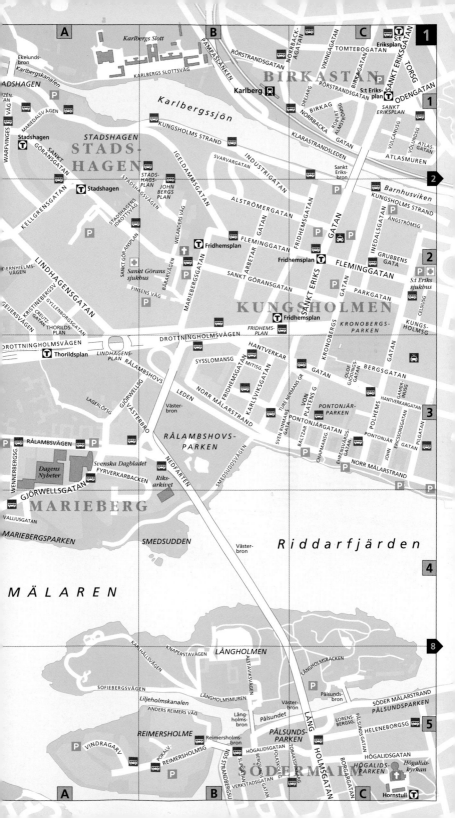

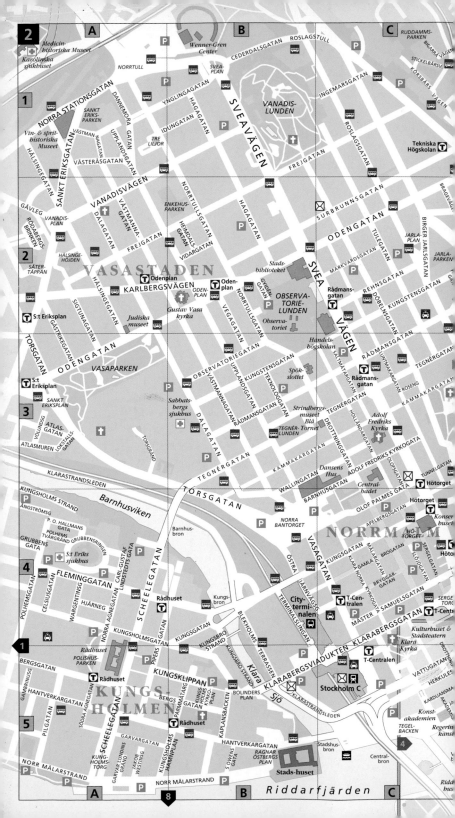